Religion, Culture and Society

Series Editors:
Oliver Davies and Gavin Flood
Department of Theology and Religious Studies,
University of Wales, Lampeter

Editorial Board:
Mashuq Ally
Chris Arthur
Paul Badham
Fiona Bowie
Xinzhong Yao

Religion, Culture and Society is a new series presented by leading scholars on a wide range of contemporary religious issues. The emphasis throughout is generally multicultural, and the approach is often interdisciplinary. The clarity and accessibility of the series, as well as its authoritative scholarship, will recommend it to students and a non-specialist readership alike.

The Coming Deliverer

Millennial Themes in World Religions

Edited by

FIONA BOWIE

with CHRISTOPHER DEACY

UNIVERSITY OF WALES PRESS
CARDIFF
1997

© The contributors, 1997

British Library Cataloguing in Publication Data
A catalogue record for this book is available from
the British Library.

ISBN 0-7083-1338-8

Cover design by John Garland, Pentan Partnership, Cardiff
Typeset at the University of Wales Press
Printed in Great Britain by Dinefwr Press, Llandybïe

Contents

Dedication to Cyril Williams

The decision to publish a collection of essays on 'The Coming Deliverer' from the standpoint of different faiths stems originally from an idea put to his colleagues by Professor Cyril Williams. It is therefore fitting that his fellow contributors and indeed his former colleagues at Lampeter and elsewhere in the University of Wales should use the occasion of its publication to pay tribute to him.

In a very real sense, the determination that this publication should see the light of day reflects three particular characteristics of Cyril's career: first, his ability to generate and respond to new ideas; second, his consistent desire to collaborate with and to encourage fellow scholars, and in particular younger scholars; third, his deep conviction that theological beliefs and religious practices are best studied in a multi-faith perspective.

Cyril Williams combines in a unique way the national and the international, the local and the global. He was born and brought up in the Gwendraeth Valley and he has never forgotten his roots in Welsh Wales; indeed, he is intensely proud of being Welsh and has retained his very close links with *Y Fro Gymraeg*, both culturally and religiously. On the other hand, he has learned to look beyond the horizon of Wales and Welsh Nonconformity to the wider world. He spent five fruitful years as a professor of religion in Canada; he has developed a specialist academic interest in Indian religions, and more recently has researched the historical links between Wales and Christianity in the Far East, particularly China and Korea.

Over a long career he has displayed a remarkable versatility. His early scholarly work, under the guidance of Aubrey Johnson, was in what Christians call Old Testament Studies, but in Cardiff he quickly responded to the challenge of learning about and teaching other faiths. His mastery of this vast subject and his determination that the Welsh should take the subject seriously led to the publication of *Crefyddau'r Dwyrain* in 1968. This publication also reflects his innovative and visionary contribution to higher education (and indeed secondary and continuing education) in Wales. Cyril Williams, beyond all others and sometimes almost single-handedly, introduced Religious Studies as a serious academic discipline into the curriculum of the University of Wales.

His pioneering work in Wales (and Canada) and its influence on developments in other parts of the United Kingdom has been recognized by his peers, who elected him to the presidency of the British Association for the History of Religions. Seldom can such an accolade have been more richly deserved. Yet for those of us who know him, Cyril remains a gentleman (in every sense), a trusted friend, a patriotic and passionate Welshman, a true Christian and a worthy example of what it means to be a human being.

D. P. Davies

Acknowledgements

This book was conceived by Cyril Williams, who has continued to direct energy and enthusiasm into the project. Without his vision the book would never have been written. All the papers were commissioned specifically for this volume, drawing widely on expertise within the Department of Theology and Religious Studies at the University of Wales, Lampeter, as well as on scholars elsewhere who, for the most part, have been former students, examiners or friends of the University. We are particularly glad to have several chapters written by postgraduate and recently graduated doctoral students, whose in-depth and up-to-date knowledge of their subjects makes an important contribution to the volume. Both staff and students in Lampeter have given their time generously to help with the editing, particularly Oliver Davies, Gavin Flood, Steve Jacobs, Sarah Lewis, and above all Christopher Deacy, who answered a plea for help and took the responsibility for producing a single coherent text from a collection of incompatible disks.

Fiona Bowie
October 1996

The contributors

Chris Arthur is a senior lecturer in Religious Studies at the University of Wales, Lampeter.

Fiona Bowie is a lecturer in Theology and Religious Studies and in Anthropology at the University of Wales, Lampeter.

Jonathan G. Campbell is a lecturer in Theology at the University of Bristol.

W. Owen Cole is Research Fellow in Religious Studies at Chichester Institute of Higher Education.

D. P. Davies is D. J. James Professor of Theology at the University of Wales, Lampeter.

Christopher Deacy is a research student in the Department of Theology and Religious Studies at the University of Wales, Lampeter.

Simon Dien is a medical anthropologist and clinical psychologist. He teaches part-time at University College, London.

Kent Eaton is a lecturer in Church History at an evangelical seminary in Spain and a postgraduate student at the University of Wales, Lampeter.

Sarah M. Lewis is a part-time lecturer in Religious Studies at the University of Wales, Lampeter.

Neil O'Connor is a lecturer in Religious Studies at the University of Cork.

David Shankland is a lecturer in Anthropology at the University of Wales, Lampeter.

Cyril Williams is Emeritus Professor of Religious Studies at the University of Wales, Lampeter.

1

Equilibrium and the end of time: the roots of millenarianism

FIONA BOWIE

1 Introduction

As human beings we live with paradox. We are conscious and self-reflective, aware of our existence, assured of our position as hunters rather than prey, without predators in the world in which we live, and yet we remain ignorant of the world – of our place in the delicate ecological balance which holds our existence in its thrall – and powerless before the reality of death, the great equalizer which puts paid to our specious notions of superiority. Human societies and individuals have historically come to two broadly contradictory conclusions concerning our predicament. These contrasting emphases may be present within each person, but the stress on each element varies from one culture to another, across time and within individuals. The first approach is to conceive of the world (the limits of which are culturally determined) as existing in a delicately balanced state of equilibrium, to which human beings, through their social and religious actions, contribute. The forces of nature and human misdemeanours constantly threaten to upset this ideal harmony, as may the actions of destructive gods or spirits, who must be constantly opposed if chaos is to be averted. Such a view may be combined with a notion of endless cosmic cycles of growth and decay, mirroring the experience of life itself within a time-scale set between the life-span of creatures on earth and the stars on which they gaze. The main thrust of such a vision tends to be this-worldly and life-affirming. Through constant struggle and vigilance human beings can and must play their part in the great drama of life on which the continued existence of the world depends. By way of contrast we have the solution of those whose eyes are set on a future utopia, or perhaps on a golden past which they seek to recreate in a transformed world. The present constraints of existence are eschewed in favour of a new world in which suffering and chaos are finally overcome. This new world, whether for the few or the many, recreated on this earth or in some future existence, demands the destruction of the old order and is therefore life-denying and transcendental. The notion of a coming deliverer belongs to the latter scheme of things – a human or divine (or divine human) saviour will come who is strong enough to take on the forces of chaos and evil and defeat them once and for all, leading the chosen few to the new world beyond the boundaries of the present age. Two quotations will serve to illustrate this contrast, despite the great variety and the cultural specificity of human societies.

The first gives the words of a Kogi *Mama*, one of the highly respected religious and political leaders of an indigenous Colombian people who, after initial coexistence with the Spanish in the sixteenth and seventeenth centuries, withdrew as far as possible from contact with the outside world by retreating into the jungles and higher reaches of the Sierra Nevada, which they regard as the heart of the world. Their self-imposed isolation was breached when the Kogi decided to co-operate with a BBC film-maker, Alan Ereira, in order to impart an important ecological message from the 'elder' to the 'younger brother' (that is, from themselves to peoples who do not belong to the First Nations). The Kogi *Mamas* were concerned at the climatic changes which threaten the continued existence of the Sierra Nevada, which stands in their eyes as a microcosmic image of the planet as a whole. The speech illustrates the biophylic, this-worldly orientation of the Kogi, and the importance as they see it of their sustaining work in making offerings to balance and harmonize the world.

> We know what is happening.
> They say that the world will end.
> But it will not end yet.
> If we behave well it will not end.
> The earth is still fertile.
> It is still growing crops.
> The crops are still growing.

When it is going to die, there it will be barren.

Father Serankua made this earth
so that it would not end
so that we could all go on living here.

Younger Brother,
your water is drying up down below.
Do not think that we are responsible,
do not think we have forgotten our work.
When will the world end?
We do not know.
Neither the Younger Brother nor us can know.[1]

The second quotation, illustrating a totally different cosmological schema, forms part of the discourse on the end of time attributed to Jesus in Matthew's gospel. The redactor comes from a tradition of apocalyptic Judaism which identifies Jesus as the coming deliverer, and the disciples are depicted as looking forward with trepidation and longing, to the ending of the present order when, after a period of increasing chaos and destruction culminating in a great cosmic battle, the faithful will be ushered into God's kingdom.

As he sat on the mount of Olives the disciples came to speak to him privately. 'Tell us,' they said, 'when will this happen? And what will be the sign of your coming and the end of the age?'

Jesus replied: 'Take care that no one misleads you. For many will come claiming my name and saying, "I am the Messiah," and many will be misled by them. The time is coming when you will hear of wars and rumours of wars. See that you are not alarmed. Such things are bound to happen; but the end is still to come. For nation will go to war against nation, kingdom against kingdom; there will be famines and earthquakes in many places. All these things are the first birth-pangs of the new age . . .

Then will appear in heaven the sign that heralds the Son of Man. All the peoples of this world will make lamentation, and they will see the Son of Man coming on the clouds of heaven with power and great glory. With a trumpet blast he will send out his angels, and they will gather his chosen from the four winds, from the furthest bounds of heaven on every side.'[2]

The contributors to this volume explore the idea of a coming deliverer in a variety of religious traditions, in some of which, as in Buddhism or Sikhism, for instance, millenarian tendencies remain marginal to the mainstream teachings. In others, particularly Christianity, millenarian thought and expectations have been a recurrent theme, inspiring Christians and groups with Christian origins and influences down the centuries. Each chapter is written by an expert in their own field, some of whom attempt to present an overview of the ways in which ideas concerning a coming deliverer have been conceived within a specific tradition or at a particular period, while others provide detailed case studies of groups for whom apocalyptic or millenarian ideas have been central, and for whom the promised deliverer may even have already come. My own training is in the discipline of social anthropology, and in this first chapter I turn to some anthropological paradigms, and to explanations from other disciplines, of the roots of millenarianism, attempting to uncover in the process the reasons for the apparent upsurge in apocalyptic fervour as the second millennium draws to a close.

2 Some definitions

As terms such as 'millenarian' and 'apocalyptic' are central to most of the papers in this volume it is as well to clarify what they mean before we go any further. The millennium (from the Latin *mille*, 'a thousand', and *annus*, 'a year') is used first of all to refer to a period of a thousand years, particularly with reference to the Western Christian (Gregorian) calendar, so that we can talk of approaching the end of the second millennium (the year 2000). Many societies have seen a hidden significance in dates, and attribute a mystical power to numbers.[3] It is often assumed that the passing of the first millennium caused widespread panic in Western Europe, but this does not in fact seem to have been the case.[4] The perception that such dates are important is, however, of significance, and the turn of the last century and approach of the second millennium do seem to have led to an increase in apocalyptic fervour.[5]

The term 'millenarian' derives from Christian usage, which should immediately alert us to the dangers of assuming that it can be applied unproblematically as a cross-cultural category (see

Chris Arthur below). While not necessarily linked to the millennium, in the sense outlined above, excitement over calendrical dates derives at least in part from the conflation of the millennium as a passage of time with Christian apocalypticism. In its original context 'millenarian' refers to the belief held by some Christians that after his second coming Christ would reign over an earthly kingdom for a thousand years before the Last Judgement. (The term chiliasm, from the Greek word for a thousand, is sometimes used in the Christian context in order to distinguish it from other usages.) In the book of Revelation in the New Testament (also known as the Apocalypse), the author has a vision in which the Devil, or Satan, is characterized as a dragon, 'that ancient serpent' who is chained for a thousand years, after which he will be let loose again for a little while (20:1–4). During this period those who died as martyrs for their faith will be resurrected and become priests of God and co-rulers with Christ. This is referred to as the 'first resurrection' (20:4–6). At the end of this millennium Satan will be loosed once more to cause chaos on earth, only to be destroyed once and for all together with all of his followers. This final defeat ushers in the 'second resurrection' and Last Judgement, when all those who have died are tried according to their deeds and flung into the lake of fire or admitted as citizens to the new heaven and new earth. This new creation was located on a cleansed earth, when God (as in the Garden of Eden) would dwell once more with his people (20:7–15). As the following verses indicate, the laws of birth and death will no longer apply, the cycle of earthly existence as we know it has been banished, found wanting and rejected once and for all:

I saw a new heaven and a new earth, for the first heaven and the first earth had vanished, and there was no longer any sea. I saw the Holy City, new Jerusalem, coming down out of heaven from God, made ready like a bride adorned for her husband. I heard a loud voice proclaiming from the throne: 'Now God has his dwelling with mankind! He will dwell among them and they shall be his people, and God himself will be with them. He will wipe every tear from their eyes. There shall be an end to death, and to mourning and crying and pain, for the old order has passed away!' (21:1–4)

Although most Christians have interpreted such passages in a figurative sense, this has not always been the case. Chapter 7 below by Kent Eaton, on the nineteenth-century millenarian preacher, John Nelson Darby and the (Plymouth) Brethren, provides an example of a strand of Christian millenarian thinking which attempts to interpret such passages literally. As Neil O'Connor's study (Chapter 8) of a Christian-inspired New Religious Movement, the Worldwide Church of God, illustrates, a fascination with apocalyptic numerology, based on the book of Revelation and the book of Daniel, remains a recurrent theme within many contemporary churches. The Mormons (the Church of Jesus Christ of Latter Day Saints) and the Seventh Day Adventists are two other groups for whom a literal interpretation of such texts has formed a central plank of their teaching. It is not only overtly religious ideologies, however, which display a fascination with apocalyptic thinking. The great scholar of medieval millenarianism, Norman Cohn, was inspired to write his seminal work *The Pursuit of the Millennium* as a result of army intelligence work at the end of the Second World War. The fanaticism of Nazi and Communist ideologues, who shared the notion of a 'prodigious last struggle with a demonised enemy' and Nazi dreams of a thousand-year Reich, struck Cohn as profoundly millenarian, convincing him that these ideologies, which justified any barbarity as a means to an end, had deep and ancient roots.[6]

In a looser sense, as employed by anthropologists, sociologists and historians of religion, 'millenarian' is used to refer to religious or politico-religious movements which have some sort of utopian ideal, usually involving the overthrow of the established order by natural or supernatural means. In many of the instances studied by anthropologists working in small-scale societies these movements envisage the defeat of dominant or oppressive groups and the re-establishment of a pre-colonial status quo.[7] Precisely what such movements have in common is not easy to define. Norman Cohn has used the term 'millenarian' to refer to 'any religious movement inspired by the phantasy of a salvation' which is 'collective, terrestrial, imminent, total and accomplished by supernatural agencies',[8] but, as Arthur (Chapter 3 below) points out, this would exclude consideration of soteriological Buddhism and the notion of Maitreya Buddha as a coming deliverer. While recognizing the necessity to look at each instance in its own historical and cultural context, there are some general points which can be made concerning millenarian movements and beliefs, both in terms of causation and in their symbolic structures as outlined below.

The term 'apocalyptic' has been used several times above in relation to millenarianism, and this word too requires clarification. As already noted the Apocalypse is another name for the Revelation of Saint John, the last work in the Christian canon of the New Testament. Deriving from the Greek word for an 'uncovering' or 'revelation', it is usually taken to refer to a disclosure of the last things, the end of time and second coming of Jesus. More generally, the apocalypse is used to describe a belief in a catastrophic end of the world which will usher in the new age, usually with reference to teachings derived from Christianity. Apocalyptic and millenarian ideas have, therefore, a strong Christian provenance and the central role of Christian doctrine when dealing with the theme of a coming deliverer is reflected in a number of papers in this volume. The chapters by D. P. Davies on the early Christian church, Kent Eaton on nineteenth-century Christian Brethren, Neil O'Connor and Sarah Lewis on the Worldwide Church of God and the Unification Church respectively, all deal with aspects of millenarianism which relate to early Jewish and Christian source documents. These texts should, however, be seen against a broader canvas, and it is to the roots of such millenarian thinking that I will now turn.

3 The roots of millenarianism

One of the best kept secrets in the history of religions is that the origins of soteriological and eschatological thinking (a concern with salvation and the end of time) can be traced to one of the least well-known and understood of the great world religions, Zoroastrianism. Cyril Williams (Chapter 2, below) locates the belief in a deliverer or *Saoshyant* in the ancient faith of the Parsis, whose ethical dualism leads them to view the world in terms of a struggle between good and evil. In his recent work, *Cosmos, Chaos and the World to Come*, Norman Cohn describes the development of Zoroastrian thought as 'a major turning point in the history of human consciousness'. Until around 1500 BCE, Cohn argues, the religions of the ancient world had an essentially static view of the cosmos. It had been set in order by the gods and, although constantly threatened by destructive forces, human, natural and supernatural, it was in essence immutable. Law, custom and stable social relations were seen as reflections of divine order and were therefore religiously sanctioned. A warrior figure, often a young hero god who might have gained power by stealth or trickery, helped keep the forces of chaos at bay. As Cohn notes, Zoroaster's thinking took him in a totally different direction:

> Some time between 1500 and 1200 BC Zoroaster broke out of that static yet anxious world-view. He did so by reinterpreting, radically, the Iranian version of the combat myth. In Zoroaster's view the world was not static, nor would it always be troubled. Even now the world was moving, through incessant conflict, towards a conflictless state. The time would come when, in a prodigious final battle, the supreme god and his supernatural allies would defeat the forces of chaos and their human allies and eliminate them once and for all.[9]

Cohn convincingly demonstrates the influence of Zoroastrian thinking on Jewish and early Christian communities and less directly, one could add, on apocalyptic Islam. One should not conclude, however, that all religions from Zoroaster onwards shared his view of an end time, with its final battle and the destruction of the present order. It is nevertheless a recurrent theme in most of the world religions.

Anthropologist Ioan Lewis focuses not on the chronological development and diffusion of eschatological faiths, but on the ways in which this-worldly and other-worldly elements are present in most religions. Lewis situates apocalyptic and non-apocalyptic faith in the human desire to build a bridge between moral evaluations and mystical forces. The eschatological solution, which postulates the existence of an after-life in which both good and bad will receive their just deserts, is 'chosen by most universalistic religions in their traditional or official forms'.[10] More immediate solutions to human problems and scapegoats for misfortune are also sought by the practitioners of all religions, whatever their formal teachings.[11]

Hinduism, Buddhism, and to some extent Sikhism, form an interesting contrast to Semitic monotheistic religions (see

Chapters 3 and 4, below). Time, in Eastern religions, is viewed as cyclical, so that any deliverer takes their place within the greater cycle of growth and decay. The notion of *karma* in Hinduism rewards individual merit not in an afterlife, but by means of a higher birth in this world, while Buddhists accumulate merit which will enable them finally to escape the round of rebirth and desire. Either way, however, gratification is delayed, and Lewis points out that the daily practice of Buddhism and Hinduism involves recourse to spirits, deities and a theory of 'contagious *karma*' which offers more immediate explanations of fortune or misfortune. Both Eastern and Semitic religions therefore have an official version of moral virtue which is rewarded in a future existence. At a popular level there is a more intimate involvement with supernatural forces which provide immediate explanations for the vicissitudes of everyday life.

The so-called 'primal religions' of small-scale societies, which characteristically focus on the nexus of human relations as opposed to a transcendent metaphysic, share a world-view which is closer to that of the ancient Near Eastern religions than to the Religions of the Book. Deities, ancestors, spirits and other mystical forces are part of the moral fabric of human social intercourse and act as regulatory agents in day-to-day relationships. This is, however, only a trend and not an absolute division. Apocalyptic and millenarian themes are to be found in a wide range of both small-scale and world religions, with 'cargo cults' in Melanesia and Polynesia providing some of the best known examples of millennial movements in a pre-industrial 'tribal' context.[12]

4 Theories of millenarianism

If both millenarian other-worldly and non-millenarian this-worldly beliefs are to be found, potentially, in all religious systems, the question arises as to which factors dispose groups and peoples towards one position as opposed to another. Diffusion and culture contact with Zoroastrianism may have been a deciding factor in precipitating the development of apocalyptic eschatology in some streams of Judaism and Christianity, but do not explain why this initial shift took place, nor why some individuals adopted such beliefs with enthusiasm, while others felt no need to anticipate the end of the present age and birth of a new order. In the case of Zoroastrianism Cohn posits two determinative factors. First, ancient Indo-Iranian religion emphasized the notion of singularity – everything was created out of one.

> Perhaps it was through reflecting on this primordial singularity that Zoroaster arrived at the conviction that in the beginning there had been only one god. Certainly he proclaimed that once upon a time Ahura Mazda, the wholly wise, just and good, had been the one and only god.[13]

This good god had a counter-creation, personified in Angra Mainyu, the forces of evil, which had to be combated. A deep dualism pervaded Zoroaster's thinking, extending to all aspects of life, including attitudes to the body. The good and bad elements of the person, of nature and of human groups were separated and set at odds with one another. Strict adherence to laws of purity aided Ahura Mazda in his battle against Angra Mainyu and the forces of chaos. The strict 'policing of boundaries', both internal and external, is characteristic of groups which feel threatened and vulnerable, and is apparent in the early experience of Zoroastrianism.[14] If Zoroaster had a religious foundation which lent itself to the development of a dualistic embattled philosophy, he also had the typical background and experiences of a millenarian prophet:

> Prophets who promise a total transformation of existence, a total perfecting of the world, often draw their original inspiration from the spectacle not simply of suffering, but of a particular suffering: that engendered by the destruction of an ancient way of life, with its familiar certainties and safeguards. Zoroaster would have been just such a prophet.[15]

This theme of eschatological religion as compensation for lack of real power and as a response to disorientation and misfortune has been explored at some length by anthropologists and sociologists. Cargo cults appear to be a case in point. When missionaries, traders and colonialists made contact with the peoples of the Pacific, particularly in areas such as highland New Guinea, hitherto isolated from the outside world, communities with a stone-age technology were brought face to face with the paraphernalia of Western culture. There developed a widespread belief that European goods (cargo) had a non-human divine source. Europeans may use ships, aircraft, guns, books and trade articles but they were never seen to manufacture them. The ancestors, according to traditional cosmologies, mediated good fortune to their descendants and the initial supposition was that the Europeans were an embodiment of the ancestors coming to bring such wealth to their children. When, however, the new-comers with their superior power and colonial attitudes failed to share the goods the conclusion was drawn that Europeans were deliberately keeping the 'cargo' from the native inhabitants. If not the ancestors, the Whites must have superior access to the ancestors, and efforts were directed to discovering the key which would unlock access to the goods. Mission education, Christianity and the adoption of Western clothes were all tried, without any obvious success. Throughout the 1940s and 1950s, in particular, various prophetic leaders announced that they had discovered the secret of 'cargo' and encouraged their followers to leave their farms and villages, often destroying their belongings, so as to await the ancestors' gifts. The new millennium which the ancestors would usher in would restore the status quo, with the indigenous inhabitants once more in control of their own destiny but enriched by Western manufactured goods.[16]

We have here a close parallel to the Zoroastrian case: a belief system which lent itself to adaptation under new conditions, feelings of disorientation and marginality at a time of rapid social change, and an inspired individual or individuals who could persuade others to follow them. Garry Trompf favours just such an analysis, claiming that:

> So-called 'cargo cults', in fact, are adjustments in the face of intrusions and rapid change, which reflect the time-honoured indigenous reliance on spirit-sanctioned dreams, visions, spirit-possession, supernatural intervention, the revelation of mythic truths or the divulging of a great secret. For significant changes of direction the role of individual leaders or purveyors of spiritual insight was fundamental.[17]

David Aberle also points to deprivation as a factor in millenarian movements. What is important is relative, not absolute deprivation, defined as 'a negative discrepancy between legitimate expectation and actuality'.[18] In order to determine what particular groups regard as deprivation it is necessary to understand the reference points they use to judge both legitimate expectations and their actual circumstances. Aberle notes three such reference points: '(1) one's past versus one's present circumstances; (2) one's present versus one's future circumstances; (3) one's own versus someone else's present circumstances.'[19] Material wealth may be a feature of relative deprivation, but Aberle also mentions behaviour, status and worth as significant, which may reflect an individual or group experience. In practice, two or more of these factors are likely to be combined. In the case of cargo cults the indigenous inhabitants *en masse* found that they suffered a loss of status and sense of worth *vis-à-vis* Europeans. They may have been materially better off than before colonization, but were relatively deprived both compared to the Europeans they met and in relation to their expectation that they too would or should share in the new wealth.

Deprivation may result in attempts at remedial action, or may conversely precipitate feelings of helplessness and despair. The presence of deprivation is not of itself, therefore, sufficient to predict whether people will seek to improve their circumstances, nor whether such attempts 'will have as aims changing the world, transcending it, or withdrawing from it, whether the remedy will be sought in direct action or ritual, and whether it will be sought with the aid of supernatural powers or without'.[20] What is significant, for Aberle, is whether there is a sense of blockage. If the democratic process or some other legitimate, easily attainable means is to hand to remedy the deprivation, millenarian movements are unlikely to occur. If human efforts prove insufficient, there is likely to be recourse to supernatural means. 'And' adds Aberle, 'difficult as it may be to anticipate whether a group's aspiration will be to return to the past, achieve the standards of the outside world, or transcend earthly standards completely, there is usually no serious difficulty in deciding whether, at a particular time, a particular group faces obstacles which are empirically unsurmountable in short-run terms.'[21]

Whether we look at cargo cults, the early Christian communities described by D. P. Davies, the example of the nineteenth-century Brethren in Kent Eaton's chapter, New

Religious Movements such as the Unification Church and Worldwide Church of God, which form the subjects of Sarah Lewis's and Neil O'Connor's contributions, or the Lubavitcher Jews studied by Simon Dien, we can detect instances of relative deprivation, a sense of powerlessness at times of rapid change and the charismatic effect of prophetic individuals who encourage their followers to isolate themselves from the wider society while awaiting the supernatural intervention which will transform their lives for ever.

Chapter 10, by David Shankland, on modern Turkey provides an interesting contrast to the examples cited above. In this case Necmettin Erbakan, the leader of the Welfare Party, the only political party specifically founded on religious (Islamic) principles, won the 1995 general elections with a distinctly millenarian agenda. Erbakan plays on anti-Semitic fears of a worldwide Zionist plot, and, like the leaders of cargo cults, persuades his voters that if they follow him riches will be theirs. 'Thus, in effect, the millennial movement is employing wishful thinking combined with religious belief to cut short what is largely the technical, and highly complicated, process of modernization'.[22]

The Turkish example, as explicated by Shankland, reminds us that while relative deprivation may be a factor in the rise of millenarian politics, with some Muslims feeling disoriented by the secularism of modern Turkey, fearful of the imagined Jewish threat and economically disadvantaged in relation to their more successful European neighbours to the West, millenarianism can also be a tool of the powerful. Conservative Americans working in the nuclear industry belong disproportionately to fundamentalist Protestant churches which look forward to the imminent end of the world, and even see their role in precipitating a nuclear 'Armageddon' as their contribution to that end.[23] Ronald Reagan sought biblical authority for his defence appropriations, quoting Luke 14:31: 'Or what king, going to war against another king, sitteth not down first, and consulteth whether he be able with ten thousand to meet him that cometh against him with twenty thousand.'[24] Reagan famously referred to the Soviet Union as 'the Evil Empire', invoking a dualistic cosmology which takes one straight back to Zoroaster. The theme of conflict between good and evil, drawing on ancient roots is, therefore, by no means confined to the weak. Unlike Erbakan, however, Reagan and the workers in the nuclear weapons programme are apocalyptic rather than strictly millennial. Although millennial movements, in which followers have been encouraged to destroy their goods, separate themselves from the wider society and even commit suicide, have flourished in North America, as elsewhere in recent years, this path is not, as Aberle predicted, favoured by those, like Reagan and his conservative followers, who can achieve their goals by readier political and economic means.

5 Millenarianism and ritual

If deprivation theory can provide some insight into the conditions under which groups are likely to resort to supernatural millenarian solutions to their problems, an understanding of rituals and their symbolic force gives us some clues as to the mechanisms at work which enable people to restructure their behaviour, beliefs and expectations. Maurice Bloch is one anthropologist who has tackled this theme in a book subtitled *The Politics of Religious Experience*.[25] Bloch focuses on the structure of rituals, first described by Arnold van Gennep in 1908. Van Gennep noted that life does not proceed at a uniform rate, but is made up of stages and life crises, such as birth, puberty, marriage, childbirth and death. These life events, calendrical cycles and occasions such as a journey or change of status are marked by rituals whose purpose is to enable the individual to pass from one recognized state to another. All these rituals of transition are marked by three fairly well-defined stages, each of which has its own characteristic form and symbolism. Van Gennep referred to these stages as 'separation', 'transition' and 'incorporation', or 'preliminal', 'liminal' and 'postliminal' (from the Latin *limen*, 'threshold').[26] Bloch, like Van Gennep, sees an irreducible core to ritual behaviour, not in some mystical archetype (as proposed by Mircea Eliade),[27] but in the ways in which human societies conceive of themselves in relation to the natural processes of birth, growth and death. The quasi-universality of the minimal ritual structures identified by Bloch derive 'from the fact that the vast majority of societies represent human life as occurring within a permanent framework which transcends the natural transformative process of birth, growth, reproduction, ageing and death'.[28] Rituals are, according to Bloch, ultimately ordered according to universal human constraints involving the 'simple transformation of the material processes of life in plants and animals as well as humans'.[29] Bloch identifies two elements this process. The first is that it is 'accomplished through a classic three-stage dialectical process, and secondly it involves a marked element of violence or . . . of conquest'.[30] This process is referred to as 'rebounding violence'.

Rituals involve entering a state in which everyday understandings and order are inverted, and notions of weakening and death often symbolize the individual's dissociation from the world, possession by or obedience to higher powers, and a stripping away of limitations. Such a passage into another state 'beyond process' can enable individuals to see themselves as part of something permanent or transcending. It is, however, a limited tactic, as Bloch observes:

> Moving out of this world into another can, however, only be a partial answer to the problem posed by the politico-social requirement of constructing a totality consisting of living beings, which is, unlike its constituent parts, permanent. The reason why the move into the beyond is ultimately politically unsatisfactory is simply that, if you leave this life, you leave this life, and so the constructed totality becomes of no relevance to the here and now.[31]

In practice, rituals allow individuals to leave this world (metaphorically), and enter another realm, and then to return once more to this life. However, as Van Gennep also noted, rituals transform those who participate in or perform them. 'In the return the transcendental is not left behind but continues to be attached to those who made the initial move in its direction; its value is not negated.'[32] Another way of looking at this is to see the return in terms of a conquest of the here and now by the transcendental. The person who has taken part in a ritual can dominate the here and now in a way not possible before the start of the ritual. It is here that Bloch's notion of 'rebounding violence' or conquest (a term which I prefer) comes into play. In many instances the conquest is moral. In Christian eucharistic theology, for instance, the communicant both eats and is absorbed by Jesus Christ, and returns to the here and now nourished and conquered by the divine, enabled to carry out Christ's work in the world. The theme of eating or conquering the vital energies of plant or animal life is characteristic of the culminating stage of a ritual. The ascended Jesus has no materiality – his power is invisible and metaphysical. The communicant must consume a *natural* material substance, taken from the physical world (the bread and wine) in order for the divine, Jesus Christ in the form of the eucharistic offering, to re-enter the world in his 'conquered' followers who are exhorted to 'conquer' in turn.[33]

In many instances, however, the third stage of ritual is marked by actual violence. Empowered by the transcendental, the individuals concerned may seek to conquer others. The 'violence' of a symbolic death of the self and of conquest by the divine is a preliminary to the 'rebounding violence' of the completed ritual: 'the third stage is not seen as a return to the condition left behind in the first stage but as an aggressive consumption of a vitality which is *different* in origin from that which had originally been lost'.[34] In other words, the individual is enjoined to separate from the world and to submit him or herself to the demands of the transcendental in order to acquire a greater power with which to return and conquer (or participate in more forcefully) the here and now.

The insight into millenarianism which Bloch's scheme contributes is that in this instance for some reason the ritual process is not completed. The third stage of re-incorporation into the everyday, renewed by the vitality of the supernatural, does not take place. Rituals are normally conservative in nature, allowing little room for individual expression owing to their formalized structure. Individuals may assent to or disassociate themselves from the symbolic and consensual meanings of a ritual while still participating in it: 'There are, however, occasions when the conditions of life are so obviously troublesome that individual doubts join together and emerge into the open, leading to fundamental and dramatic changes in the rituals and in the images they evoke.'[35] Bloch's language reminds us of the conditions for millenarian movements described by Aberle and others. What can happen when the world is perceived so negatively that people do not want to return to it, is that rituals are aborted at the second stage. The participants submit themselves to the gods or higher powers, partake of the transcendental divine vitality, but do not seek to complete the ritual and reconnect with the here and now. This suggests that millenarian tendencies are politically neutral or disempowering. Millenarians, whether medieval Christians or twentieth-century cultists, characteristically abandon normal economic and reproductive activity, and choose supernatural (or unrealistic) means to achieve their ends. Symbolically, Bloch adds, 'the millennium would be the occasion of a world-wide funeral which all should welcome as it would herald a rebirth in another non-vital and immortal existence'.[36]

Bloch applies his theory of ritual structure to a wide range of examples, including the early church, contrasting the Epistle of Paul to the Romans with later teaching on the virgin birth. Romans, arguably one of the earliest documents in the Christian New Testament canon, is full of suggestions that Paul expected an imminent end to the world. Paul de-emphasizes the role of reproduction, 'Those who have wives should live as though they had none . . . I say this because the world as we know it is passing away' (7:30–31). Christians are asked to share in Christ's death, in the expectation that they will also rise with him, changed into an immortal form: 'I will tell you something that has been secret: that we are not all going to die, but we shall all be changed' (15:51). Although a Jew, Paul argued strongly against compulsory circumcision for Gentile converts. Circumcision rituals contain a strong reaffirmation of life, fertility and the continuation of human society. If Paul expected the imminent end of the world and second coming of Jesus his attitude towards circumcision, marriage, and women more generally, is logical and comprehensible.

As the expectation of the second coming was delayed, and Christian communities established themselves as mainstream social and political units, and not just marginal religious entities, their theology developed accordingly. Paul does not mention the virgin birth, which reflects a very different emphasis from his Epistle to the Romans and other Pauline letters. The belief that Mary was penetrated by the Holy Spirit, rather than by an earthly man, is a powerful statement about the conquest of this world by the divine. Christianity had moved from a millenarian stage, in which Christ's crucifixion and the second coming were prioritized, to a more affirmative state in which 'the re-entry of the divine into the vital through conquest of a woman'[37] was celebrated. Yet again we discover that those who feel that they have a stake in society, or who feel able to fulfil their expectations by political and social means, are likely to develop a theology and ritual expressions which reconnect them to the here and now, whereas those suffering 'relative deprivation' are susceptible to millenarian beliefs, and are likely to develop rituals which emphasize death and a move to the transcendent, without the final conquest of vitality and return to the everyday world. Seen in this light the isolationism, and occasionally self-destructive behaviour of millenarian groups can be understood as an effort to maintain their separation from the rejected world and to hasten their final and unequivocal entry into the transcendent.

6 Counter-trends

The end of the second millennium is perceived by many people as a significant event, with expectations of change and the accompanying uncertainty such change evokes. While we can expect to witness a rise in millenarian anxieties and rhetoric, there are also strong counter-trends. This-worldly, ecologically based religions, whether of Western origin or of indigenous peoples in small-scale societies, are receiving increased attention from a Western populace unhappy with a 'use it, discard it' view of the creation. Space technology and the dream of leaving our fragile planet for a new world 'out there' competes in the popular imagination with community-based action aimed at conservation and the maintenance of sustainable eco-systems. The moving speech of Chief Seattle (1786–1866), a Suquamish leader from the Puget Sound region of the Pacific north-west coast of America, has attracted widespread attention. In 1855 Chief Seattle addressed the Great Tribal Assembly of the Suquamish and sent a letter based on his speech to the President of the United States, referring to a request, which they were hardly in a position to refuse, to sell their land and accept relocation to a reservation. In his speech and letter, Chief Seattle contrasts the attitudes of his own people with those of the white man:

> How can you buy or sell the sky – the warmth of the land? The idea is
> strange to us. Yet we do not own the freshness of the air or the sparkle

of the water. How can you buy them from us? We will decide in our time. Every part of this earth is sacred to my people.[38]

Similar sentiments are attributed to numerous Native Americans faced with the loss of their land from the middle of the nineteenth century onwards. Interestingly, such ecological statements were often made in a millenarian context. Smohalla, a Wanapum man from Washington Territory, which was formed in 1853, is reported to have said,

> You ask me to plough the ground. Shall I take a knife and tear at my mother's bosom: You ask me to dig for stone. Shall I dig under her skin for bones: You ask me to cut grass and make hay and sell it, and be rich like white men. But how dare I cut off my mother's hair?[39]

Smohalla was associated with a millenarian movement of non-treaty Indians known as the 'Dreamers' who looked forward to a return to the pre-contact status quo with the ejection of the whites from the land they sought to control. A common threat to their way of life led to numerous widespread nativistic movements among Native Americans, such as the Ghost Dance Movement of the 1880s and peyote religion of the twentieth century, as well as to the development of theme of a sacred earth mother.[40] Sam Gill argues that there is little evidence of a Mother Earth deity among Native Americans before the twentieth century, and that it should be seen as the result of contact between the First Nations and white Americans, particularly as a reaction to loss of land and the traditional way of life. In a conflict over mineral rights on Navajo land an eighty-four-year-old woman, Asa Bazhonoodah, uses the image of Mother Earth to differentiate Navajo attitudes to the land from those of the white prospectors:

> The Earth is our mother. The white man is ruining our mother. I don't know the white man's ways, but to us the Mesa, the air, the water, are Holy Elements. We pray to these Holy Elements in order for our people to flourish and perpetuate the well-being of each generation.[41]

While the notion of the earth as a female deity may be relatively new, it has become a defining feature of the spirituality of First

Nation peoples in the Americas, and there is no reason to believe that such statements do not draw on pre-contact values regarding the use of the earth's resources.

The rise in interest not only in the spirituality of the First Nation peoples of the Americas, but also in witchcraft, shamanism, druidism and other contemporary forms of paganism, is a sign that many people in Europe and America are actively seeking an ecological spirituality which regards the earth, and not some transcendental realm 'beyond', as their sacred focus. Reward for a good or bad life, and explanations for fortune and misfortune are brought into the warp and weft of day-to-day human relations. The notion of a cosmic battle in which the forces of good will conquer the forces of evil, leading to a time of everlasting peace and goodness, is rejected in favour of an intimate involvement with the sacred in the self and in the world, held in an eternal cycle of birth, growth and decay. Salvation is not sought in a coming deliverer who will gather his (for he is almost invariably male) forces for the final conflict and grant his followers a privileged place in the new order. Instead, there is emphasis on the older idea which holds that human beings are co-responsible for maintaining a divinely appointed social, natural and cosmic harmony. The appointed order may include a religious hierarchy, as among the Ancient Egyptians or Kogi today, or be more egalitarian as in most contemporary forms of (neo)-paganism, but in both instances the health and equilibrium of the present world is the goal.

An article in a recent edition of *Pagan Dawn: The Journal of the Pagan Federation* illustrates this desire of many people for an immediate, intimate and embodied participation in the transcendent.

Last year at Beltane, when most of my Pagan friends were dancing round their Beltane fires, altars and getting up to Goddess-knows-what in the woods and fields, my husband and I were experiencing it slightly differently than in years past . . . we were becoming parents.

Up to my chin in the calming waters of a birthing pool, focusing each contraction on a small Sheila-na-gig given to me by my best friend, I came face to face with the Goddess in a way that I never thought possible while still rooted in flesh . . . I relied on Jim's sometimes gentle and sometimes compelling encouragement and support, and when things reached a point where even he could not help me, I was received by the Great Mother. We were in a space more sacred to me than any physical place on earth, full of light and power and pain and blood, and any woman who has given birth knows that this is a communion like no other. As my daughter emerged from my body, I was myself in that instant born into the Mother Aspect.[42]

If soteriological beliefs have an official status in most world religions, and millenarian doctrines are orthodox within Christianity, this is not to deny that here too there are counter-trends. Both process theology and feminist theology emphasize a contingent creation, and are oriented towards a this-worldly metaphysic. Within the bastions of the Christian academic establishment there are also stirrings. Keith Ward, the Regius Professor of Divinity at Oxford, is described in a review of his book *Religion and Creation* as giving 'overriding importance to setting out his ideas about God the Creator, to certain human values, in particular the need to preserve creaturely freedom in reciprocal interaction with God'. This perspective is deemed to lead to a theology with 'a remarkably anthropomorphic God, who has a history, whose will can be thwarted, and who consequently has feelings of frustration as well as of delight'.[43] A rather anthropocentric view of the world in which '[T]he cosmos, events in nature, and particularly their impingement on human affairs through fortune and mishap, all unfold inexorably in response to man's behaviour towards his fellows' and in which '[N]ature, and the mystical forces which animate it, respond dutifully to whatever dramas occur in social relations', is regarded by Ioan Lewis as a 'profoundly humanitarian view of life' as it focuses on the way in which men and women behave towards one another, and towards other creatures, as the major cause of present and future happiness or despair.[44]

The papers in this volume include both synoptic overviews of millenarian thinking and belief in a coming deliverer in various religious traditions and case studies which allow the dynamics of millenarianism to be explored in more detail. Whether the major religions described, the many different groups within them, and their various offshoots, emphasize or marginalize millenarianism, we cannot afford to ignore the phenomenon. The longing for a coming deliverer and for a final solution to the problems of existence remains seductive, and can give coherence and a sense of common identity to believers. But by staking too much hope on a future existence and a new world order, the exigencies and possibilities of living in the present, in the 'real' world, are undermined. As the various contributions in this book illustrate, there are difficulties in attempting to generalize on a theme which has been taken up and elaborated in such a wide variety of historical and cultural circumstances, but as a response to the human condition millenarianism remains a popular option. It is, however, only one possible reaction, a reaction which is ultimately reductionist and potentially amoral as its focus is directed upward and outward, rather than being centred in the created world in which we live. A theology and spirituality which seeks the imminent in the day-to-day world, and which reinforces human responsibility towards maintaining a sacralized earth is, I would argue, an urgent necessity as we enter the twenty-first century.

Notes

[1] A. Ereira, *The Heart of the World* (London, Jonathan Cape, 1992), 226.

[2] Matthew 23:4–8, 30–1. All biblical quotations are from the *Revised English Bible*.

[3] A succinct account of different calendrical systems is given in M. Westrheim, *Calendars of the World: A Look at Calendars and the Ways We Celebrate* (Oxford, Oneworld, 1993).

[4] See Norman Cohn, *The Pursuit of the Millennium* (London, Secker & Warburg, 1957).

[5] Cf. J. F. C. Harrison, *The Second Coming* (London, Routledge & Kegan Paul, 1979) on eighteenth- and nineteenth-century millenarianism and Damian Thompson, *The End of Time* (London, Sinclair-Stevenson, 1996) on contemporary millennial movements.

[6] 'Pre-millennial tension', interview with Professor Norman Cohn by Derek Thompson, *Fortean Times*, 88 (July 1996), 24.

[7] Cf. C. Seymour-Smith, *Macmillan Dictionary of Anthropology* (London and Basingstoke, Macmillan, 1987), 191–2, and K. Burridge, *New Heaven New Earth* (Oxford, Basil Blackwell, 1969).

[8] N. Cohn, 'Medieval Millenarism', in S. L. Thrupp (ed.), *Millennial Dreams in Action* (The Hague, Mouton & Co., 1962), 31.

[9] *Cosmos, Chaos and the World to Come* (New Haven and London, Yale University Press, 1993), 227.

[10] I. M. Lewis, *Social Anthropology in Perspective* (Cambridge, Cambridge University Press, 2nd edn., 1992), 145.

[11] B. R. T. Wilson draws on many instances from both 'tribal' and 'non-tribal' religions in his book *Magic and the Millennium* (St Albans, Palladin, 1975).

[12] See for instance Burridge, *New Heaven New Earth.*

[13] Cohn, *Cosmos, Chaos,* 81.

[14] See Mary Douglas, *Purity and Danger* (London, Routledge & Kegan Paul, 1966) for examples of this type of boundary maintenance via food taboos and ritual.

[15] Cohn, *Cosmos, Chaos,* 95.

[16] Major studies of such cargo cults include Peter Worsley, *The Trumpet Shall Sound* (London, MacGibbon & Key, 1957) and Peter Lawrence, *Road Belong Cargo* (Manchester, Manchester University Press, 1964).

[17] G. W. Trompf, *Melanesian Religion* (Cambridge, Cambridge University Press, 1991), 26.

[18] D. F. Aberle, 'A note on relative deprivation theory as applied to millenarian and other cult movements', in Thrupp, *Millennial Dreams in Action,* 209.

[19] Ibid.

[20] Ibid., 211.

[21] Ibid., 212

[22] Shankland, below, p. 230. See also Shankland, 'The demise of republican Turkey's social contract?', *Government and Opposition,* 31, no. 3 (Summer 1996), 304–21.

[23] Cf. Brian Gates, 'Nirvana, nukes and nothingness', in *The Shap Handbook on World Religions in Education* (London, Shap Working Party on World Religions, Commission for Racial Equality, 1987), 154–5. He points out that Robert Oppenheimer made a deliberate connection between the *Bhagavadgita*'s vision of 'a great melt down' and the first nuclear explosions in 1945 in which he himself had had a decisive role (p. 155).

[24] K. C. Boon, *The Bible Tells Them So: The Discourse of Protestant Fundamentalism* (London, SCM, 1989), 21.

[25] M. Bloch, *Prey into Hunter: The Politics of Religious Experience* (Cambridge, Cambridge University Press, 1992).

[26] Van Gennep's ideas have been elaborated by Victor Turner, who focused particularly on the middle or liminal stage of a rite of passage. Turner used the term 'communitas' to describe the bonds commonly formed between neophytes in the liminal stage of a rite of passage, whether they are Ndembu boys secluded together during initiation, pilgrims on a common journey or the hippies of the 1960s and 1970s who sought to extend the stage of liminality and communitas

indefinitely. See Turner, *Dramas, Fields and Metaphors: Symbolic Action in Human Society* (Ithaca, NY, Cornell University Press, 1974) and *The Ritual Process: Structure and Anti-Structure* (Ithaca, NY, Cornell Paperbacks, 1977).

[27] M. Eliade, *The Myth of the Eternal Return* (Princeton, Princeton University Press, 1974).

[28] Bloch, *Prey into Hunter*, 3.

[29] Ibid., 4.

[30] Ibid.

[31] Ibid.

[32] Ibid., 5.

[33] The theme of sacrificing oneself to God, sharing in the crucifixion of Christ, and being empowered in turn by him to be his vehicle in the world is made explicit in most Christian eucharistic liturgies. One of the post-communion prayers in the Anglican Church in Wales liturgy contains the words: 'Wherefore, we offer and present unto thee, O Lord, ourselves, our souls and bodies, to be a reasonable, holy and living sacrifice unto thee, beseeching thee to keep us by thy grace, in this holy fellowship and to enable us to do all those good works which thou has prepared for us to walk in . . .' Another reads, 'we thank thee for feeding us with the Body and Blood of thy Son Jesus Christ through whom we offer to thee our souls and bodies to be a living sacrifice. Send us out in the power of thy Spirit to live and work to thy praise and glory'. *The Book of Common Prayer for Use in The Church in Wales* (1984), 16–17.

[34] Ibid., 6.

[35] Ibid., 85.

[36] Ibid., 90.

[37] Ibid., 95.

[38] From Chief Seattle's speech and letter to the President of the United States in 1855, published by USPG as a resource pack, *Testimony–Chief Seattle* (n.d.). An imaginative version of a speech by Chief Seattle delivered in 1854, much embellished by Ted Perry, a Hollywood scriptwriter, achieved a wide circulation in the United States and Europe, testifying to the considerable interest and investment many white Americans and Europeans have had in 'discovering' an ecologically sustainable 'authentic' Native American spirituality.

[39] Cited in S. D. Gill, *Earth Mother: An American Story* (Chicago and London, University of Chicago Press, 1991), 40.

[40] See S. D. Gill, *Native American Religions: An Introduction* (Belmont, CAL, Wadsworth, 1982), 166–71.

[41] Gill, *Earth Mother*, 142.

[42] Lisa Bennett, 'The concerns of a pagan parent . . . children of the Great Mother', *Pagan Dawn: The Journal of the Pagan Federation*, 120 (Lammas 1996, London), 14.

[43] Paul Helm, 'Smoothing out the creases with too much panache', review of *Religion and Creation* by Keith Ward, *The Tablet* (19 October 1996), 1270.

[44] Lewis, *Social Anthropology*, 148.

Further reading

Bloch, M., *Prey into Hunter: The Politics of Religious Experience* (Cambridge, Cambridge University Press, 1992).

Bull, M. (ed.), *Apocalypse Theory and the Ends of the World* (Oxford, Blackwell, 1995).

Burridge, K., *New Heaven New Earth: A Study of Millenarian Activities* (Oxford, Basil Blackwell, 1969).

Cohn, N., *The Pursuit of the Millennium: Revolutionary Millenarians and Mystical Anarchists of the Middle Ages* (London, Secker & Warburg, 1957).

——, *Cosmos, Chaos and the World to Come: The Ancient Roots of Apocalyptic Faith* (New Haven and London, Yale University Press, 1993) .

Harrison, J. F. C., *The Second Coming: Popular Millenarianism 1780–1850* (London, Routledge & Kegan Paul, 1979).

Lawrence, P., *Road Belong Cargo: A Study of the Cargo Movement in the Southern Madang District New Guinea* (Manchester, Manchester University Press, 1964).

Lewis, I. M., *Social Anthropology in Perspective: The Relevance of Social Anthropology* (Cambridge, Cambridge University Press, 2nd edn, 1992).

Thompson, Damian, *The End of Time: Faith and Fear in the Shadow of the Millennium* (London, Sinclair-Stevenson, 1996).

Thrupp, S. L. (ed.), *Millenial Dreams in Action: Essays in Comparative Study* (The Hague, Mouton & Co., 1962).

Trompf, G. W., *Melanesian Religion* (Cambridge, Cambridge University Press, 1991).

Turner, V., *Dramas, Fields and Metaphors: Symbolic Action in Human Society* (Ithaca, NY, Cornell University Press, 1974).

——, *The Ritual Process: Structure and Anti-Structure* (Ithaca, NY, Cornell Paperbacks, 1977).

Van Gennep, A., *The Rites of Passage* (London, Routledge & Kegan Paul, 1960).

Westrheim, M., *Calendars of the World: A Look at Calendars and the Ways We Celebrate* (Oxford, Oneworld, 1993).

Wilson, B. R., *Magic and the Millennium* (St Albans, Paladin, 1975).
Worsley, P., *The Trumpet Shall Sound: A Study of 'Cargo' Cults in Melanesia* (London, MacGibbon & Key, 1957).

2

Deliverance and human destiny in Zoroastrianism

CYRIL WILLIAMS

Zoroaster has been described as the first apocalypt. The term 'apocalyptic' generally indicates revelatory disclosure of what was previously veiled from human knowledge and has to do with events surrounding the fate of humanity and the last things. It has been used to designate a type of literature and also the kind of religion or ideas which found expression in such literature disclosing the secrets of the beyond.[1] The prophet, Zoroaster, it is claimed, was 'the first to teach the doctrine of individual judgement, Heaven and Hell, the future resurrection of the body, the general last judgement, and life everlasting for the reunited soul and body'.[2]

Zoroastrianism, the religion of ancient Iran, is practised today only by the Parsis of India, some in Pakistan, and a few pockets in eastern Iran. Yet, at one time, it is presumed to have been the state religion of three empires: the Achaemenian (c.550–300 BCE), the Arsacid or Parthian (c.141 BCE–224 CE) and the Sasanian (c.224–439 CE). Today, Zoroastrians are principally associated in popular thought with fire-worshipping in their fire temples and as people who dispose of their dead by exposure on *dakhmas* or towers of silence. It is not generally realized that the sacred fire is for them the symbol of Truth and that it was their strict laws governing pollution, still surviving in the Vendidad, a section of the sacred scriptures, which eventually led them to forsake the practice of interment. Zoroastrianism is a mono-theistic religion with a strong moral emphasis in the context of an ethical dualism, namely the struggle between good and evil. Everything in the Gathas, its earliest scriptures (being hymns ascribed to the prophet Zoroaster himself), is regarded in the context of a struggle between Ahura Mazda, upholder of *asha* ('the right'), and Dregvant who opposes the right and supports *druj* ('lie' or 'falsehood'). Most scholars are now prepared to believe that this religion has exercised an influence upon the Abrahamic faiths of Judaism, Christianity and Islam, particularly in the doctrines of the last things and the destiny of humankind, while in its expectation of a deliverer it has also influenced Buddhism, another of its rivals at one time. Yet, it has not received the attention it deserves, probably primarily because of the daunting linguistic challenges it presents and the lacunae in our knowledge concerning its 'lost' scriptures. Of those who have challenged the claim of Iranian influence on Judaism in recent times none has written as forcibly as Jacob Neusner in a well-documented article where he remarks that 'Iranian "influences" on the culture and religion of Babylonian Jewry, have been for the most part exaggerated and overrated'.[3] Of course, influence need not all be in one direction, and Zoroastrianism itself was probably influenced by other cultures including Judaism. In fact, Zoroastrianism has been compared to an artichoke, each layer has external influence overlaid.

Zoroastrians believed in the inseparable unity of sound and sense and for long centuries eschewed the transcription of sacred matters. In fact, their scriptures were not committed to writing until the fifth century CE. Prior to that, the tradition had been an oral one and when Alexander the Great in the fourth century BCE conquered Persia many of the priests were slaughtered. A major part of the oral tradition died with them, but fortunately the liturgical elements have survived in the Vendidad.

The scriptures of Zoroastrianism are known as the Avesta, the earliest part of which, as mentioned, are the Gathic hymns. These were most carefully preserved in the oral liturgies by the priests who officiated in the temples and performed the rituals. The language of the Gathas differs somewhat from the remainder of extant Avestan literature and contains terms which are not encountered elsewhere and may well have had a technical significance which eludes modern investigation. Many words, however, have affinities with expressions in the Rig-Veda, the earliest Hindu, or any, scriptures, and strongly indicate at some stage a common Indo-Iranian background and maybe even an earlier Indo-European heritage. This background already had notions of heaven and hell and of a golden age. Similarly, the Yashts (hymns in praise of minor divine entities), which were composed in the various periods of Zoroastrianism, reflect Aryan traits. Studies have been undertaken which compare the Avesta and the Vedas, resulting in attempts at the reconstruction of a common heritage before the separation of Iranians and Indians.

Zoroastrian studies make many linguistic demands on the student: Gathic Avestan (Avestan of later literature), Middle Persian or Pahlavi (the official language of the Arsacid dynasty of Persia), and Sasanian Pahlavi (the official language of the Sasanian dynasty before Islamic conquest), not to mention Arabic and modern Persian and some languages of northern India of more recent times. In addition to sacred writings there are inscriptional texts, some in cuneiform, such as those of Darius (521–486 BCE) at Behistan and Xerxes (485–465 BCE) at Persepolis. While there is no way of assessing what was lost in the silencing of a great part of the oral tradition during the Greek conquest, Zoroastrianism suffered a further loss of a major part of its written Avesta during subsequent Arabian, Turkish and especially Mongolian invasions, when many libraries which included precious books were destroyed. Fortunately, however, in the ninth century CE a wave of literature written in Pahlavi reached final redaction and some of these books, such as the Denkard and Bundahishn, offer summaries of commentaries (*Zand*) of some of the lost Avestan books (*nasks*). They also provide selections worked into sustained themes, but this literature, of course, depends on the veracity of the previous oral repetitions. To complicate matters still further there was a change of language when Arabic replaced Persian as the medium in the tenth century.

Yet, from the Gathas to the Pahlavi Bundahishn, representing a span of more than fifteen centuries, in spite of inevitable modifications, one can find a continuity of tradition, especially in its eschatology. We continue to hear, for instance, of a *Saoshyant* ('Deliverer'), the Bridge of Separation, the resurrection of the dead, the reward of the good and the punishment of the wicked, a trial by molten metal and the ultimate triumph of good over evil. Naturally, as one would expect, new aspects or emphases are introduced and greater detail advanced in the Middle Persian literature, but there is a solid core of expectation in early

Zoroastrianism which adumbrates several aspects in later eschatology and enables one to speak of continuity. In the Gathas the idea of salvation tends to be negative and construed as deliverance from evil perils, but the idea of *Saoshyant* as bringer of benefit is also present.[4] The word occurs several times in the Gathas, and is translated 'Saviour' or 'Redeemer', but since it had not acquired a technical meaning, and because of the Judaeo-Christian connotations of the terms Saviour or Redeemer, I prefer to employ the word 'Deliverer' for *Saoshyant*. It is found in both singular and plural forms, and in this oscillation a singular may have a corporate or communal connotation but there is no doubt that in certain contexts it refers to a definite individual deliverer. As Hinnells reminds us,[5] even in some of the older Avestan texts such as the Zamad Yasht he has defined functions, one of which is the restoration of the world. Hinnells is convinced that many of the beliefs concerning the Saoshyant which are found in later Pahlavi books are indeed Avestan and combine selections from the earlier scriptures in sustained themes. This is all the more remarkable when one considers the early date which must be assigned to the Gathas if they are to be attributed to Zoroaster himself.

Classical writers like Aristotle gave the prophet an impossibly early date of 9000 BCE, while early Western investigators tended to make him a contemporary of the Hebrew prophets of the seventh–sixth centuries BCE, but a recent scholar, Mary Boyce, argues for a much earlier date, placing him *c.*1500–1200 BCE. These differences of time-scale serve to underline the hazards of attempting to speak of influences when our dating is so uncertain. Yet similarities offer a fascinating attraction and have generated much speculation.

A student of Zoroastrianism soon experiences the frustrations caused by the apparent lack of order in the accounts given of final events in the various documents. Just as the origin of Zoroaster's cosmogony could be sought in his eschatology, the two being closely interdependent, so, in studying Zoroastrianism, a good case could be made for a methodology of 'advancing backwards'. Commencing with what is known of the rituals and practices of a traditionally conservative community like the Parsis, what has been preserved and regarded as central to the faith by its modern practitioners in their liturgies can be noted, for the act of worship has evolved over many centuries, and some of the material derives from the ancient Yashts. While proselytism has not been entirely unknown in Zoroastrianism in the past, few non-Zoroastrians have had the privilege of entering their temples. It is possible, however, to examine prayers in daily use such as the selections contained in the Khorda, which is known as the Little Avesta. Moreover, I maintain that the Pahlavi religious system reflects the ideas of the Gathas, which are accessible in translation.

Attempts to arrange the Gathas in proper chronological order have failed, for additions seem to have been made on various occasions even by the prophet himself. Mary Boyce has offered a rearrangement which seeks to elicit the doctrinal content of the Gathas as clearly as possible.[6] As mentioned, some of the notions encountered in the Gathas have their roots far back in time, so that one could speak of an Indo-Iranian culture and even earlier. For instance, the idea of a difficult crossing, such as over a bridge, to a post-mortem existence is encountered in many ancient cultures and preliterate communities. It takes various forms, of course. Among some Native Americans, for instance, the trial consists of crossing over a slippery log. The expression 'House of Song' in the Gathas, the abode of the blessed, occurs also in Vedic literature (Rig Veda 10:135) which shows other affinities such as the conception of *rta* ('order') corresponding to *asha* ('right') in Zoroastrianism. In the Gathas, there are references to both individual and collective judgements. At the end of life the individual has to cross the Bridge of Separation and Zoroaster himself will accompany the righteous across and lead them to the House of the Good Mind. The fate of the wicked differs, for their own souls and consciences torment them and their destiny is a life of darkness and woe in the House of the Lie. Zaehner, however, contrasted the Gathic view regarding the fate of the wicked and that found in later Zoroastrianism. He states that the Prophet seems to have regarded the torments of the dead as being eternal, while in later Zoroastrianism the souls of the dead are released in the last days.[7] In both versions, people's fates relate to past morality. Those who have chosen to follow *asha* go to the abode of light while the followers of *druj* go to the dwelling of darkness. Another feature in effecting the separation is introduced in the Gathas, without dispensing with either the idea

of the Bridge of Separation or the notion of Ahura Mazda as the
agent of retribution, that is the trial by a river of molten metal
which will separate good men from the evil. As Duchesne-
Guillemin remarks, the separation is made by Ahura Mazda
himself in a way 'in which divine preference traditionally
manifests itself – by the ordeal of fire and molten metal'.[8] The
duplication of the trials is proclaimed without comment.

Zoroastrianism has been described by some as 'optimistic'
since it teaches the triumph of good over evil, while others
disagree since the triumph is delayed until the end of time and,
meanwhile, many vicissitudes are to be encountered. The promise
of future recompense, they argue, does not minimize the
tribulations of the interim period. There is also an ambivalence in
Zoroaster's expectation; on occasion he believes the end is
imminent and that he himself will see the establishing of Ahura
Mazda's kingdom, and at other times the end is in a far-off
future. In Yasna 48, Zoroaster himself enquires of Ahura Mazda
as to when the righteous will triumph, and his words could be
construed as meaning that he regards himself as the future
Saoshyant or another: 'May the future Deliverer know what his
destiny will be' (v. 9). Again (v. 2),

> Tell me the things which thou knowest, O Lord,
> Shall the righteous man defeat the wicked one, O Wise One,
> Even before the coming of the punishments which thou hast
> > conceived?
> For this is known as the good renewal of existence.

The answer given is veiled in obscurity, like much else in the
Gathas, but it is clear that Dominion, Devotion and Righteousness will have their part to play, and in verse 12 the Deliverer is
thought of collectively in terms of the community of the
righteous, that is, persons who embody the qualities inspired by
the divine entities in their acts. They are referred to as the future
deliverers (*saoshyants*) and the foes of Fury. Any person, therefore, who follows the path of righteousness participates in the
work of the *Saoshyant*. In Yasna 43, however, the reference is
presumably to the *Saoshyant* as a single individual (v. 3):

> And may that man attain the better than good, he who would teach us
> the straight paths of salvation – those of the material world and of the

mind, leading to the true heights where dwells the Lord; a faithful man, of good lineage, holy like Thee, O Mazda.[9]

Zoroaster, probably experiencing doubt caused by the delay in the coming of the Deliverer, asks that visible signs be given him to know the judge that shall heal existence (Yasna 44:16) and an indication of the deeds he will perform (Yasna 31:16). Doubt is short-lived and confident faith restored in the rightness of his forecast of deliverance for the godly and doom for the wicked, who are deemed punished by their own soul and their own conscience and to become inmates of the house of Evil (Yasna 46:11, cf. Yasna 51:13). Zoroaster intercedes on behalf of members of his own family, in spite of their previous hostility towards him, and they too shall dwell with the Lord amid abundance (v. 16). This spirit of forgiveness is by no means universally sustained by the Prophet and there is one episode which reminds one of the New Testament reference which could be considered as a lapse in the case of the regenerated St Paul: 'Alexander the coppersmith did me great harm; the Lord will requite him for his deeds' (2 Timothy 4:14). In Zoroaster's case, the misdeed of the minion of the *kavaya* ('sorcerer prince') at the Bridge of the Winter is linked with his punishment at the Bridge of Separation (Yasna 51:12,13):

> The minion of the sorcerer prince, at the Bridge of Winter,
> Offended Zarathustra Spitama by refusing him shelter,
> Him and his beasts of burden who came to him shivering with cold.
> Thus does the evil one's conscience forfeit the assurance of the straight (path);
> His soul (?) Stripped naked (?) Shall be afraid at the Bridge of Separation,
> Having strayed from the path of Righteousness
> By its deeds and those of his tongue.[10]

These passages clearly illustrate that Ahura Mazda is a god of justice, retribution is a crucial and dominant factor in the future hope of the devotee and that the Prophet himself has confidence in the ultimate triumph of good over evil. His God brings hurt to the wicked and benefit to the righteous. He gives salvation or

perdition and, in the Gathas, immortality to the righteous and
torments which are everlasting for the wicked (Yasna 45:7).
Those who withstand the foes of Ahura Mazda and the enemies
of the Deliverer will find the latter as a friend, a brother or father
(Yasna 45:11).

While the Gathas frequently refer to the Last Day and the final
judgement, and even anticipate in embryonic fashion the
resurrection of the dead, the ninth-century Pahlavi literature
gives a more detailed description of what is to come. This
literature, produced under Islamic rule, when Zoroastrianism was
becoming, increasingly, a minority faith, contains selections from
the Zand (commentary) of lost Avestan works, and by comparing
these with the commentary of extant Avestan texts, investigators
have surmised the content of some of the missing material. The
method, of course, lends itself to much speculation, but where
the teaching elaborates on what is already incipient in the Gathas,
we can be reasonably sure in speaking of a degree of continuity of
thought. In the Bundahishn, for instance, Zoroaster's concepts of
a Last Day, a final judgement and the resurrection of the dead are
set out more distinctly. The Prophet's eschatology is related to his
cosmogonic ideas, which in turn indicate indebtedness to ancient
creation myths. In Iranian eschatology, the final events will see
the establishing of Ahura Mazda's kingdom on earth which will
again attain its pristine state as when it was first created.

The nature of these coming events, however, cannot be fully
appreciated without reference to the Zoroastrian conception of
time – its notion of a world year and the significance of the
coming *Saoshyants* within it. According to Boyce, it was during
the Achaemenian period that Persian scholar priests encountered
the theory held by Babylonian astronomers about the cosmic year
and its division into three eras. It is further suggested that it was
probably Zurvanites, worshippers of Zurvan, the divinization of
Time, who first sought to adapt it to Zoroastrianism.[11] In this
scheme, known history is divided into three millennia, the first
one being ushered in by Zoroaster himself, the next two by the
first and second World Deliverer respectively, namely, Ukshyat-
ereta (Ushedar, Pahl.) and Ukshyat-nemah (Ushedarmah, Pahl.).
Characteristic of these millennia is that a period of goodness and
prosperity is in each case followed by anarchy and decline.
However, when the true *Saoshyant*, the third World Deliverer,

appears, he will begin the work of world renewal (Frasho-kereti, Pahl. Frashegird) with the resurrection of the dead, the Last Judgement and the conquest of evil. History will cease when Ahura Mazda establishes his kingdom here on earth and he will reign for ever and ever.

Certain apocalyptic texts sought to elaborate this hope in a coming World Deliverer. In expansions of legendary material each of three *Saoshyants* are presented as sons of Zoroaster born in a miraculous manner from three virgins. A Bundahishn account mentions how Zoroaster's seed when he went 'near unto (*his* wife) Hvovi . . . had dropped on *the* earth', and another tells of the miraculous preservation of the seed in the depth of the sea Kayansah (now identified as Lake Kasaoya). The account reads:

> As regards these three sons of Zaratust, such – as Usetar, Usetarmah and Sosiyans, *one* – says: 'Before Zaratust wedded, they *had* – consigned *the* glory *of the* waters, that is *to the* yazat Anahit.' *They* say: 'Even – now *they* are seeing three lamps glowing at night, in *the* bottom of the sea; and each one *of them* will – arrive, when *it is* their – own cycle'. *It* – *will* so happen that a virgin will – go to the water of Kayansah in order to – wash *her* head; *the* glory will – mingle within her body, *and she* – will be pregnant; they will, one *by* one, be – born thus in *their* – own cycle.[12]

In the tradition, each Deliverer born ushered in his own millennium. The third and last to be born would be the true *Saoshyant*, whose coming would herald the end of time and the conquest of evil. The Bundahishn mentions that the sun will stand at the zenith of the sky at the coming of Sosiyans, *son of* Zaratust. The Bahman Yasht repeats many of the same predictions with some variations of detail – for instance at the coming of the *Saoshyant* the sun shall stand for thirty days, people will turn to the true faith and become vegetarians. Noxious creatures will be destroyed and the dead resurrected. One cannot fail to notice similarities in the Zoroastrian eschatology to features in the Judaeo-Christian literature, and even those who claim a special development in the latter's doctrine of the Last Judgement allow that it may have derived from Zoroastrianism. In the case of Zoroaster, while he looks forward to a coming age of bliss, in spite of the certainties advanced as in passages in the Zervaniteinfluenced Bundahishn, it remains unclear whether this golden age will be terrestrial or in an afterworld beyond death. The fact is that ancient features remain alongside new traits in thought about renewal of existence and the conquest of evil. The question of Zoroastrian influence on other faiths cannot be explored here, but two features which found favour in apocalyptic literature in more than one culture can at least be mentioned – namely, the allegory of a sequel of dynasties in terms of various metals, and the doctrine of the resurrection of the body. On the former, one can find similarities between the Bahman Yasht – where Zoroastrian teaching comes interwoven with much older material – and the biblical book of Daniel, which has been hailed as the first great apocalyptic work in the literature of Judaism. This is not to say that the scheme wherein four metals correspond to empires or dynasties does not have parallels in other cultures also, both Eastern and Western, but the opportunity of historical diffusion in other instances would not be as likely. In the Bahman Yasht, which is probably based on an even earlier Yasht, the vision of the dynasties employs the analogy of a tree with four branches:

> Auharmazd spoke to Zaratust the Spitaman thus:
> That root of a tree which thou sawest, and those four branches, are the four periods which *will* come. That of gold is when I and thou converse, *and* King Vistasp shall accept the religion, and shall demolish the figures of the demons, *but* they *themselves* remain for . . . concealed proceedings.
>
> And that of silver is the reign of Ardakhshir the Kayan king (Kai shah), and that of steel, is the reign of the glorified (anoshakruban) Khusro, son of Kevad, and that which was mixed with iron is the evil sovereignty of the demons with dishevelled hair of the race of Wrath, and when it is the end of the tenth hundredth winter (*sato zim*) of thy millennium, O Zaratust the Spitaman.[13]

The names which appear are of known real personages, which underlines the fact that Zoroastrianism was a world-affirming religion at this stage. Apocalyptic patterns occur likewise in the Apocryphal Enoch literature and in the Dead Sea texts, and Zoroastrian influences have been claimed, for instance, in a correspondence between the Amesha Spentas (the Holy Immortals, and helpers of Ahura Mazda) and Jewish angelology, while the concept of Angra Mainyu, the evil one later known as

Ahriman, has been compared to the Antichrist of Christian apocalyptic. A previous generation of scholars, remarkable though their contribution was, were perhaps too prone to speak of influences wherever they detected similarities. One has to concede, however, that the passage in Bahman Yasht and the account of the vision in Daniel 2 seem to have shared a similar allegorical method. There, Daniel recounts for the king, Nebuchadnezzar, his dreams and provides an interpretation of the image seen by the monarch: 'As for this image, his head was of fine gold, his breast and his arms of silver, his belly and his thighs of brass, his legs of iron, his feet part of iron and part of clay.'

Then Daniel proceeds to describe the stone 'cut out without hands', which smote and broke the feet of the image into pieces. In his interpretation, the stone signifies the setting up of a kingdom of God 'which shall never be destroyed', and 'shall stand for ever' (Daniel 2:44). Commentators have understood the allusions in Daniel as references to specific eras in history – Assyria, Media, Persia, Macedonia – and champions of Iranian influence have seen in the sequence support for their claim. The triumph of the kingdom of God over the kingdoms of the world, a basic idea in the book of Daniel, recalls the final conquest of evil associated in Zoroastrianism with Ahura Mazda's establishing of his kingdom and the coming of the third Saoshyant. However, influence cannot be determined without being sure of the dating of the documents concerned. Furthermore, it seems futile to endeavour to determine the precise reference and chronology of the expectations described in Zoroastrian apocalyptic literature, especially the timing of the final event. Like so many modern-day prophets predicting the end of time, Zoroastrians often had to postpone the advent of the events associated with a Deliverer!

More intriguing, in my view, is that the Iranian literature advances a doctrine of the resurrection of the body. Zoroastrianism, in contrast to Zervanian-Manichaeism, the pessimistic world-renouncing faith of Sasanian times with its hostile attitude to the physical, has a high regard for the body as well as the soul. It is more akin to the Hebraic view of a person as an animated body, rather than the Orphic idea of an incarnate soul. Apocalyptic sources in Jewish literature, especially in post-exilic times, also refer to bodily resurrection. For instance, it is explicit in the book of Daniel already mentioned. There we read (12:2): 'And many of them that sleep in the dust of the earth shall awake, some to everlasting life, and some to shame *and* everlasting contempt.'

In some canonical Hebraic scriptures, as in Isaiah 26:19, resurrection was restricted to the righteous, but here, the resurrection of both wicked and righteous is proclaimed, and again – as in Zoroastrianism – a different fate awaits them. What is implicit in the early Gathas becomes central in the Pahlavi literature. Even so, as in the Bundahishn, there are discrepancies between the various accounts – for example, of the nature of the resurrection – which challenge attempts at producing a coherent rendering. However, at Bundahishn 30:7, *all*, good and bad, will be raised up. This account is in response to the question addressed by Zoroaster to Ahura Mazda as to how the resurrection occurs. In reply, Ahura Mazda declares that surely it must be easier to recreate what was once than to create *de novo*:

> First, the bones of Gayomard are roused up, then those of Mashya and Mashyoi, then those of the rest of mankind; and in the fifty seven years of Soshyans they prepare all the dead *and* all men stand up; whoever is righteous *and* whoever is wicked, every human creature, they rouse up from the spot where its life departs.[14]

Again, it is virtually impossible to give an ordered account of the various trials which will befall both righteous and wicked before their final separation. Suffice to say that the delights of the righteous are represented, as is the terrible plight of the wicked. In the first separation of the good and the bad, their sojourn in heaven and hell, respectively, is only for a short period of three days and nights, for it is followed by another trial, namely, that of molten metal, which seems to the righteous as warm milk. In the renovation of the universe initiated by the *Saoshyant*, by order of the creator, he has his assistants, fifteen righteous men and the same number of righteous damsels, who perform a sacrificial ceremony in the slaughter of the ox Hadhayos, and from it prepare hush, a sacred beverage which they give 'to all men, and all men become immortal for ever and everlasting'. In the restoration, families are reunited and 'they act as now in the world, but there is no begetting of children' (30:26). Every individual is given by *Saoshyant* and his assistants, by the order of the creator Ahura Mazda, 'the reward and recompense suitable to *his* deeds', whether it be the bliss of paradise or the stench and pollution of hell. Finally, the evil powers are vanquished and even hell becomes purified in the molten metal. It is brought back for the prosperity of the world, and the renovation arises in the universe by the will of Ahura Mazda, and the world is immortal and everlasting (30:32–3). It is interesting to note, in view of the prophecy of Isaiah 40:4 about making every mountain and hill low, and the readiness of Hebraic and other cultures to regard certain mountains as sacred, that mountains here are regarded as the work of the evil spirit and will disappear with their author in the renovation, and so will cold and ice.

If the chronology of the Bundahishn is accepted, the millennium of Zoroaster ended in 593–635 CE, which would place our present age in the millennium of his second posthumous son, Ushedharma. The Denkard, like the Bundahishn, assigns the renovation to the time and coming of the Saoshyant, the last of the posthumous sons of Zoroaster, at the end of the third millennium. In considering the fate of individuals the Denkard recalls the Gathic trial of the Chinvat Bridge as the means of separating the righteous and wicked. According to Zoroastrian soteriology only those deemed just will be able to cross the bridge; for the evil, it will become narrow as a razor's edge and they will fall into hell. In the case of the just, three days after the separation of soul and body in death, they will meet their *daena*, their 'conscience' or 'true self', in the form of a young maiden of fifteen, the age of maturity in ancient Iran. While the Denkard speaks of grades of position and places in heaven and hell it also introduces 'between the two, the place of the ever-stationary, those having good works *and* sin' (8:14.8).

The notion of experiencing heavenly relations through dreams and induced ecstasies was not unfamiliar in the Zoroastrian tradition. The vision of Zoroaster himself recounted in Yasna 43 has been so explained. Accounts of heaven and hell derived from visionary experiences seem to have exercised profound influence in the later Zoroastrian tradition. In this later development, one which gripped the popular mind was the *Ardā Wirāz Nāmag* which has been compared to Dante's *Divine Comedy*. It is assigned to the late Sasanian period.[15] Wirāz's account of his out-of-body experiences has been said to represent the culmination of all the Middle Iranian apocalyptic tradition both in the content and technique. Here, the bliss of Paradise is vividly described, but the torments of Hell even more so. It also refers to another trial in the Zoroastrian catalogue of events at the Chinvat Bridge, namely, the weighing of the just and the wicked in the scales held by the righteous Rashn in his hand. The work was written at a time when the old religion was in a declining condition, and the intention was to restore the hold of the ancient faith and its moral code. It would seem that the horrors of hell so vividly described had a greater effect than the attractions of heaven, and induced strong men to cry. Previously, for instance, the Chinvat Bridge had been understood by interpreters symbolically, but in later Zoroastrian literature it is real and the places on which it stands identified.

Another text, probably Persian, which needs to be taken into account in any discussion of the coming deliverer in Zoroastrianism, is the oracle of Hystaspes, a reconstruction of which has been offered by Professor John Hinnells.[16] Having assessed the evidence for and against, his conclusion is that the saviour expected here is the Zoroastrian *Saoshyant*:

> . . . there are three facts which suggest that the figure was the Soshyant [*sic*]: the thoroughly Zoroastrian nature of the apocalyptic imagery; the plausibility of the idea of Zoroastrian texts or oracles containing anti-Roman sentiment; and the fact that the person and work of the Soshyant were known to the West.

Some earlier commentators who had placed Zoroaster in the sixth century BCE identified Hystaspes with Vishtaspa, the patron king of the prophet. Modern critics reject such an allusion and Hinnells is probably nearer the mark when he assigns the oracle to a first-century date, 'if not earlier', and regards its dating as significant for the studies of Zoroastrian apocalyptic and for theories of the latter's influence on Judaeo-Christian traditions. Without developing that theme further, one can nevertheless declare that the disasters and vicissitudes predicted for the earth and its inhabitants in the oracle make biblical and present-day forecasts of doom quite innocuous.

In conclusion one can state that any discussion of millenarian hope cannot ignore Zoroastrianism, and maybe our indebtedness will acquire greater recognition as our knowledge of the Prophet and his teaching increases.

Notes

[1] Tord Olsson, 'The apocalyptic activity', in David Hellolm (ed.), *Apocalypticism in the Mediterranean World and the Near East* (Uppsala, 1983), 21; 2nd edn. (Tübingen, Mohr, 1989).

[2] M. Boyce, *Zoroastrians: Their Religious Beliefs and Practices* (London, Routledge & Kegan Paul, 1979), 29.

[3] Jacob Neusner, 'Jews and Judaism under Iranian rule: bibliographical reflections', in *History of Religions*, viii, ch. 1 (1968), 159–77. Neusner asserts (p. 171): 'The history of Judaism in Babylonia is yet to be written. I do not know of a single, systematic, methodologically sophisticated, and historically reliable account.'

[4] Of course, the context needs to be considered in each case. However, it is at the heart of Zoroastrian soteriology, whether it is the result of a secondary development or, as I prefer to believe, the reappearance of an old belief. See, further, Jean Kellens, 'Saosiiant', in *Studia Iranica*, 3 (1974), 187–209.

[5] J. Hinnells, 'Zoroastrian saviour imagery and its influence on the New Testament', *Numen*, 16, No. 3 (1969), 167.

[6] M. Boyce, *Textual Sources for the Study of Zoroastrianism* (Manchester, Manchester University Press, 1984), 35ff.

[7] R. C. Zaehner, *The Dawn and Twilight of Zoroastrianism* (London, Weidenfeld & Nicolson, 1961), 20.

[8] Jacques Duchesne-Guillemin, tr. M. Henning, *The Hymns of Zarathustra* (London, John Murray, 1952), 20.

[9] Boyce, *Texts*, 40.

[10] Duchesne-Guillemin, *Hymns*, 145.

[11] Boyce, *Texts*, 20f.

[12] B. T. Anklesaria (ed.), *Zand-Ākasīh: Iranian or Greater Bundahishn, Transliteration and Translation in English* (Bombay, 1956), 283.

[13] F. Max Müller (ed.), tr. E. W. West, *Pahlavi Texts* (*SBE* 5, Oxford, 1880), 192–3.

[14] Gayomard is the first man created, Masha and Mashyoi the first couple (Dēnkard 8:13.1). J. Duchesne Guillemin, *La Réligion de l'Iran Ancien* (Paris, Presses Universitaires de France, 1962), 54.

[15] Fereydun Vahman, *Ardā Wirāz Nāmag* (Scandinavian Institute of Asian Studies Monograph Series, 53, London and Malmo, Curzon Press, 1986).

[16] E. J. Sharpe and John Hinnells (eds.), *Man and his Salvation* (Manchester, Manchester University Press, 1977), 125ff.

Further reading

Baron, W., *A Social and Religious History of the Jews*, vol. 2 (Philadelphia and New York, Columbia University Press, 1952).

Boyce, Mary, *A Persian Stronghold of Zoroastrianism* (Oxford, Clarendon Press, 1977).

——, *Zoroastrians: Their Religious Beliefs and Practices* (London, Routledge & Kegan Paul, 1979).

——, *Textual Sources for the Study of Zoroastrianism* (Manchester, Manchester University Press, 1984).

Brandon, S.G.F., *Man and his Destiny in the Great Religions* (Manchester, Manchester University Press, 1962).

Duchesne-Guillemin, J., *The Hymns of Zarathustra*, tr. M. Henning (London, John Murray, 1952).

——, *La Réligion de l'Iran Ancien* (Paris, Presses Universitaires de France, 1962).

Hellolm, David (ed.), *Apocalypticism in the Mediterranean World and the Near East*, 2nd edn. (Tübingen, Mohr, 1989).

Saggs, H. W. F., *The Greatness that was Babylon* (London, Sidgwick & Jackson, 1962).

Sharpe, E. J. and Hinnells, J. (eds.), *Man and his Salvation* (Manchester, Manchester University Press, 1977).

Zaehner, R. C., *Zurvan: A Zoroastrian Dilemma* (Oxford, Clarendon Press, 1955).

Zaehner, R. C., *The Teachings of the Magi: Ethical and Religious Classics of East and West* (London, Allen & Unwin, 1956; Sheldon, 1975).

3
Maitreya, the Buddhist Messiah

CHRIS ARTHUR

Let me begin this chapter in the wrong place, with the kind of
bare bones of information favoured by popular encyclopedias:

> 'Maitreya' ('loving or kindly one'). The future Buddha, believed by
> Buddhists to be presently living in the Tusita ('joyful') Heaven,
> temporary access to which is possible through advanced meditation.
> Maitreya will remain in this particular heavenly realm until the time
> comes for his descent to earth. This is variously calculated as being
> anything from 500 to many millions of years after the death of
> Siddhartha Gautama, the historical Buddha (*c.*566–486 BCE). Belief in
> Maitreya (known as Miroku in Japan) extends throughout the
> Buddhist world and occurs in all three major strands of this tradition
> (Theravada, Mahayana and Vajrayana). Before Maitreya's descent to
> earth, Buddhist teaching will disappear as the world passes through a
> periodic phase of decline, at whose nadir human life-span will be
> reduced to only ten years. As time continues to pass through the
> enormous cycles of growth and decay posited by Buddhist cosmology,
> things will gradually improve. Eventually a paradisal state will be
> reached where human life-spans will extend for thousands of years
> and a great monarch will usher in a period of universal wellbeing. The
> pinnacle of this golden age will be marked by the appearance of
> Maitreya, who will teach the same great dharma (fundamental truths
> about human existence) as that offered by Gautama Buddha. The
> extreme difficulty of achieving Nirvana, their ultimate soteriological
> goal, is widely acknowledged by Buddhists. Instead of aiming for it
> directly in this life, many pin their hopes on rebirth either in the Tusita
> Heaven or on earth during the dispensation of Maitreya, when
> conditions will put salvation more easily within their grasp.

Anyone who likes to chew on such comfortable facts without
the irritations of complication and qualification should read no

further. For, in a sense, the rest of this chapter involves taking away the bones I have just given and fleshing them out into something at once more complex, confusing and difficult to digest, but also – hopefully – more closely attuned to the nature of this important aspect of Buddhist belief. In doing so, I will be trying to contribute (albeit on a small scale and in a very modest way) to what is surely *the* great task of religious studies in the modern period. Namely, taking our understanding of human religiousness beyond the level of the obvious; moving away from a precritical use of language to a more sophisticated appreciation of the limitations and possibilities of the descriptive terms we use.

The right place to start this chapter (or a least a better place) is with three warnings designed to alert readers to some of the pitfalls which attend the attempt to write about Maitreya, particularly when this is done in some kind of comparative perspective.

1. In a book like this, which sets up the notion of 'the coming deliverer' as a kind of conceptual magnet with which to extract the metal of particular ideas from a range of different faiths, it is important to remember three things. That not all metals are magnetic; that magnets can repel and disrupt as well as attract; and that just because one can draw out certain themes which may appear similar when laid side by side, this does not necessarily mean that they possess the same valency within that complex metallurgy of history, practice and belief which constitutes a religion. This is to stress metaphorically the risks implicit in looking at different religions through a lens which has been ground and polished according to the vision of a single faith tradition. For those who prefer to have their warnings served up more literally, Alan Sponberg, one of the editors of the key source of recent scholarship on Maitreya, is adamant that whilst it is quite legitimate to include Maitreya in 'any discussion of messianism in world religions',[1] the point of doing so 'must be to expand and modify our concept of messianism, not simply to plug Buddhism into it'[2] and this also applies to terms like 'millennial', 'eschatological', 'apocalyptic' and so on. We must, in other words, try to ensure that our descriptive categories are sensitively malleable and open to the revision and nuance which their application to new subjects may suggest. It will prove only

that our methodology is barbaric if we attempt to force phenomena to fit the procrustean bed of a rigidly inflexible typology.

2. My second warning has simply to do with the vastly disparate scale of subject-matter, Maitreya, and the medium through which it is being viewed, namely, this one short chapter. Belief in Maitreya was established by 100 BCE (or earlier) and has continued to flourish right up to the present day. It is a key aspect of Buddhism as a living religion, an important element characterizing the day-to-day faith of millions of people throughout the world. Spreading with Buddhism into most of Asia, belief in Maitreya can be found in various forms in China, Japan, Tibet, Korea, Thailand, Vietnam and elsewhere. As Buddhism has begun to take root in the West in the modern period, belief in Maitreya has also spread to Europe and America. It is no exaggeration to say that 'Maitreya has been a significant figure in Buddhist thought wherever the religion has found support'.[3] Indeed the founder members of the Princeton Maitreya Project, whilst allowing that 'many developments of the Buddhist tradition have been more prominent than the Maitreya legend at any given time or place',[4] hold that 'there is perhaps no other, save the cult of Sakyamuni (i.e. the historical Buddha) that has been as universal and pervasive'.[5] Given the scale of Buddhism – one commentator has estimated that 'over fifty per cent of the population of the world live in areas where Buddhism has at some time been the dominant religious force'[6] – something deemed universal and pervasive within it is something which occurs on the grand scale.

In writing on Maitreya we could focus on textual sources. Though the Pali canon contains comparatively little material, two non-canonical works, the *Anagatavamsa* and the *Maitreya-vyakavana*, are substantially devoted to Maitreya. However, 'the tendency to confuse "scriptural Buddhism" with the "religion of the Buddhists"',[7] often a weakness in the academic study of religion, is one which we must take particular care to avoid in dealing with Maitreya, given the importance of this figure in *popular* religious practice. Independent of any formal status which may be accorded to Maitreya within 'orthodox Buddhism' (whatever we may take this highly questionable concept to be),[8] Maitreya has profound significance for the religiosity of millions of ordinary Buddhists. We could, for example, focus on the way in which Maitreya plays an important part in Korean fertility practices,[9] something which does not have any scriptural sanction but which can shed light on one of the ways in which people view this multi-faceted figure. Or we might look at the way in which Maitreya became a favourite subject for Buddhist art, focusing on the scores of statues which depict him and in whose aesthetic and iconographic dimensions we can find considerable insight into both the affective and cognitive impact which Maitreya has had on the minds of devotees. Or we could consider those individuals scattered through history who have considered themselves, or have been considered by their followers, to *be* Maitreya, for example the Empress Wu in seventh-century China,[10] or U Nu in twentieth-century Burma, who 'tried to combine a fervent Buddhism with democratic and socialist politics'[11] and was 'considered by many Burmese as a saint and as the long awaited messianic ruler, Maitreya'.[12] The point I am stressing here is that Maitreya constitutes a huge and varied subject area, open to numerous different avenues of approach. If we are not profoundly to misrepresent it, we need to remain aware throughout of the danger of oversimplification and omission. This is a massive, diverse and untidy topic which could not be encompassed in a book, let alone in a single chapter.

3. The third warning is at once the most straightforward and the most easily forgotten. It can be issued quite briefly. The act of naming something or someone often carries with it an unnoticed ontological cargo whose weight has the effect of making it appear that the thing or person named is real and actually exists. We need to ensure that in talking about Maitreya, referring to him as 'he' and discussing his various characteristics, we do not end up giving the impression that he exists in the same sort of straightforward sense in which the authors and readers of this book exist. Clearly, Maitreya is real and does exist in terms of constituting an important aspect of Buddhist belief. It is equally clear that to millions of Buddhists he is considered as real an entity as God is considered to be by those within the theistic religions. But it would be quite mistaken to let these commonsense acknowledgements of an easily observable religious reality slide towards an uncritical acceptance of theological (or buddhalogical) assertions. Whether or not Maitreya actually exists as an ontologically real being outwith

Buddhist thought and practice, is not something on which I wish to comment here. Instead of describing Maitreya as 'the Future Buddha', I should, therefore, refer to 'him' in much more circumspect terms – 'the name given by Buddhists to a figure they believe to be the future Buddha'. However, although such locutions might not build into the discussion the same temptations to assume reality as their abbreviated siblings, they are simply too cumbrous to be a serious option. Instead, this assertion of 'metaphysical neutrality' will have to suffice.[13]

With these three warnings kept firmly in mind, I want to consider the extent to which 'messiah', the term that comes most immediately to mind with the idea of a coming deliverer, can be applied to Maitreya. I hope that this exercise will not only cast light on the nature of this important Buddhist figure, but that it will also illustrate (in however inchoate and imperfect a manner) the way in which religious studies needs to sharpen its basic descriptive terms.[14]

   T. W. Rhys Davids (1843–1922), one of the most perceptive of the early Western scholars of Buddhism, struck the note of comparison between Maitreya and messiah which many others have followed. However, although descriptions of Maitreya as 'the Buddhist messiah' are now more or less routine,[15] Rhys Davids' treatment is notable for the way in which he highlights differences as well as similarities:

> There is sufficient justification for the comparison between Maitreya and the western idea of a messiah. The ideas are, of course, not at all the same; but there are several points of analogy. The time of Maitreya is described as a Golden Age in which kings, ministers and people will vie with one another in maintaining the reign of righteousness and the victory of truth. It should be added, however, that the teachings of the future Buddha also, like that of every other Buddha, will suffer corruption and pass away in time.[16]

In this passage Rhys Davids deftly identifies two key interrelated features of Buddhism as they find expression in ideas about Maitreya. Both serve to give the notion of a Buddhist messiah a resonance which sets it apart from traditional Judaeo-Christian understandings of this term.

First, what he says about the teaching of the future Buddha passing away, 'like that of every other Buddha', indicates the way in which Buddhas are viewed in the plural. They are a regular phenomenon, repeated over the vast aeons of time which are mapped by Buddhist cosmology, rather than a single never-to-be-repeated instance of one particular individual biography. The man we think of today as 'the' Buddha, Siddhartha Gautama, may be historically unique, but in the ontological/mythological economy of Buddhism, the definite article is a misnomer which can mask the important fact that he is viewed as one in an ever-recurring series. Buddhas are seen in serial not singular terms. They are considered to be an inevitable part of the fundamental fabric of existence, rather than an unforeseen and unrepeatable result born of the unpredictable contingencies of one person's life. Their existence is viewed as much in cosmological as in biographical terms. Whilst I would agree with Michael Pye that 'Buddhism is most easily understood through the story of its founder',[17] if we fail to see the Buddha as one of a type, rather than as a unique individual, we will have failed to grasp an important aspect of the Buddhist world-view and one which is essential for any understanding of Maitreya. Richard Gombrich offers a useful contrast between the way in which the Buddha tends to be viewed by Buddhists and by non-Buddhists:

> Outsiders see him as the founder of Buddhism; for Buddhists the matter is slightly more complicated. As they see it, the Truth is eternal, but not always realized. Time has no beginning or end but goes through vast cycles. Every now and again there arises in the world a religious genius, a Buddha, who has the infinite wisdom to comprehend the Truth and the infinite compassion to preach it to the suffering world, so that others too may attain Enlightenment. Gautama is the most recent Teacher in the infinite series of Buddhas.[18]

Clearly an infinite series has no beginning or end, but Dipankara, the name given to the first of twenty-four Buddhas who are said to have preceded Gautama, is sometimes treated (particularly within Chinese Buddhism) as the archetypal Buddha of the past. Likewise, though the future Buddha is said to be Maitreya, he is the next in line rather than the end of the line; he is the future Buddha, not the final Buddha, *a* messiah not *the* messiah. In a sense, the three figures of Dipankara, Gautama and Maitreya, in a potent blend of mythology, history and eschatology, could be seen as constituting that tiny part of the massive soteriological scaffolding undergirding time which is conceptually 'visible' from our present temporal location.

Secondly, in making clear that the teaching of Maitreya 'will suffer corruption and pass away in time', Rhys Davids reminds us of the centrality of anicca, or impermanence, in the Buddhist outlook.[19] Before the time of Maitreya, the teachings of the historical Buddha will gradually decline and be forgotten. The dharma will disappear as the world passes through a period of degeneracy and decay. When the new golden age finally dawns and Maitreya offers the teaching again, this too will be subject to anicca. Though the reign of Maitreya may last for many thousands of years it is not seen as something eternal. *Everything* (other than nirvana) is subject to the remorseless rhythm of arising and cessation, through which impermanence eats away at everything we know (our bodies, our consciousness, the whole fabric of the world from mountains to mayflies). The pictorial representation of the Buddhist world-view known as the *Bhavachakra*, or Wheel of Life, shows the different realms of existence into which it is possible to be reborn. Each realm – whether heavenly, earthly or hellish – is subject to impermanence. Neither the gods nor the demons of hell will occupy their stations for ever. Even the teachings of a Buddha are subject to periodic rise and fall.

If Maitreya can indeed be viewed as 'the Buddhist messiah', it is therefore important to recognize that he is a messiah who is not unique and who will not bring time to an end, but will instead act as a punctuation mark in the great cycles of time in which all beings are caught up and from which, according to Buddhist soteriology, they ought to seek release in the form of nirvana. The golden age of Maitreya will itself dim and darken into another long cosmic night, which in turn will be broken after millions of aeons by another manifestation of the dharma. The Buddhist messiah is not a judge sent by some deity to sentence humanity according to their just desserts, but simply part of the process of arising and cessation, the very heartbeat of existence, to which the gods themselves (minor figures within Buddhism) are subject, along with everything and everyone else.[20]

In a recent issue of the journal *Concilium* devoted to the topic of 'Messianism Through History', Alister Kee considers the messianic elements in the thought of Karl Marx. He concludes that far from it being a case of Marx's philosophy being 'but a distorted and truncated version of the true and final faith found within the church',[21] in fact Marx's version points to 'embarrassing gaps in Christian messianic faith'.[22] Commenting on this finding, Sean Freyne suggests that it is 'one of the ironies of the history of ideas'[23] that the contemporary reawakening of interest in messianic ideas within Christianity should have been prompted by an encounter with *secular* messianism. Looking at how Marxist thinking, together with the work of the Jewish historian Gershom Scholem, have had an impact on the way in which Christian theologians understand messianism, Freyne notes the way in which some scholars have seen the need 'to speak about messiahs in the plural in order to underline the fact that it is improper to think about *the* messiah, as though only one account of the expectations engendered by that figure was either possible or legitimate'.[24] One wonders what impact an encounter with the messiah of Buddhism might have on contemporary Christian, Jewish, Muslim and Hindu thinking about the coming deliverer in their respective traditions.[25] This takes us back to Alan Sponberg's point, quoted earlier, that looking at Maitreya may help to expand and modify our concept of messianism. One of the values of a book such as this is that it exposes what may be quite insular religious concepts to enriching and refining from cognate ideas in other faiths. The creative potential which such a multi-faith context may hold for religious thinking would seem to be considerable (if also daunting).[26]

In the same way that testing 'messiah' for fit against Maitreya can be an instructive exercise in terms of furthering our understanding of both of these topics, we might likewise usefully apply 'millenarianism', 'eschatology' and 'apocalyptic'.[27] It would, for instance, be interesting to compare Norman Cohn's five-point characterization of the way in which millenarian movements picture salvation as being collective, terrestrial, imminent, total and miraculous,[28] with how various Buddhist groups have interpreted the salvific potential of Maitreya. At first sight Cohn's five-point scheme seems quite inappropriate to Buddhism. Maitreya's coming is not usually seen as imminent, his 'millennium' (if we can call it that) is not total in the sense of bringing a once and for all radical transformation, nor is it miraculous in terms of being reliant on any supernatural agency. For all that, Maitreya *has* inspired various millenarian movements.[29] So, rather than withholding all application of 'millenarianism' from a Buddhist context, it would seem more appropriate to amend our understanding of this term, avoiding the simplistic notion of a linear flow of time leading to a final and irrevocable future. One sympathizes with Kitsiri Malalgoda's view that claims of the absence or unimportance of millennialism in Buddhism should be discounted as premature 'until a thorough examination of the Buddhist tradition from this point of view has been accomplished'.[30]

As well as matching Maitreya-influenced millenarianism against Cohn's schema, it would also be fascinating to see whether the dynamics of religious disappointment in those Buddhist groups whose predictions of a new age have not materialized could be mapped in the same way that Leon Festinger and colleagues have proposed for Judaeo-Christian instances where prophecy fails.[31] However, to pursue such possibilities with millenarianism, or to consider the way in which (if at all) 'eschatology' or 'apocalypse' might be applied to Maitreya, would very quickly lead to a book-length rather than a chapter-length venture. I can do no more than mention them here as avenues for further research.

Having deliberately begun this chapter in the wrong place, let me end it in what some would no doubt consider to be a mistaken manner. One of the most fascinating aspects of Maitreya is, arguably, the way in which he has been transformed (some would say corrupted) into the figure of a pot-bellied laughing Buddha, which is such a favourite subject for popular religious art in many Buddhist countries and is fast becoming a familiar object in the West too. (Though no doubt few of the purchasers of the crude porcelain statues of rotund jovial Buddhas which can increasingly be found in British shops will have the remotest inkling of its connection with the Buddhist messiah!)

A Maitreya cult had been established in China as early as the fourth century.[32] This flourished for the next two hundred years or so, buoyed by the belief of many Chinese that such was the state of affairs in their country that the time was ripe for the coming deliverer. When Maitreya did not appear, his cult was gradually replaced by that of Amitabha and Avalokitesvara, two of Mahayana Buddhism's most popular bodhisattvas (Maitreya, incidently, is the *only* bodhisattva accepted by Theravada Buddhism). Although 'majestic images of Maitreya disappeared from the repertoire of artists'[33] during this time and devotion to him was generally in decline, Maitreya reappeared in the eleventh century in a wholly new guise, transformed into what Lewis Lancaster has described as 'a folk deity of great importance'.[34] This folk deity seems very largely to have been the result of a historical figure, Pu-tai, falling victim to what Ferdinand Lessing has aptly termed 'idealization through religious fiction'.[35]

It seems that this unlikely, but hugely popular, manifestation of Maitreya was based on the superimposition of Buddhist messianic thought on to the intriguing figure of one Pu-tai, the 'Hemp Sack Monk', so called because he carried a large hemp sack wherever he went. The real name of this individual is unknown to us,[36] but he is thought to have been a native of Chekiang who lived sometime in the tenth century and was made popular both by his apparent ability to predict the weather and by his enigmatic Zen-like behaviour. For instance, on one occasion, asked how old his hemp sack was, 'he replied that it was as old as space'.[37] On another he was found lying in the snow, apparently quite oblivious to the cold. Given his eccentricity it comes as no surprise to learn that this individual acted as a magnet to the curious. Children in particular were fascinated by him, 'they would chase him and climb all over him, and force him to open his bag. On such an occasion he would put the bag on the ground, empty the contents one by one, and just as methodically put them back into the bag',[38] asking 'what is this?', 'what is this?' After his death, poems written very much in the spirit of Zen began to be attributed to Pu-tai and people took to drawing portraits and making statues depicting him. In one legend about him 'it was said that Maitreya appeared on earth and wandered about in the appearance of a fool, with his protruding belly uncovered and a smile on his face. No one knew his true identity. He appeared undignified and eccentric in his conduct. But when he spoke his words were filled with wisdom.'[39] At this point Ch'en sees the identification of the Hemp Sack Monk and

Maitreya as complete, though rather than straightforward identification it might be better to follow Lessing's more cautious suggestion that Pu-tai came to be seen as a kind of 'preincarnation' of Maitreya.[40] Whatever the precise provenance of the Laughing Buddha may be, it is clear that a number of important Chinese life-ideals are contained in this figure:

> The huge protruding stomach and the hemp bag denote prosperity and a wealth of material goods. The reclining figure is indicative of the spiritual contentment and relaxation of one who is at peace with himself and the world. The large number of children surrounding him are illustrative of another Chinese virtue – a large family.[41]

The Hemp Sack Monk and his subsequent metamorphosis into Mi-lo, the Laughing Buddha, provides an excellent illustration of the fact that belief in Maitreya is diverse and liable to a wide range of expression in different cultural settings (as is Buddhism itself). Given his acknowledgement of the fact that it is figures of the (to his mind) gross Mi-lo that 'have come in recent times to be *the* representations of Buddhism in the general consciousness'[42] (rather than more aesthetically pleasing manifestations of Maitreya), it is interesting to note that Arthur Wright is prepared to condemn this figure in no uncertain terms. 'The total effect no longer suggests spiritual grace or aspiration but rather gross jollity and the satisfaction of fleshly appetites'.[43] Likewise Joseph Kitagawa seems dismayed by Mi-lo: 'It is tragic that popular minds have associated Maitreya with the jovial laughing Buddha, an image which has lost the historic meaning of the lofty Bodhisattva who was expected to become the future Buddha.'[44] Why should this be considered tragic? Such assessments seem intent on measuring an important and flourishing aspect of popular religiousness against some kind of unstated normative standard. Comparing Maitreya as he is depicted in, say, the famous statue known as the Chugu-ji Miroku (a sculpture which has been described by Sherman Lee as displaying 'infinite grace'[45]), with a contemporary popular rendering of Mi-lo, one might, on an aesthetic level, be forgiven for expressing a preference. But it would surely be highly questionable to let such artistic judgements become theological ones. In considering the kind of criticism which Wright and Kitagawa offer we need to be careful not only of casually condemning a key icon of popular piety, but of obscuring one of Maitreya's most fundamental characteristics, namely the exuberant diversity of forms in which he is found. As Alan Sponberg puts it, 'Perhaps the most striking characteristic of Maitreya, in contrast to other mythic figures of the Buddhist tradition, is his multivalence, the fact that his characterisation allows such rich variation . . . By necessity, any study of Maitreya must be as multifaceted as the figure himself.'[46] If we are to understand the full range and depth of this important strand of Buddhism, we must take care that we do not dismiss those aspects of it that are simply not to our taste.

George Steiner once suggested that when we use a word 'we wake into resonance its entire previous history'.[47] Few language-users are likely to be as aware as Steiner is of the complex of echoes and nuances of meaning, past and present, which words bear. None the less, his remark conveniently provides two useful reminders with which to conclude. First, in trying to understand Maitreya we should *attempt* 'to wake into resonance' the entire spectrum of occurrence past and present within which this aspect of Buddhism has found expression, rather than confining ourselves to whatever segment of its meaning happens to appeal to us. This is, of course, an enormous undertaking, arguably tantamount to trying to understand Buddhism *per se*. But religious studies is nothing if not heroic in the scale of its endeavour. Only by trying patiently to unravel the whole tangle of threads which make up this particular part of the fabric of Buddhist religiousness, will we be able to grasp something of its nature.[48] Secondly, Steiner's remark should remind us of a key point which I stressed at the outset. Our words can often carry hidden cargoes of assumption and evaluation. In the study of religion it is particularly important to have in place some effective means of verbal quarantine and customs, otherwise when we use terms from one religio-cultural context ('messiah', 'millennial' and so on) to talk about things in a different context, we may find our attempted intellectual commerce disrupted by a black economy, where contraband meanings will soon bankrupt what we want to say.

Notes

[1] Alan Sponberg and Helen Hardacre (eds.), *Maitreya: the Future Buddha* (Cambridge, Cambridge University Press, 1988), 295.

[2] Ibid.

[3] Lewis R. Lancaster, 'Maitreya', in *The Encyclopedia of Religion*, editor-in-chief Mircea Eliade (New York, Collier Macmillan, 1987), ix, 140.

[4] Sponberg and Hardacre, *Maitreya*, xi.

[5] Ibid.

[6] L. S. Cousins, 'Buddhism', in John R. Hinnells (ed.), *A Handbook of Living Religions* (Harmondsworth, Penguin, 1984), 278. Cousins's account of Buddhism (pp. 278–343) is highly recommended to readers unfamiliar with this religion. It provides a first-rate introduction.

[7] Kitsiri Malalgoda, 'Millennialism in relation to Buddhism', *Comparative Studies in Society and History*, 12, No. 4 (1970), 440.

[8] At one point in his insightful and incisive article, Malalgoda asks, 'who would expect "orthodox Buddhism" to be the religion of all, or for that matter, even the majority of Buddhists?' (ibid., 441). A powerful corrective to the tendency which academic studies have towards elevating 'scriptural' Buddhism into some sort of normative or orthodox form, against which all other varieties of Buddhism may be judged, is given by Gregory Schopen in 'Archaeology and Protestant presuppositions in the study of Indian Buddhism', *History of Religions*, 31, No. 1 (1991), 1–23.

[9] On this see Lewis Lancaster, 'Maitreya in Korea', in Sponberg and Hardacre, *Maitreya*, 145f.

[10] Although political rather than religious motives may seem paramount in this case, Daniel L. Overmeyer suggests that since the Empress Wu had been raised by a pious Buddhist mother, had supported the carving of Buddhist sculptures and had become a nun after her father's death, 'there may have been an element of sincere belief in her devotion to Maitreya'. (*Folk Buddhist Religion: Dissenting Sects in Late Traditional China* (Harvard East Asian Series 83; Harvard: Harvard University Press, 1976), 226 n. 38).

[11] S. J. Tambiah, *World Conqueror and World Renouncer: A Study of Buddhism and Polity in Thailand Against a Historical Background* (Cambridge Studies in Social Anthropology Series, 15; Cambridge, Cambridge University Press, 1976), 517.

[12] Ibid., 483.

[13] For some perceptive comments on the use of metaphysical neutrality in the study of Buddhism see Richard Gombrich, *Theravada Buddhism: A Social History from Ancient Benares to Modern Colombo* (London, Routledge & Kegan Paul, 1988; in the Library of Religious

Beliefs and Practices series, ed. John Hinnells and Ninian Smart), 9.

[14] Writing twenty years ago, Ralph Wendell Burhoe delivered a damning assessment of the academic study of religion, suggesting that it is 'in a more primitive state than was biology two centuries ago'. According to Burhoe 'we have not yet had our Darwin; we have hardly had our Linnaeus to sharpen our basic descriptive terms and their classifications' ('The phenomenon of religion seen scientifically', in Allan W. Eister (ed.), *Changing Perspectives in the Scientific Study of Religion* (New York, Wiley International, 1974), 15). Though the situation has undoubtedly improved, the fact remains that the kind of 'basic descriptive terms' we might reach for in discussing Maitreya – 'messiah', 'millennial', 'eschatology' etc. – still need to be handled very carefully if we are to avoid simply imposing religious and cultural assumptions where they do not belong.

[15] For instance, to take a varied handful of examples, such descriptions can be found in W. Y. Evans Wentz (ed.), *The Tibetan Book of Great Liberation* (London, Oxford University Press, 1954), xxvii; Sir Charles Eliot, *Japanese Buddhism* (London, Routledge & Kegan Paul, 1935), 119; Yoneo Ishii, 'A note on Buddhist millenarian revolts in northeastern Siam', *Journal of South East Asian Studies*, 6 (1975), 125; Erik Zürcher, 'Beyond the jade gate: Buddhism in China, Vietnam and Korea', in Heinz Bechert and Richard Gombrich (eds.), *The World of Buddhism* (London, Thames & Hudson, 1984), 209; Charles Luk (tr. and ed.), *The Vimalakirti Nirdesa Sutra* (Boston, Shambhala, 1990), 148.

[16] T. W. Rhys Davids, 'Anagata Vamsa', in James Hastings (ed.), *Encyclopedia of Religion and Ethics*, xix (Edinburgh, T. & T. Clark, 1908), 414. Rhys Davids uses the Pali form, 'Metteyya'. In the interests of simplicity I have changed this to 'Maitreya', preferring to keep to the Sanskrit form alone.

[17] Michael Pye, *The Buddha* (London, Duckworth, 1979), 1.

[18] Gombrich, *Theravada Buddhism*, 1–2.

[19] *Anicca*, 'impermanence', is one of the 'three marks of existence' (*trilakshana*). Along with *dukkha* ('unsatisfactoriness', 'imperfection', 'suffering') and *anatman* ('egolessness', 'no self') it is held to characterize all phenomenal existence. Meditation on any of the three marks of existence (in their various guises) is an important strategy for securing insight into the true nature of things. That impermanence is absolutely fundamental to the Buddhist world-view, and that it is intimately connected to the unsatifactoriness from which human beings seek to escape, is summed up in the Buddha's last words before he died: 'Decay is inherent in all compound things, work out your own salvation with diligence.'

[20] Perhaps it should be stressed that in Buddhism there is no place for God, in the singular overarching sense understood within the Semitic family of faiths. Arguably, though, at least to some extent, the cult of Maitreya might be seen as something which 'offers its devotees the advantages of theism and Buddhism combined' (Richard H. Robinson and Willard L. Johnson, *The Buddhist Religion: A Historical Introduction* (Encino, CA, Duxbury Press, 1977), 103). Whilst the Buddha, having entered nirvana, is beyond the entreaties of the faithful, Maitreya as the next Buddha is, by that logic, currently existent as a bodhisattva and is considered very much as a compassionate interceding saviour whose help may be sought.

[21] Alister Kee, 'Marx's messianic faith', in Wim Beuken, Sean Freyne and Anton Weiler (eds.), *Concilium 1993/1: Messianism Through History* (London, SCM Press, and New York, Orbis Books, 1993), 113.

[22] Ibid.

[23] Ibid., viii.

[24] Ibid.

[25] A clue may perhaps be found here in the possible impact on Christian theology of the Buddhist idea of sunyata (nothingness or emptiness). According to one assessment, 'a close encounter with the nothingness of Buddhism will effect noteworthy changes in every recognizable form of contemporary discourse about God': Langdon Gilkey, 'God', in Peter Hodgson and Robert King (eds.), *Christian Theology: An Introduction to its Traditions and Tasks* (London, SPCK, 1983), 86.

[26] For some ideas about this creative potential, see my 'Utility, understanding and creativity in the study of religions', *New Blackfriars*, 74, 867 (1993), 14–20.

[27] These terms are all suggested by Alan Sponberg in his excellent 'Prospectus for the study of Maitreya', which suggests a methodologically sophisticated framework for further research in this area. See Sponberg and Hardacre (eds.), *Maitreya*, 285–97, esp. 295. Melford Spiro's identification of 'eschatological' and 'millennial' Buddhism also offers some useful points of reference. See his *Buddhism and Society: A Great Tradition and its Burmese Vicissitudes* (London, George Allen & Unwin, 1971), 164–80.

[28] This can be found in Cohn's superb study of revolutionary millenarians and mystical anarchists in Europe's Middle Ages, *The Pursuit of the Millennium* (London, Temple Smith, 1970), revised and expanded edition, 13. On some of the problems and possibilities facing cross-cultural studies of millenarianism, see S. L. Thrupp (ed.), *Millennial Dreams in Action: Essays in Comparative Study* (The Hague, Mouton, 1962), and Bryan Wilson, 'Millenialism in comparative perspective', *Comparative Studies in Society and History*, 6 (1963–4),

93–114. A concise but superb overview of millenarianism (which usefully locates 'two constellations of millenarian thought about an epochal pulsing of time, one Zoroastrian-Jewish-Greek-Christian, the other Hindu-Buddhist-Taoist-Confucian') is given in Hillel Schwartz's essay in *The Encyclopedia of Religion*, ix, 521–32.

[29] Hue-Tam Ho Tai has described how 'the Maitreya theme inspired two recent millenarian movements in Vietnam, both founded in the first half of the twentieth century' ('Perfect world and perfect time, Maitreya in Vietnam', in Sponberg and Hardacre (eds.), *Maitreya*, 154); Kitsiri Malalgoda identifies Buddhist millennial movements in Ceylon, 'Millennialism', 431f. For further examples see Daniel Overmeyer's *Folk Buddhist Religion* (referred to in n. 10 above); Charles F. Keyes, 'Millenialism, Theravada Buddhism and Thai society', *Journal of Asian Studies*, 6 No. 2 (1977), 283–302; and Erik Zürcher, 'Prince Moonlight: messianism and eschatology in early medieval Chinese Buddhism', *T'oung Pao*, 48 Nos. 1–3 (1982), 1–75. Zürcher identifies a type of sectarian Buddhism in which belief in Maitreya inspired messianic movements and rebellions, 'a phenomenon that is attested from the late fifth century onward and that was to continue throughout Chinese history till modern times' (p.14).

[30] Malalgoda, 'Millennialism', 440.

[31] Leon Festinger's ideas about the religious applications of 'cognitive dissonance' are expounded in the fascinating (if methodologically reprehensible) study which he co-wrote with Henry Riecken and Stanley Schacter, *When Prophecy Fails, a Social and Psychological Study of a Modern Group that Predicted the Destruction of the World* (New York, Harper & Row, 1956).

[32] Kenneth K. S. Ch'en, *Buddhism in China, a Historical Survey* (Princeton, Princeton University Press, 1962), 405. In what follows I draw heavily on Ch'en's account, 405–8. See also his *The Chinese Transformation of Buddhism* (Princeton, Princeton University Press, 1973), 7–8.

[33] Lewis Lancaster, 'Maitreya', in *The Encyclopedia of Religion*, ix (New York, Collier Macmillan, 1987), 138.

[34] Ibid.

[35] Ferdinand Lessing, *Yung-Ho-Kung: An Iconography of the Lamaist Cathedral in Peking* (Sino-Swedish series, 18, Stockholm, 1942), 27.

[36] Pu-tai's family name is not known, but he sometimes called himself Chi'tzu, which may mean either 'dependant on this' or 'independent of this', both variants having important resonances with key Buddhist teachings. On Pu-tai's names and biographical details, see Helen Chapin, 'The Ch'an Master Pu-tai', *Journal of the American Oriental Society*, Vol.53 no.1 (1933), 49–52.

[37] Ch'en, *Buddhism in China*, 406.

[38] Ibid.

[39] Ibid., 407.

[40] Lessing, *Yung-Ho-Kung*, 29.

[41] Ibid.

[42] Arthur F. Wright, *Buddhism in Chinese History* (Stanford, CA, Stanford University Press, 1959), xiv. Wright's book contains an excellent illustration of a twentieth-century example of the (offending?) figure in question (facing p.115).

[43] Ibid.

[44] Joseph M. Kitagawa, 'The career of Maitreya, with special reference to Japan', *History of Religions*, 21 No.2 (1981), 117.

[45] Sherman E. Lee, *A History of Far Eastern Art* (London, Thames & Hudson, 1975, revised edn.), 151.

[46] Sponberg and Hardacre (eds.), *Maitreya*, 286.

[47] George Steiner, *After Babel: Aspects of Language and Translation* (Oxford, Oxford University Press, 1977), 24.

[48] Such unravelling will lead us to some topics even more likely to outrage our sensibilities than the fat laughing figure of Mi-lo. What are we to to make, for example, of the claims of Scottish painter Benjamin Creme, who in 1980–2 travelled round the world with the message that the coming of 'Maitreya the Christ' was imminent? In 1982 Creme identified a Pakistani leader in London as 'Maitreya the Christ', but the individual in question declined to accept this 'honour'. See Linda W. Duddy, 'Benjamin Creme and Maitreya the Christ', *Update: A Quarterly Review of New Religious Movements*, 6 No. 4 (1982), 42–5, and R. Kronenborg, 'Benjamin Creme and Maitreya the Christ', *Update* 9 No. 1 (1985), 50–5.

Further reading

A range of reading is suggested in the notes. Three important and readily accessible sources are:

Lancaster, Lewis R., 'Maitreya', *The Encyclopedia of Religion*, editor-in-chief Mircea Eliade (New York, Collier Macmillan, 1987), ix, 136–41.

Sponberg, Alan and Hardacre, Helen (eds.), *Maitreya: the Future Buddha* (Cambridge, Cambridge University Press, 1988).

Sayagyi U Chit Tin (with Pruitt, William), *The Coming Buddha Ariya Metteya* (The Wheel Publication, 381/383, Colombo, Buddhist Publication Society, 1992). Usefully, this booklet contains a complete English translation of the *Anagatavamsa* (The Chronicle of the Future Buddha).

4

The coming deliverer – a Sikh perspective

W. OWEN COLE

1 Introduction

Sikhism is one of the most recent religions to have originated in India. It is still little studied in the West even though there are Sikhs in every English-speaking country as well as in many others. Reasons for it being ignored lie beyond this present study but one that might be mentioned is the continuing erroneous tendency to class it as a form of *bhakti* Hinduism. Sikhs claim it to be a distinct revealed religion and that is how it should regarded by anyone who wishes to understand it. Because of lack of knowledge about Sikhism a brief introduction is provided.

Guru Nanak (1469–1539) was the first person to proclaim the tenets of the Sikh faith. Nine other Gurus who succeeded him continued his work, developing the community Panth in many ways but preaching essentially the same message. Finally, the teaching, the *gurbani,* expressed in poetry, was embodied in a corpus of scripture known as the Guru Granth Sahib which is now the spiritual authority for Sikhs, interpreted by the Guru Panth.

Besides possessing a scripture Sikhism has distinct beliefs, practices and values. Its close linguistic and cultural links with the Punjab continue despite the diaspora. To an increasing extent English has become the medium of scholarship though not of worship.

2 Sikh beliefs

The coherence of Sikh teaching lies in the belief in one God, who is beyond gender and should not be described as male or female, though it has been customary among writers in English to use the pronouns 'he' and 'him', a habit which is only slowly being broken. The oneness of God, the essential unity of the divine, is the starting-point of all Sikh theology. From the One came the many life forms. God chose to create male and female forms and it is through their interaction that the various species multiply and evolve but a consequence of that physical process has been a human tendency to forget or neglect unity and stress duality. The repeated message of the Gurus is that God is the only One, there is no second.

Sikh teaching also stressed the oneness of humanity, rejecting ideas of class or caste and affirming the equality of women and men. Teachings which emphasize distinctions of race, gender, class or even religion, just as much as those which speak of the plurality of gods, are encouraging people to exchange the truth of unity for the illusion of duality. Guru Nanak teaches in Adi Granth 433, that 'The One God is all-pervading and alone dwells in the mind' and 'The One takes away; the One gives. I have not heard of another, a second'. The first statement is not only a strong monotheistic declaration; it is also an affirmation that God is immanent in creation and in humanity. The God-realized person is aware of the Being Beyond Time, Akal Purukh, God, as One and of the unity of the universe. It has to be admitted, however, that the ideal of social unity is one which Sikhs have never achieved, since they tend to live in predominantly Hindu cultures and often have relatives who are Hindus. The five evils of lust, covetousness, attachment, wrath, and pride have to be overcome. A casteless community in which women enjoy actual equality with men is still not a practical reality. In worship (*diwan*), however, Sikh places of worship, gurdwaras, are open to everyone, including non-Sikhs, and women may be seen sharing fully in leading it and serving on committees.

Guru Nanak was born in the Punjab. Non-scriptural stories of his life known as *janam sikhs*, describe the rejection of what he regarded as the ritualistic formalism of Hinduism and Islam from an early age. Sikhs believe that he was born in accordance with divine will (*hukam*) and not the consequence of the karmic process which determines the birth of most mortals. At around thirty he experienced being taken to God's court where he was commissioned to proclaim knowledge of *Nam*, the nature of God and the means of God-realization. For twenty years he travelled far and wide preaching this message to everyone. His followers became known as Sikhs from the Punjabi word *sikhna*, to learn. Before he died it was clear that his work was not complete and the community or Panth which he established became so focused upon him as well as his teaching that he found it necessary to provide them with a successor. There were ten Gurus in all.

The last preceptor, Guru Gobind Singh, whose impact upon the Panth was such that the form of present-day Sikhism owes much to him, was notable for four reasons.

1. In 1706 he made a recension of the Adi Granth, the scripture which had been compiled by Guru Arjan, the fifth Guru in 1604. He inserted the hymns, *bani*, of his father Guru Tegh Bahadur but none of his own. (These are included in the Dasam Granth, a collection compiled some years later by one of his disciples.)

2. He sanctioned the use of military force in defence against oppressors and promulgated a just war theory.

3. He declared the line of human guruship to be at an end.

4. As he lay dying he installed the scripture as Guru, hence its title Guru Granth Sahib (although Adi Granth is still used). This has become the focus of Sikh worship, as can be seen immediately by anyone who enters a gurdwara. Naming, wedding and initiation ceremonies also take place in the presence of the scripture. There is probably no other religion in which the scripture plays such a central role liturgically and doctrinally. The ten Gurus were united in their message. Two bards writing in the time of the fifth Guru said: 'The divine light is the same, the life form is the same. The king has merely changed the body' (AG 966).

Thus, for example, although it was Guru Gobind Singh who affirmed the right of Sikhs to take up arms, Sikhs would claim that he was only maintaining the principle of resisting social injustice which began when Guru Nanak demanded the end of the ill-treatment of captives and their release after the siege of Saidpur by the Mughal invader Babur in 1520. Briefly, the message of the Gurus was that God is latently immanent in all human beings and may be experienced through moral effort and divine grace, though the emphasis is strongly upon grace. Guru Nanak said: 'God is attained by grace. All other boasted ways and means are vain and false' (AG 7). God is truth and spiritual and moral truth must operate together in those who have forsaken the path of self interest (*manmukh*) for that of being God-orientated (*gurmukh*). Self-centredness, *haumai*, which means literally 'I-I', is the great obstacle to liberation. In the ignorance which characterizes unregenerate humanity the pursuit of material goals prevents realization of the truth that bliss (*anand*) can only be obtained when God's will (*hukam*) is obeyed. Liberation is not earned, however, as the verses quoted above demonstrate, but the enlightened person naturally seeks to serve God through humanity. God realization comes from meditation upon the divine word (*shabad*), the *bani* of the Guru Granth Sahib, and *seva*, the altruistic service of one's fellow beings. Asceticism has no place in Sikh teaching. The true Sikh belongs to a human family and a family of faith. The *grihastha* stage of life is the one ordained by God. Consequently, there is room in Sikhism only for moral purity and impurity. Beliefs in auspicious times, holy places and the impurity of women or people of lower caste are dismissed as superstitious.

3 Sikhism and Hinduism

One aspect of Sikh teaching which is relevant to our subject is the rejection of a number of Hindu concepts and principles. There is a denial of the authority of the Vedas, the *varnashramadharma*, the Manu Smirti and the necessity of a priestly class, the brahmins, to interpret scripture and perform rituals which were essential for a successful life here and in the hereafter. There is no belief that liberation is open only to the three castes of twice-born *varnas* or that women must be reborn as men before they can attain *moksha*. Liberation is open to everyone and not only through being a member of the Sikh Panth. Most relevant of all, the doctrine of avatar is particularly rejected. All this means that there is no belief in the Guru Granth Sahib about such things as the return of Yudhisthira or the coming of Kalki, the final avatar of Vishnu.

4 Liberation in Sikh thought

Mukti, spiritual liberation, is possible here and now. Indeed, it is this hope that Sikhs should take seriously, and the Gurus continually rail against the lack of concern with it. Such was the emphasis upon making an immediate response to their message that it could be a matter of debate whether Guru Nanak accepted the idea of rebirth or supported the notion of one life followed by judgement. In fact, Sikhism teaches the former and evidence for it is adduced from the word spoken by Guru Nanak, but the point is that he refused to debate the issue, and discouraged speculation, warning women and men to respond immediately to divine grace. Otherwise, whatever lay beyond death was catastrophic, neither hell nor rebirth was a consoling prospect. The good news was that death need not be faced with that uncertainty. God is immanent, not far away or beyond human experience in this present life. As Guru Nanak said: 'The Sovereign Parmeshur (God), maker of the world, beholds it, sees and understands everything, and pervades all, within and without' (AG 433). The ineffable and inexpressible realm of truth is the final stage which the soul attains. It is 'the home of eternal bliss'. The tragedy of the human predicament was never so clearly or poignantly expressed as by Guru Amar Das:

> Humanity is brimful of the nectar of God's Name. Through tasting it its relish is known. Those who taste it become free from fear and find that God's elixir satisfies all their needs. Whoever is made to drink it through divine grace is never afflicted by Death. (AG 1092)

This truth is hidden by human attachment to *maya* which, in Sikh teaching, is the deluded state of regarding the material world, real as it is, for it is God's creation, as eternal. In their natural or unregenerate state human beings do not perceive the One who is within but seek for comfort and satisfaction elsewhere, in family, material wealth or fame, for example. Such actions or relationships need not be immoral, but they are means of gaining only temporary respite. Such unenlightened persons are unable to guide themselves or others: 'The mind is unstable, it does not know the way. One who trusts in his/her own self is as one befouled; s/he does not recognise the Word (*shabad*)' (AG 415). The word for 'mind' or 'self' is *man*, which is difficult to translate or interpret. Its meaning may become clearer as we consider the opposite to someone who is *manmukh*, ruled by self, *gurmukh*, one who is God-oriented, a person whose being is focused on God.

The Gurus taught that to become *gurmukh* a number of things were necessary. They were: effort, grace, a guru and the community of believers.

1. *Effort.* The third Guru, Amar Das, outlined human development in these words: 'When it pleases God a child is born and the family is happy. Love for God departs, greed attaches itself to the child and *maya*'s writ begins to run. God is forgotten and one becomes attached to the love of another (instead of God)' (AG 921). This process has to be reversed through an act of will. It would be immoral if liberation were given without any human longing for it or search after it. Effort is a prerequisite.

2. *Grace.* It is grace alone which enables a person to be liberated. The passage just quoted continues: 'Those who enshrine love for God, by grace obtain the divine being in the midst of *maya*. Nanak says, those who enshrine love for God in their hearts, through the Guru's grace obtain God even in the midst of mammon.' A popular Sikh saying is: 'If you take one step towards God, God will take a hundred steps towards you.'

3. *A guru.* The word 'Guru' in Sikh teaching refers to the ten human Gurus who lived between 1469 and 1708, to the scripture, the Guru Granth Sahib, to the community, the Guru Panth, and to God, the Sat Guru. It is this last concept which is most important. God is beyond human knowledge but is self-revealing as teacher. The divine means of communication is the Word, *shabad*, which was revealed to the human Gurus and through them to humanity. These utterances were compiled in the scripture. The Sat Guru was the only Guru of Guru Nanak.

4. *The community of believers*, the Panth or its local manifestation, the sangat. Sikhism is a religion which emphasizes assembling together. In a very significant verse Guru Ram Das, the fourth Guru, noted its salvic effect: 'Just as the castor oil plant imbibes the scent of the nearby sandalwood, so the fallen become emancipated through the company of the faithful' (AG 861).

The tense is present. Spiritual liberation is offered here and now. The Gurus did not speak about something which would be experienced beyond death, still less of the notion of the soul sleeping in some way to be awakened at the end of time. There was an urgency in the Gurus' preaching. The *janam sakhis* describe journeys to such diverse places as Tibet, Sri Lanka, and Makkah. These were undertaken in response to the divine command that he should 'spread God's glory in the world' (AG 150). A person who becomes fully God-realized in this present life is called *jivan mukt*. The Gurus themselves were in this state and Sikhism has always taught that 'the Guru is the *chela* and the *chela* is the Guru'. The words are actually those of Guru Amar Das (AG 444). He goes on to say: 'Both preach God's mission which is God's Name and placing the *shabad* in human hearts.'

However, the Gurus never taught that liberation was possible only through their preaching or that of their disciples. Their concept of *shabad* allowed for the Vedas and Qur'an to be the means of enlightenment. In fact, the Guru Granth Sahib has as one of its distinctive features the inclusion of the utterances of the outcaste Ravidas, the brahmins Jaidev and Ramanand, Sheikh Farid the Muslim and Kabir who would not be pleased to be ascribed to any religion or sectarian group. Together with vast numbers of other preachers and scriptures, they point to God's will that humanity should hear the divine call and respond to it. Perhaps the greatest note of urgency was sounded by the third Guru, Amar Das, who cried to God: 'The whole world is ablaze. Save it by showering your blessing upon it. Deliver it through whatever way it can be delivered' (AG 853). He continued: 'The Sat Guru shows the path of peace, meditation on the true Word. Nanak sees no other pardoner.'

5 The demand for social justice

Truth is the chief characteristic of God. Guru Nanak warned:

> Having come (into the world) one must depart again. This world is but a fleeting show. The abode of Truth is found through serving the True One. Truth is attained only by living in accordance with Truth, by following the path of Truth. One is disqualified by falsehood and covetousness and has no place in the hereafter. No one is invited to enter and take rest. They are like crows in a deserted house. The cycle of birth and death is the great separation and in it all are destroyed. People are led astray by being involved in the concerns of *maya* through greed. Death standing over them makes them weep. (AG 581)

Truth, as the above quotation states, is an ethical concept. 'Truth is the highest of all virtues, but higher still is truthful living' (AG 62). It is realized 'through purity of heart' (AG 472). This insistence on truth has led Sikhs to demand a just society as well as high personal standards and individual lives dedicated to the service of God (*seva)* through care for the rest of humanity and the whole created world.

Guru Nanak uttered four verses known as the Babur *bani* which seem to differ considerably from his traditional message addressed to individuals or religious groups (such as a body of Nath Yogis). These are found on pp. 360, 417–18 and 772–3 of the Adi Granth. They have a message to society in general. One reads:

> When they heard of Babur's invasion thousands of *pirs* tried to stop Mir (Babur), by prayers or magic when they heard of his invasion. Resting places were burnt, rock-like temples destroyed, princes hacked in pieces and trampled in the dust. (In spite of the *pirs'* efforts) no Mughal was blinded. None of the spells had any effect . . . You sent the Mughal as the messenger of Death.[1]

God's omnipresence is frequently mentioned by Guru Nanak:

> If God wills tigers, hawks, kestrels and falcons can be made to eat grass. Grass eating animals can become carnivores. Life's pattern is created as God wills. Mounds may appear in the streams and deserts be turned into oceans. A worm may become a king and armies be reduced to ashes. All creatures live by breathing but if God so wills it they can be sustained by some other means. Life is sustained as the True One pleases. (AG 144)

In the Japji (AG 6), Guru Nanak describes God as the 'king of kings'. Usually these expressions are not put into historical context. In the Babur *bani* they are. Here we read explicitly that God is sovereign, the ruler of history.

Thus, when we turn to the Sikh theory of the Just War, the *dharam yudh*, we find that it should not be fought for gain or even for self-defence; the only cause for which a Sikh should take up arms is in the defence of righteousness. Perhaps the best example of a Sikh protesting against injustice is the martyrdom of Guru Tegh Bahadur in 1675. Kashmiri brahmins came to him because they were being harassed by the Emperor Aurangzeb's governor of the province. Temples were being demolished and conversion strongly encouraged. The ninth Guru took their case to the Emperor, was arrested and was executed in the market place at Delhi.

The Sikh prayer known as Ardas which is offered daily in private devotions and on all public occasions such as the opening of the Guru Granth Sahib in the morning, at the close of worship, or at weddings and funerals, ends with the words: 'Raj karega Khalsa yaqi rahe na koi'. This was a slogan used by the followers of Banda Singh Bahadur, leader of the Khalsa army after the death of Guru Gobind Singh. In full the verse reads: 'The Khalsa shall rule, no hostile refractory shall exist. Frustrated, they shall all submit, and those who come for shelter shall be protected.' In their original context the words refer to the struggle for survival when Emperor Bahadur Shah issued an edict 'to kill the disciples of Nanak wherever they were found' (10 December 1710). Khalsa Raj was an aspiration of independence, which was realized with the establishment of the Sikh empire by Maharajah Ranjit Singh in 1801. It effectively ended with his death in 1839 after which the British imposed their influence upon Sikh policy before annexing the province in 1849. The slogan continued to be used by Sikhs. Those loyal to the British tended to explain it inclusively as the rule of the pure, as Khalsa can be given that meaning. 'Pure' could then refer to the just British rule of law in India. Later, it could be applied to independent India. In 1978 the eminent Sikh scholar, Professor Ganda Singh, could write:

> *Raj karega Khalsa* is an inseparable part of the Sikh prayer and of their past aspirations and traditions to serve their countrymen, and its recitation reminds them of their duties and responsibilities not only towards their own people but also to the entire family of Mother India whose own flesh and blood they are.[2]

A few years earlier, in 1966, Sikhs had commemorated the tercentenary of the birth of Guru Gobind Singh. Writing in the *Sikh Courier*'s special volume, one of their leaders, Taran Singh, explained the Khalsa in these words:

> The doctrine of the Khalsa or the Universal Brotherhood of the Pure, proceeds from the doctrine of the all-pervasive and indivisible

ultimate Reality . . . the brotherhood of the Pure is the brotherhood of entire humanity . . . It is a society of humanity so that they might transform the world into the Kingdom of Heaven.

There is no attempt here to think in the eschatological terms of Christian theology, though the seed growing secretly, or the 'leaven', may come to the mind of Christian readers.

The same is also true of the ideas of Gopal Singh in his beautiful poem inspired by Jesus, *The Man Who Never Died*, written in 1969 (published by Macmillan, India). There are abundant allusions to biblical passages and Christian ideas but the prevailing idiom is Sikh. The opening words are:

> This is the story of the Man
> Who never died;
> and Who proclaimed
> that he who's born
> must be re-born
> and he who's dead
> must rise from the state
> of death.
>
> For it is not in the nature of
> man to die
> but to live from no-time
> to not time.

The poem ends:

> But, he said unto those that believe
> that nothing dies in the realm of God-
> neither seed, nor drop, nor dust, nor man.
>
> Only the past dies or the present,
> but the future lives for ever.
>
> And I'm the future of man.
> To me, being and non-being were always one.
> I always was and never was!

Besides the interesting link with Vedic teaching (Rig Veda 10:129), Jesus is placed in an eternal context which is beyond time. This is in keeping with a religion which can call God Akal Purukh, which therefore preaches that as the believer becomes one with Akal Purukh and enters eternity the goals which other systems consider to be important cease to be a matter of ultimate concern. Sikhs do attach great importance to righteousness and justice as the virtues which the devotee should espouse and demand of others. They will only fill the earth as they are manifested in the lives of its inhabitants.

Towards the end of the 1970s the word 'Khalistan' came to be prominent in the speech of Sikhs. It signifies an independent Sikh state in which the code of Khalsa discipline will be law. It was originally used thirty years earlier when Muslim demands for Pakistan were voiced. It referred to a buffer state between that country, should it be created, and India. The revival of the demand for a Sikh homeland grew and some Sikhs became violent in their opposition to the Congress government of Indira Gandhi. In 1983 they began to fortify the precincts of the Golden Temple at Amritsar and in June 1984, on the anniversary of the martyrdom of Guru Arjan, soldiers of the Indian army stormed it. The Khalistan movement is significant in our present context because, although the great preacher who led the Sikh militants spoke of defending Sikh freedoms and saw the struggle as a *dharam yudh*, it never seemed to be accompanied by the idea that, if successful, it would inaugurate an age of righteousness. Though he preached to the religious sentiment of Sikhs, Bhindranwale's aims were political rather than religious. There is, however, some evidence that preaching about Khalistan may have had an eschatological element. During research into the beliefs of Sikh children growing up in Coventry, England, Dr Eleanor Nesbitt was told of a *katha* tape which said:

> When a lot of Sikhs are going to die the tenth Guru will come again . . . He's going to live again because he didn't go to Anandpur Sahib, the Harmandir Sahib [*sic*], so he's coming back to faith for what it is . . . and he's going to fight for Khalistan.

Beyond the obvious confusion of Anandpur Sahib and the Harmandir Sahib (Golden Temple) at Amritsar, there is awareness of the kind of ideas mentioned above, linked this time with Khalistan. Unfortunately, it has not been possible to locate the taped talk *(katha)* to which the boy refers. A careful analysis of Sant Jarnail Singh Bhindranwale's addresses, if recordings of them are still extant, may provide further evidence for the use of eschatology to motivate his supporters.

6 Popular Sikh thought

There are several stories in history of deliverers whose return is predicted. The British king, Arthur, sleeps with his knights under Richmond Castle (among other places) and will awaken to deliver his people at some time of great crisis. Frederick Barbarossa is said to be in a cave in Germany ready to come to the rescue of the German nation. There is also a Spanish tradition of the return of St James of Compostella. The history of the Sikhs for a hundred years from the end of the seventeenth century until the success of Maharajah Ranjit Singh was one in which they faced a constant threat of extinction. The Sikh psyche can only be understood if this is clearly recognized. Gurdwaras are full of pictures of heroic suffering and sermons rehearse the ordeal of Sikhs to keep the memory alive. In this context it is not surprising to find Sikhs believing stories about the return of Guru Gobind Singh.

One describes him as surviving the assassination attempt at Nander in 1708 and returning to Punjab where he lived for many more years. Popular art[3] depicts him flying on a white horse with two Rajput chieftains whom he freed from Satara fort, Rustam Rao and Bala Rao, clinging to his stirrups. A gurdwara at Marimarh commemorates the tradition. Belief in the survival of Guru Gobind Singh is fundamental to the teaching of Namdhari Sikhs with which this essay will end, but meanwhile we will pursue the line of popular thought.

Guru Gobind Singh was a prolific poet skilled in many languages. In 1730, some years after his death, Bhai Mani Singh, one of his close followers, collected his compositions and assembled them in what is now known as the Dasam Granth. Much of the material in the volume, 1428 pages long in the printed edition, still awaits careful study and translation into English. Scholars disagree about the authenticity of some of its contents and their meaning. It is generally accepted that one of the Guru's motives in writing some epics was to encourage Sikhs in times of crisis, particularly during the last decade of his life. To this end he did not hesitate to employ the mythology of Hinduism, especially concerning the doctrine of avatar, though in one of his most important passages he firmly denounced anyone who declared him to be an incarnation of Vishnu. In Vachitar Natak, one of his most influential hymns, a kind of celestial autobiography, he describes his non-karmic birth, the consequence of God's command, using ideas and language which must have reminded some of his audience of the concept of avatar. He continues:

> Those who call me Parmeshur shall fall in to the pit of hell. Know me as his servant only – have not the least doubt of that . . . For this purpose we have been born, all you saints understand this in your hearts, to spread the faith, to protect *dharma* and to extirpate evil doers.[4]

A description by Bhai Santokh Singh of the death of Guru Gobind Singh, written in the first half of the nineteenth century, states that he ordered a tent to be erected over his sandalwood cremation pyre and rode into it on a blue horse. He was wearing an aigrette of jewels as a façade to his turban, carrying a lance of pure steel and a white hawk in his left hand. His own clothing was also blue as it had been ever since the Vaisakhi gathering of 1699 when he established the order of the Khalsa.[5]

Kapur Singh describes this as the archetypal form of Guru Gobind Singh and discusses it in the context of Vishnu.[6] In the pages which follow he develops the comparison in detail, ending with a discussion of the blue horse. It is the Guru's vehicle (*vahana*) corresponding to the vehicles associated with Hindu deities. It was, he asserts, to dissociate himself from the mythology of Kalki, the tenth incarnation of Vishnu, the one who is to come, who will be seated on a white horse. Blue was the colour of the Khalsa and Kapur Singh speculates that the affinity of Guru Gobind Singh for the colour is because it is symbolic of the Absolute, being the only primary colour which 'can absorb without blemish the red, yellow and green, of the mighty spiritual movements of the Aryan and Semitic races of mankind'.[7] Guru Gobind Singh, he argues, was eager to elevate the Sikh movement into the status of the 'Third Path' between Hinduism and Islam.[8]

The stories outlined above, with Kapur Singh's comments, demonstrate how the life of Guru Gobind Singh – who was the tenth Guru as Kalki is the tenth avatar of Vishnu – could be conceived of in terms related to Hindu mythology. He does not mention a passage in the Dasam Granth in Chaubis Avatar where the Guru is said to appear, riding on a horse, as Kalki, above the Harminder Sahib. This idea is sometimes found among Sikhs today.

A number of points must be made concerning the link with Kalki. First, as Kapur Singh himself is the first to affirm, Guru Gobind Singh repudiated any notion of being an avatar. In addition to the quoted passage, there is a verse in his Krishna Avatar where he states: 'I never gave a thought to Vishnu and his human creations, such as Krishna; for though I had heard of them I do not possess even a passing acquaintance with them.'[9] Secondly, the popular pictures of Guru Gobind, found in Sikh homes or painted by eminent artists such as Kirpal Singh and Sobha Singh, do not always depict him riding a blue horse, and where they do the colour's significance does not always seem to be appreciated by other Sikhs. If there is a popular association of Guru Gobind Singh and Kalki it is certainly not acknowledged by Sikh scholars and is frowned on by Sikh orthodoxy, which categorically rejects the concept of avatar, as the Gurus themselves did. As early as the days of Guru Arjan the admonition was given: 'Burnt be the tongue which says that God takes birth. God is not born and does not die; does not come and does not go.' (AG 1136)

7 Namdharis

There may be as many as 70,000 Namdhari Sikhs in a population of about sixteen million. They originated as a reform movement within the Panth. Initially, their opposition was to moral laxity, the use of drugs and alcohol, and personal extravagance in the celebration of marriages. They also denounced dowries, the observance of caste in arranging marriages and the practice of forbidding widows to remarry. In all these matters they were upholding the known teaching of the Gurus. Their social concern was expressed in the independence struggles and a number of them were executed by the British in the 1870s for attacking

Muslim slaughterhouses and butchers' shops in a campaign to purify Punjab and restore Sikh rule. Their leader was not implicated in the disturbances, but nevertheless, was exiled to Rangoon.

A distinctive aspect of Namdhari doctrine is the belief that Guru Gobind Singh did not die at Nander but went back to Punjab as described by Bhai Santokh Singh, where he continued to live for some years, dying in 1812. During this time he met Balak Singh (1799–1861) whom he initiated as eleventh Guru. He, in turn, conferred guruship upon Bab Ram Singh (born 1816), the leader who was sent into exile. According to the British he died in 1884. Namdharis believe that he still lives and will return at a time of crisis in world history. Meanwhile a series of vice-regent Gurus has led them since the exiling of Guru Ram Singh in 1872.

Guru Ram Singh said that Russia would invade and rule India (a very strong fear among the British at that time), and that the Punjab would be utterly destroyed, so that only one light would be seen in the space of eighteen miles (a reference to the resulting depopulation of the region). Bhaini Sahib, the headquarters of the Namdhari movement, would itself be destroyed. Its location would only be recognized by the remaining stumps of two pipal trees which Guru Ram Singh had planted there.

Although Namdharis believe in the return of Guru Ram Singh they do not appear to regard him as a saviour figure, a deliverer of the Sikhs. In fact, Guru Partarp Singh (1890–1959), in a tape-recorded discourse, said that it was not enough to be a Namdhari. A good Muslim, Hindu or Christian would survive the disaster before an evil Kuka. 'The Almighty is One, so anyone who believes in God will survive', is how a devotee at Bhaini Sahib expressed the view in conversation with the present writer.

The Namdhari form of Ardas includes the names of their Gurus after those of the earlier ten, and recalls the heroic self-sacrifices of those who died at the hands of the British in resisting cow-slaughter and in the cause of Indian independence. Another passage reads:

All in this assembly pray that you will mercifully reveal yourself in all your glory. Bring to an end the killing of the poor and the cow, extend the true faith over the earth, free all who are imprisoned, destroy those who are evil, and exalt your True Khalsa.[10]

8 Conclusion

The conclusion of our study must be that the idea of a coming deliverer has a place in Sikh teaching for some members of the Panth. However, the Gurus offered people of all classes, women and men, the hope of immediate spiritual liberation through God's grace and this is a rich message which all Sikhs value and emphasize. Everyone should practise *nam simran* daily, an act of meditation which develops unity with God. Such access to eternity could not be bettered by the prospect of some divine or human intervention in time.

However, Sikh insistence upon the world as God's creation and sphere of continuous activity and a concern for social as well as individual justice, and the importance of the concept of the service of humanity, *seva,* as a way of worshipping God, requires them to take history seriously and work to bring about the actual rule of God in human affairs. For some people there is a belief that the glories of the past personified in Guru Gobind Singh will be experienced again in the future and will be realized through his return. The Namdhari Sikh hope gives purpose to belief that as in the days from Guru Arjan to Guru Gobind Singh, there is both the guidance of the scripture and the human Guru and adds a notion of destiny to it.

Eschatology, a concern about last things, is not, apart from the examples given, a predominant aspect of Sikh thought. Most studies of Sikh dharma do not mention it and many Sikhs are alarmed by any tendency to deflect the devotee from the prospect of God realization in their present existence. Time is cyclical and will continue *ad infinitum* according to God's will.

God is the One Ultimate Being. This earth and humanity may pass away if that is God's will but human beings should not speculate upon things which are known only to God. Even those who do expect a return of Guru Gobind Singh or Guru Ram Singh do not look for portents, although – in common with adherents of other religions – when wickedness seems to them to be most manifest, promises of return and the hope for the establishment of justice become strongly remembered. However, for everyone to know God now is most important. Such is the message of the Guru Granth Sahib which is the basis of all Sikh theology. As Guru Nanak said: 'If one listens to the Word the power of Death is overcome. The devout, Nanak says, live in eternal bliss, suffering and sin depart from those who hear the Word' (AG 2).

Notes

1 AG 417–18, as translated in W. H. McLeod, *Guru Nanak and the Sikh Religion* (Oxford, Clarendon Press, 1968).
2 *Punjab Past and Present* (April 1973).
3 W. H. McLeod, *Textual Sources for the Study of Sikhism* (Manchester, Manchester University Press, 1984; repr. University of Chicago Press, 1990).
4 Vachitar Natak, 6:1–28, 42, 43. The poem is most easily found in M. A. Macauliffe, *The Sikh Religion: Its Gurus, Sacred Writings and Authors* (Oxford, Oxford University Press, 1909; repr. frequently), v. 286–306.
5 Kapur Singh, *Parashaprasna* (1959), 164, 166.
6 Ibid., 167.
7 Ibid., 189.
8 Ibid., 224.
9 Ibid., 225.
10 Quoted in McLeod, *Textual Sources*, 131.

Further reading

Cole, W. Owen and Piara Singh Sambhi, *The Sikhs: Their Religious Beliefs and Practices* (Brighton, Sussex Academic Press, 1985).
MacAuliffe, M. A., *The Sikh Religion: Its Gurus, Sacred Writings and Anthems* (Oxford, Oxford University Press, 1909; repr. frequently).
McCleod, W. H., *Guru Nanak and the Sikh Religion* (Oxford, Clarendon Press, 1968).
——, *Textual Sources for the Study of Sikhism* (Manchester, Manchester University Press, 1984; repr. University of Chicago Press, 1990).
——, *Who is a Sikh?* (Oxford, Clarendon Press, 1989).
Singh, Harbans, *Encyclopaedia of Sikhism* (Patiala, Punjabi University, 1992; further 4 vols. in press).
——, *Heritage of the Sikhs* (New Delhi, Manohar, 1995).
Singh, Nikky-Guninder Kaur, *The Name of My Beloved: Verses of the Sikh Gurus* (London, Harper Collins, 1996).

5

Messianic hope in Second Temple Judaism

JONATHAN G. CAMPBELL

1 Introduction

This chapter takes as its subject the fascinating array of hopes for the future that existed among Jews in the last two centuries BCE and the first century CE.[1] By examining these beliefs, we shall learn something about the nature of Judaism in this period. We shall also come to realize that Jews and Christians of later times have often oversimplified or misunderstood the evidence under the influence of doctrines developed after 100 CE.

The three centuries concerned, roughly 200 BCE to 100 CE, are part of what scholars name the Second Temple period, a designation marking out Jewish history from the rebuilding of the Temple in Jerusalem in the late 500s BCE until its destruction by the Romans in 70 CE.[2] This interval of time overlaps with what may be called the biblical period. The Hebrew Scriptures deal with Israelite and Jewish history up to 400 BCE and beyond, and, in fact, it is now clear that several biblical books were composed well after this date, while the youngest of all, Daniel, was penned in the 160s BCE. It makes sense for us to concentrate on Judaism during the three hundred years specified, whilst early Christianity, a Jewish sect which arose towards the end of this period, will be tackled in Chapter 6.

The first task we face is to find a path through the bewildering set of terms scholars use when studying ancient Jewish hopes for the future. In particular, it is common to come across interrelated references to 'eschatology', 'apocalypses', 'apocalyptic thought', 'apocalypticism', 'the messiah' and 'messianism'. Because writers employ these words with differing or even contradictory nuances, it is worth saying a few words on each of them before going any further.[3]

Let us look at 'eschatology' first. Derived from the Greek adjective *eschatos*, meaning 'last' or 'final', it is a word used by modern scholars to denote beliefs about the future as they are found in biblical religion and in Judaism throughout Second Temple times (including early Christianity). In view of the vast period of time involved, as well as the amount of literature, the term is loose enough to encompass a thoroughly this-worldly expectation, as well as hopes for the imminent arrival of a more other-worldly age of blessing. The former looks ahead to God's blessing of the ordinary life of the nation, and it is sometimes labelled 'prophetic eschatology' because it tends to be associated with the prophetic books of the Bible. The latter, often called 'apocalyptic eschatology', designates the sort of hopes that became increasingly common after 200 BCE, concentrating on an 'apocalyptic' crisis of the 'last things' as the end of the world, or 'eschaton', draws near and the era of salvation dawns.

'Apocalyptic' here denotes the overwhelmingly supernatural or dramatic character of elements in God's plan for the future, including such varied features as a final cosmic battle, unprecedented persecution of the righteous, direct divine intervention and judgement, or the miraculous creation of a new heaven and earth to replace the existing order. Most often, such 'apocalyptic' themes occur in works which are set in the genre of an 'apocalypse'. Indeed, this link explains the related terminology. Strictly speaking, however, an 'apocalypse' is simply a book which takes the form of a divine 'revelation' (Gk., *apocalypsis*) and which is usually linked pseudonymously to some pious hero from Israel's past such as Enoch, Daniel or Moses.[4] To avoid confusion, therefore, it is important to realize that some books which are apocalypses in form (that is, presented as divine revelations about any given subject) do not have much that is apocalyptic (that is, concerned with a dramatic end to the world) by way of content. For example, Jubilees claims to be an apocalypse about important legal matters, additional to those in the Bible yet also revealed to Moses on Mount Sinai. But it contains only a small amount of apocalyptic thought about the eschaton. On the other hand, some texts do speak of apocalyptic matters but are not set in the form of a revelation to an ancient figure like Moses. Here, for instance, the War Rule (1QM) among the sectarian Dead Sea Scrolls is important.

In any case, scholars nowadays tend to use 'apocalypse' to designate any ancient text which claims to be a revelatory book, while 'apocalyptic' is a more general term describing dramatic ideas about the end of the world. We can tell that both were popular among Jews in the second half of the Second Temple period, because a lot of apocalypses have survived and apocalyptic motifs appear in a range of texts. However, we should not think that there was ever an identifiable religious movement which might be dubbed 'apocalypticism', as some used to suggest. On the contrary, apocalypses were written and apocalyptic themes were employed over a long stretch of time by a variety of religious groups which, in other respects, may often have had little in common.

The English word 'messiah' and the related 'messianism' derive from *messias*, a Greek transliteration of the Hebrew word *mashiach*. The latter means 'anointed (one)' and may also be translated into Greek as *christos*. Of course, Christians have traditionally held that Jesus was the 'anointed one', Messiah or Christ sent by God to redeem the world. This has led some scholars to an anachronistic preoccupation with the role of the Messiah in Jewish thought before the rise of Christianity. However, it is now increasingly recognized that *mashiach* is never used in the Hebrew Scriptures of a future saviour in the way envisaged by later Christians. More significantly, the term does not occur frequently in Jewish writings from Second Temple times to denote a figure whom God will deploy to usher in the era of salvation. Where it does crop up, it is best to adopt the translation 'anointed one' or 'messiah', rather than 'the Messiah', in order to avoid confusion. To complicate matters further still, others have used the term 'messianism' to denote general beliefs about God's future plans for his people, even when a specific anointed figure is not mentioned!

In view of the above discussion, we should make clear how terms will be employed in this chapter. 'Eschatology' or 'eschatological' will be taken to denote both general and specific hopes about the future of all kinds; 'apocalypse' will be reserved solely for works which are presented as divine revelations (whether they contain apocalyptic themes or not), while 'apocalyptic' will describe dramatic or supernatural events at the end of time (as found in some apocalypses and elsewhere); 'messiah' and 'messianism' will only be employed when individual anointed figures are expected. Furthermore, because our main topic is Jewish beliefs about the future in the last two centuries BCE and the first century CE, we need to endeavour to enter more fully into this complicated world. First, the biblical background to the general unfolding of Jewish expectations about the future in the post-biblical period will be discussed. Secondly, we shall look at Jewish eschatological hopes in a range of material that has come down to us from the period *c.* 200 BCE to 100 CE. Then, evidence for a belief in the advent of a messianic figure as the agent of God's redemption will be considered more specifically. Finally, an attempt will be made to draw some conclusions.

2 Biblical perspectives on the future

The basic eschatological hope, that God will ensure a better state of affairs dawns for his people in the future, is found in portions of the Hebrew Scriptures, in Second Temple Jewish texts and in the New Testament. Since it is the subject of another chapter, we shall leave the New Testament to one side. But some comments on eschatology in the Hebrew Scriptures will serve to clarify our discussion of later Second Temple material. One cautionary note should be sounded immediately, however, for scholars are not as keen as they were even a generation ago to systematize any aspect of the thought of the Bible.[5] This reluctance is due to an increasing awareness of the diversity of religious practice and belief in the biblical period. Indeed, various individuals or groups living side-by-side within Israel, both before and after the exile, may well have had different or even opposing views about what the future might hold. Also, such ideas as there were will have evolved as circumstances and needs altered. At the same time, some biblical writers, like those who composed the Wisdom literature (Proverbs, Ecclesiastes, Job), seem to have had little interest in eschatological matters at all.[6]

Nevertheless, it is possible to isolate two pre-exilic beliefs which to a large degree shaped expectations for the future in the biblical period. The first concerns what may be called the powerful David-Zion tradition. This theme, finding characteristic expression in 2 Samuel 7, centres on the divine promise to ensure that a descendant of the royal line of David will always sit on the throne in Jerusalem. Various Psalms express the related conviction that, when this Davidic king is righteous, his position on Mount Zion, which is also God's special dwelling-place, will be inviolable and the people of Israel will enjoy abundant divine blessing. The promises of progeny and land to the Patriarchs in the narratives of Genesis 12–50 are also closely bound with this tradition, for they assume that Israel's true destiny lies in the future as a 'great nation' (12:2) in the period of the monarchy.

The second tradition concerns the nature of the covenant made between God and Israel as mediated through Moses on Mount Sinai, and as repeated by Moses prior to the conquest of the land; see Exodus 19–24 for the former and Deuteronomy 26–32 for the latter. The conditions of this agreement stipulate that the future lot of the people of God depends on their obedience or otherwise to the dictates of the covenant. Such a choice opens up two basic possibilities: blessing in reward for obedience or punishment for disobedience. Indeed, the whole history of Israel up to the exile, as set forth in what scholars call the Deuteronomic History (Joshua–2 Kings), is presented on the assumption that such a schema controlled the nation's fate. Whatever is to be made of the historical accuracy of this long narrative, the writer or writers believed in a correlation between the present/future and the past/present. In other words, God is pictured as dealing with his people in the present according to the extent of their faithfulness to him in the past, while their future predicament will equally depend on their obedience to God's will in the here and now.[7]

It is against the background of these two central traditions in ancient Israelite religion that the pre-exilic prophets of Israel and Judah levelled their devastating criticisms of both the king and the people for their lack of faithfulness to God, as recorded in the likes of Isaiah 1–12, Hosea, Amos and Micah.[8] In the same passages, we also encounter pronouncements that, given the lamentable state of the nation's moral and spiritual health, the imminent future entails a scenario so different from the common expectation that it can be pictured as 'final' or as 'an end' – with the resultant loss of nationhood, monarchy, Zion and Temple. A good illustration here is Amos 8:1, with a deliberate pun on the Hebrew *qayits* and *qets*:

This is what the Lord GOD showed me – a basket of summer fruit [*qayits*]. He said, 'Amos, what do you see?' And I said, 'A basket of summer fruit [*qayits*].' Then the LORD said to me,
> 'The end [*qets*] has come upon
> my people Israel, I will never
> again pass them by.'[9]

However, despite the tone of the final phrase in this citation, it is important to note that there is usually also an open-endedness in such proclamations so that, should the people unexpectedly change their ways, disaster may be averted right up to the last moment.

But according to the biblical writers, such repentance was not forthcoming. Instead, the disappearance of the northern kingdom of Israel (722 BCE) and the exile of the people of Judah in the south to Babylon (587 BCE) were interpreted as punishments for sin. Nevertheless, the positive elements in both the David-Zion and Sinai Covenant traditions enabled the exilic prophets like Jeremiah, Deutero-Isaiah (Isaiah 40–55) and Ezekiel to hold out the hope of a new age in which God's blessing would materialize in an unprecedented way and in which the people's faithfulness would be unparalleled. The details of this restoration vary considerably from writer to writer. Hence, while Jeremiah and Ezekiel assume that divine redemption will include a restoration of all twelve tribes of Israel to form a united monarchy as in the days of King David, Deutero-Isaiah sees such restoration as applicable only to the people of Judah. Or again, in contrast to the new righteous Prince presented in Ezekiel, Deutero-Isaiah democratizes the Davidic promises, so that in the new order they will apply to the whole of the populace. But these variations are subsumed under a common overview which, with the exile understood as due punishment for past transgression, holds out the hope of redemption. This will take place in the near future, it is promised, so that what had not been realized in pre-exilic times would be more than fulfilled in the age of God's approaching restoration of his people to their land. Such ideas of a restoration to the land, accompanied by a new obedience and consequent divine blessing, are expressed in Jeremiah 31:31–3, which states:

The days are surely coming, says the LORD, when I will make a new covenant with the house of Israel and with the house of Judah. It will not be like the covenant I made with their ancestors when I took them by the hand to bring them out of the land of Egypt – a covenant that they broke, though I was their husband, says the LORD. But this is the covenant that I will make with the house of Israel after those days, says the LORD: I will put my law within them, and I will write it on their hearts; and I will be their God, and they shall be my people.

Somewhat in contrast to these bright pictures of hope are the prophetic and other writings of the post-exilic age: Haggai, Zechariah 1–8, Third-Isaiah (Isaiah 56–66), Malachi, Ezra and Nehemiah.[10] These texts show that the experience of those who returned to the land of Judah in the late 500s and in the 400s BCE, as well as of those who had remained there all along, did not live up to the glorious expectations of the exilic prophets. Once again, however, this common theme of disappointment is handled differently when it comes to detail. Hence, Haggai and Zechariah 1–8 lament the fact that initial rebuilding of the Temple in Jerusalem has come to a halt. The reinstatement of this project, it is argued, will have cosmic consequences and will lead to the fulfilment of everyone's expectations for a restored community headed by the rightful successor to the Davidic throne, Zerubbabel, and his high-priestly counterpart, Jeshua. Third-Isaiah blames the non-fulfilment of Deutero-Isaiah's vision on the continuing faithless state of the community which, at the time of the author, seems to have been divided over issues that are no longer entirely clear. These chapters promise both salvation from this predicament and judgement on those who are responsible; the language is dramatic and assumes a radical break between the evil present and the new heaven and earth that God will soon create (see especially Isaiah 65–6).

Although they do not appeal directly to the earlier expectations of the exilic prophets, Malachi, Ezra and Nehemiah are also concerned with the less-than-ideal situation prevailing in post-exilic times. It seems clear that, for some reason, the hope for a continuation of the Davidic line had disappeared by the time reflected in these works (*c.*450–350 BCE). Blame for a more general lack of divine blessing is placed on various sins committed by the people, including defilement of the Temple and priesthood (Malachi) and mixed marriages (Ezra and Nehemiah). As a result, the writers of these books call for repentance and promise that a whole-hearted devotion to the laws of God on the part of the people, including proper attention to priestly and Temple matters, will lead to an outpouring of the covenant's blessings. Malachi 4:1–2 is informative here:

> See, the day is coming, burning like an oven, when all the arrogant and all evildoers will be stubble; the day that comes shall burn them up says the LORD of hosts, so that it will leave them neither root nor branch. But for you who revere my name the sun of righteousness shall rise, with healing in its wings. You shall go out leaping like calves from the stall.

Further, Malachi 4:5–6 envisages the advent of a messenger figure who, following in the footsteps of the prophet Elijah of old, will inaugurate divine reward and punishment for the righteous and the wicked, respectively.

This biblical passage shows that new projections into the future were having to be made in post-exilic times. The necessity of such speculation arose largely from the fact that the prophetic promises of exilic times had gone unfulfilled. Thus, just as Deutero-Isaiah, for instance, had sought to convince the exiles that an age of restoration was about to dawn, so too the post-exilic authors were forced by their circumstances to focus their promises of salvation in the future rather than in the disappointment of the present. This had the effect of putting on hold the ancient promises which, doubtless for good reasons, were now thought to be delayed until such time as their proper fulfilment was deemed appropriate by God.

Alongside this development, one practical factor should be noted. Between *c.*400 and 300 BCE, most of the books that later came to form the canon of the Hebrew Scriptures reached their final shape – with the chief exception of Daniel which stems from the mid-second century. This means that by the middle of the Second Temple period, the Law and a core of prophetic writings were gaining an ever-wider circulation among the Jewish populace – that is, the Torah, the Deuteronomic History, Isaiah, Jeremiah, Ezekiel, the Twelve Minor Prophets and the Psalms.[11] Any observant reader of these works would realize that they contained promises which patently had not been met in their entirety. In particular, we may imagine that many Second Temple Jews would have asked what was to be made of the promises of land and progeny to the Patriarchs, or of Deutero-Isaiah's images of a blessed life in the land. Or again, what about the powerful images associated with the Davidic king as pictured in the so-called Royal Psalms (for example, Psalm 20 or 110), or the coupling of the king and the high priest in a blessed dual leadership as portrayed in Haggai and Zechariah 1–8? These various idealized expectations, which had obviously still to be attained, must have made an impression on many Jews in the last two centuries BCE and the first century CE.

3 Eschatological hopes in Second Temple Judaism

Before we survey the relevant literature from this period, it will be useful to mention three further developments which influenced the way hopes for the future took shape.[12] The first concerns the Law-centred nature of Judaism. By 200 BCE, there can be no doubt that the Law or Torah (Genesis, Exodus, Leviticus, Numbers, Deuteronomy) was universally acknowledged by Jews as the summation of God's revelation to Israel; obedience to its rules was required as the response of faith and as the way of receiving divine blessing. But, as we have observed, it must have seemed to many that this blessing was not forthcoming. Much of the religious output of the period, therefore, calls for proper observance of the Law and then speculates about the future that will unfold following obedience. However, it is important to remember that it was the adherence to the Torah alone which held binding force in Judaism at this time, leaving plenty of room for divergence of thought when it came to reflection about the future.

Another factor concerns the domination of Palestine by successive world powers – Babylon and Persia (in the fifth and sixth centuries BCE), and Greece and Rome (from *c.*300 BCE to 70 CE and beyond). For many this must have been one of the chief signals that God's blessing of the nation was being held in check. Nevertheless, it had the effect of broadening the political and religious horizon, so that God was no longer seen simply as the God of Israel but as the God of the whole universe. Moreover, some Jews began to envisage a time when the last such world power and its earthly ruler would be succeeded by God and the advent of his kingdom, which would have universal consequences for the entire cosmos and all peoples, not just the Jews.

Thirdly, we may note a growing concern for the fate of the individual. The evolution of Jewish religious consciousness might have resulted in such individualism, regardless of historical circumstances. But this tendency may be explained in part by the practical fact that it was not easy to treat the Jewish people of the last two centuries BCE and the first century CE as a single entity. Indeed, various sects and parties came into being from the second century BCE onwards, while many Jews lived outside their traditional homeland – whether in Rome or Babylon or Egypt. Such realities made it simpler to focus on the individuals that made up one's own group, leaving the future fate of the nation as a whole in God's hands.

It was against the background of these varied factors, then, that speculation about the future took shape, founded upon the scriptural traditions already outlined. We may detect an increasing tendency towards favouring dramatic or apocalyptic motifs, allowing us to distinguish an older, biblically based hope from later biblical and post-biblical ideas. In the former, it was held that the purified nation would one day flourish in the midst of the vanquished Gentiles, ruled by an upright Davidic king in peace, justice and harmony with nature. But later works exhibit a gradual shift towards a more other-worldly or supernatural orientation. Ultimately, texts from the end of our period, like 4 Ezra and 2 Baruch, envisage a transcendent future, descended intact from heaven and thoroughly divorced from historical processes.

A number of works from the early decades of the second century BCE contain related apocalyptic motifs in a less developed form. They reflect what scholars have called the Hellenistic crisis, a period of upheaval and dissension among Palestinian Jews caused by the influx of Greek ideas and customs, culminating in the persecution of Judaism by the foreign king Antiochus IV in the mid-160s BCE. His behaviour led to the Maccabean revolt which reasserted Jewish identity and resulted in an independent Jewish state in Palestine for some 100 years. However, the conduct of its leadership in turn acted as a catalyst for dissent and the formation of various religious sects and parties.[13]

We shall mention two important apocalyptic works belonging to this category. The first is 1 Enoch, a collection of five books which were once independent, presented as a revelation to Enoch about a range of topics.[14] In fact, four of the books come from the the first few decades of the second century BCE or earlier and try to encourage the reader in two ways. First, assurances are given that, notwithstanding the turmoil of the times, history is unfolding in line with what is written on God's heavenly tablets (see 1 Enoch 93:2). Indeed, numerous apocalyptic details are prominent, and the author clearly views his own day as part of the final stage in the history of the world. In various parts of the collection, he looks forward, therefore, to imminent vindication for the righteous, a new heaven and earth, a new Jerusalem and Temple, the advent of a messiah, and a reversion to the primordial bliss of creation.[15] Secondly, through Enoch's guided tour of the cosmos as described in 1 Enoch 17–36, the reader is reassured that, despite appearances to the contrary, the wicked will certainly be punished and the righteous vindicated.

The book of Daniel, presented as a series of revelations to a pious Babylonian exile of the 500s BCE, was specifically written to encourage those experiencing the persecutions of Antiochus IV. Hence, the prediction of the exilic prophet Jeremiah (25:11) that the sixth-century exile would last '70 years' is reinterpreted in Daniel 9:24 to mean '490 years'. This figure has the effect of bringing the reader into the second century BCE and demonstrates that everything is taking place according to God's overall plan. In a similar vein, Daniel 7 promises that God's oppressed faithful people, personified as an angelic 'one like a son of man' (7:13, 14), will eventually triumph over their enemies. Further, Daniel 10–12 contains a detailed historical schema which, when the author's own day has been reached (11:39), moves into an apocalyptic prediction of future salvation and resurrection. These chapters assume the beginning of Antiochus IV's persecution in 167 BCE but not the victory of the Maccabees in 164 BCE. Thus, although he knows of their initial military success, the author of Daniel feels safer putting his hope in a dramatic divine intervention as the solution to the troubles of the time.[16] This can be seen most clearly in Daniel 12:1–3, predicting divine assistance through the archangel Michael, as well as a resurrection of the dead:

At that time Michael, the great prince, the protector of your people, shall arise. There shall be a time of anguish, such as has never occurred since nations first came into existence. But at that time your people shall be delivered, everyone who is found written in the book. Many of those who sleep in the dust of the earth shall awaken, some to everlasting life, and some to everlasting shame and contempt.

Several other writings of a similar age reflect a more traditional outlook, akin to that which predominates in the Bible. One of them, Ecclesiasticus, or Sirach – a book following in the biblical Wisdom tradition – was originally written in Hebrew around 180 BCE and then translated into Greek by the author's grandson soon after 132 BCE. Although a glorious future for the Jews is expected, it is presented in a rather sober manner when compared with 1 Enoch or Daniel. Indeed, the author is something of a scholar, for he realizes that the biblical prophets spoke primarily to their own day. However, he holds that some of their words still await fulfilment. Accordingly, Sirach 36:1–7 bemoans the state of Jerusalem and the dispersion of the Jews. Yet the writer's hope for the future is thoroughly this-worldly in orientation. While he predicts that the appearance of a successor to Elijah will bring repentance and restoration (48:10), there is no belief in a resurrection but only the expectation of a mere shadowy existence after death in the biblical Sheol (41:1–4). It is against this background that the promise of a new Davidic ruler should be understood (see 47:11, 22). A closer look shows that this expectation is theoretical. Rather, it is in the High Priest that the writer invests his real hope (45:23–4), so that a recent incumbent of this office, Simon II, is eulogized in Sirach 50. Such a this-worldly concern may be explained partly by the predilections of the author and partly by the time of writing, for we may imagine that the temptation to engage in apocalyptic speculation was much less pressing than in the heat of the persecution under Antiochus IV.[17]

Moving on to the beginning of the first century BCE, several works look back with hindsight on the victories of the Maccabees and the ensuing Hasmonean dynasty. One of these is 1 Maccabees, written *c.*100 BCE and clearly intended as propaganda for the Hasmoneans.[18] Drawing on the terms of the biblical Sinai covenant to describe second-century matters, the persecution under Antiochus IV is interpreted as divine punishment for the faithlessness of the people. However, the reader is reminded that the brave activities of the Maccabees turned God's anger into deliverance, so that their Hasmonean successors are rightful High Priests (see 2:19–26) and rulers of the Jews (see 2:68; 3:8; 5:62). In this way, the period of the author is presented as enjoying the covenant's full blessings with no need for future salvation. Indeed, it has already arrived in the form of the Hasmonean dynasty. This is why 1 Maccabees 14 describes Simon Maccabee in clichés which suggest the fulfilment of biblical prophecies of Israel's future glory.[19] In particular, verses 11–12 echo traditional motifs:

> He established peace in the land,
> and Israel rejoiced with great joy.
> All the people sat under their own vines and fig trees,
> and there was none to make them afraid.[20]

In contrast, an altogether negative response to the Maccabees and their Hasmonean successors lies behind the sectarian Dead Sea Scrolls, which probably reflect the beliefs and practices of a branch of the Essenes.[21] This important body of material contains works written by a religious community living beside the Dead Sea from towards the end of the second century BCE until 68 CE.[22] Although various factors contributed to the formation of the sect, opposition to the Maccabees' assumption of high-priestly office seems to have been a major element. The community retreated to the site of Qumran in the Judaean desert, believing it lived in the final 'age', during which it alone was in receipt of God's blessing and knew how to interpret the scriptures. As for eschatology, several scrolls state that God has predetermined the history of the world (1QS 3–4, CD 2:3–10, 1QpHab), which will end in a final cosmic battle, as described in apocalyptic detail in the War Scroll (1QM). God, his angels and the sect will, of course, win this war. The salvation, of which the sectarians already had a foretaste, would then be consummated. However, it is not clear what their experience after this would be, for while one text speaks of resurrection (4Q521), others merely describe the hope of a long and blessed life. For now, we may note a recent description by Sanders of the sect's eschatological hopes:

> they would fight a great battle and win; all of God's adversaries would
> be destroyed; they would rebuild the temple and run it correctly; they

would observe the right calendar; they would live in peace, love, and joy . . . [but] We do not learn just what happened to dead sectarians.[23]

Similarly, it is not easy to work out the community's expectations regarding the advent of a messiah or messiahs, despite numerous references to anointed figures. We shall, however, return to this topic in the next section.

At this point, it is also worth taking note of the Psalms of Solomon.[24] Written in the late 60s BCE, in the aftermath of the Roman rise to power in Palestine, they too are extremely critical of the Hasmoneans. Indeed, the Roman General Pompey's success is interpreted as divine punishment for the Hasmonean pollution of the Temple and Davidic pretensions, while the writer looks ahead to the proper fulfilment of the Davidic promises in the future. This will materialize when a future figure arises who, although fully human, will possess miraculous powers and be without sin. He will act as judge, succeed in war, gather the tribes of Israel together and be served by the Gentiles. A future judgement is also anticipated when God visits the earth, including the resurrection of the righteous and damnation of the wicked, although it is unclear how such divine activity relates to the role of the messianic figure himself.

All of the works considered so far constitute Jewish responses to the historical realities of Palestine in this period – whether Antiochus IV's persecution, the Maccabean uprising, the Hasmonean dynasty, or the Roman conquest. A text with another perspective is the Wisdom of Solomon. It probably dates from not long after the Psalms of Solomon but, although pseudonymously attributed to the same Israelite king, its provenance has rendered it very different in other respects. Almost certainly composed in Egypt, the Wisdom of Solomon mixes Jewish and Greek traditions and takes the form of a warning against the folly of idolatry. It is shown that, although the wicked may seem to flourish for a time, they will eventually perish. The righteous, on the other hand, even if suffering at the hands of the ungodly, can be sure of eternal life in the form of immortality of the soul under the care of God. This will be experienced at an individual level after death and the author, therefore, has no need for a wider eschatological belief nor for any physical resurrection of the body.[25]

Returning to Palestine, different yet again in its outlook is a work composed in the aftermath of the destruction of the Temple by the Romans in 70 CE. 4 Ezra intensifies the themes of earlier apocalyptic writers, exhorting patience amid suffering and promising that God's eventual miraculous intervention into the historical process is guaranteed. The original Jewish form of the book, consisting of 4 Ezra 3–14, contains three dialogues and four visions purportedly derived from the Ezra of the fifth century BCE.[26] Overall, they ask a series of penetrating questions, intended to refer indirectly to Jewish defeat and suffering at the hand of the Romans in the first century CE. The writer asks whether the end of the world is near, what the signs of its approaching advent might be and, if it is delayed, whether the ongoing sins of the people are to blame. The answers given are only partial and are not always expressed in terms of the question. Nevertheless, it is stated that the time of the end is fixed in accordance with God's will. As it happens, it is near and the number of righteous souls that will be saved is predetermined. Moreover, it is promised that, after a period of distress, God's messiah will appear. He will be attacked but will destroy the ungodly from Mount Zion with the Torah. Then he will rule over a new Jerusalem for 400 years, at the end of which he will die. A seven-day primordial silence will usher in the final resurrection and a judgement for seven years. The wicked will be assigned to the abyss, while the righteous will enjoy paradise. Thus, a new age, returning to the bliss of primeval times, will dawn.[27]

It is fitting that we should conclude our brief survey of literature from the Second Temple period with 4 Ezra. Indeed, it marks a high point in the development of apocalyptic thought, culminating in a hope for the future which is thoroughly transcendent and divorced from history.[28] Of course, works from the second century BCE, like 1 Enoch or Daniel, contain related themes in a less developed form. But, as we have seen, it should not be forgotten that a more mundane or this-worldly expectation also continued to exist throughout the centuries we have been looking at.

4 Messianic hope in Second Temple Jewish texts

The above review has amply demonstrated the diversity of hopes for the future current in the second half of the Second Temple period, even if biblical precedents and the Torah-centred nature of Judaism shaped the outer limits of what was acceptable. It is appropriate now to turn our attention more specifically to the notion of a messianic figure.

In a broad sense, the hope for a messiah covers a range of possibilities – from the portrayal of Judas Maccabee in 1 Maccabees through the image of the warrior-hero in the Psalms of Solomon to 4 Ezra's transcendent 'figure of a man'. But, as will be clear by now, the messianic motif in all its forms is only one of a number of themes that we could distill from the multifarious expressions of future hope in Second Temple times. Indeed, taking 4 Ezra and 2 Baruch as a guiding model, Schürer has isolated eleven such motifs, most of which draw on either general or specific scriptural promises:[29]

1. There will be a final period of wickedness and tribulation as the eschaton approaches (4 Ezra 6:24; cf. 1 QM 1:11, 12).

2. Elijah will appear, or a 'prophet' like Moses (Deuteronomy 18:15), to make preparations for a better time (cf. Sirach 48:10–11 and 1QS 9:11).

3. A special anointed figure or messiah will come who will play a vital role in the establishment of God's kingdom (4 Ezra 7:28–9; 12:32; cf. CD 12:23; Psalm of Solomon 17:36).

4. Gentile powers will make a final attack against God's anointed (4 Ezra 13:34; cf. 1 Enoch 90:16; 1QM 15–19).

5. These wicked powers will be defeated by God's anointed or by God himself (4 Ezra 12:33; cf. 1 Enoch 90:18–19; Psalm of Solomon 17).

6. Jerusalem will be renewed or replaced by a heavenly city (4 Ezra 7:26; cf. Psalm of Solomon 17).

7. There will be a gathering together of dispersed Jews and the ten lost tribes to the land of Israel (4 Ezra 13:45; cf. Sirach 36:14; Psalm of Solomon 11).

8. A glorious kingdom will be established, ruled by God or his anointed in justice and righteousness (2 Baruch 73:1–7; cf. Psalm of Solomon 17:4).

9. Heaven and earth will be renewed (4 Ezra 7:30; cf. 1 Enoch 91:16–18).

10. There will be a general resurrection of the dead in preparation for judgement (4 Ezra 7:32; cf. Daniel 12:3; 2 Maccabees 7; Psalms of Solomon 3:12);

11. Everlasting bliss or damnation will be the reward or punishment for a person's deeds (4 Ezra 7:36–8; cf. Daniel 12:3; 1 Enoch 98:7–8).

We have noticed that various combinations of these items appear in most of the books we have surveyed. Naturally, however, because this catalogue is based on late and fully developed books like 4 Ezra, we should not think that each element occurs in every Second Temple work with an interest in the future.

A more recent study of late Second Temple Judaism has proposed a simpler list, isolating only four major themes in people's future expectations as they existed in the first century BCE and first century CE:[30]

1. The dispersed Jews and the lost tribes will be gathered together (see 2 Maccabees 1:27; Psalm of Solomon 17:28–31).
2. Gentile nations will be subjugated, destroyed or converted (Sirach 36:1–9; Psalm of Solomon 17:31).
3. Jerusalem and the Temple will be purified and glorified (Tobit 13:16–17; 11QT 29:8–10).
4. The people will become righteous and worship in purity (1QM 7:5–7; Jubilees 33:11,20; Psalm of Solomon 17:26).

Within this basic framework, Sanders acknowledges that there is, of course, room for a messianic figure to play an important part. But, as it happens, this was in practice a relatively infrequent facet of future hope.

For reasons of his own, Sanders limited his study to the period from 63 BCE to 66 CE.[31] Even taking a wider view, however, it is certainly true that the expectation of a messianic figure is not as pervasive as many scholars have often assumed. Rather, it was only one of a number of important motifs which might – or might not – be drawn upon by a given writer, depending on his imagination, the circumstances of the time, the traditions available to him and the predilections of the group to which he belonged. With this in mind, it will be useful to turn again to some of the main texts in which a special anointed figure does feature, leaving to one side the broadly messianic tone of 1 Maccabees. Therefore, we shall reconsider 1 Enoch, the sectarian Dead Sea Scrolls, the Psalms of Solomon and 4 Ezra.

In 1 Enoch, it is part of the Animal Vision, found in 1 Enoch 90:16–38, which stands out for consideration here. It contains several of the elements isolated by Schürer, although the whole passage is presented in the cryptic language of 'shepherds', 'sheep', 'stars' and 'white bulls'. Nevertheless, the expectations of the author are relatively clear. The last Gentile assault will be put down by God, who will then sit in judgement, casting wicked angels and evil Israelites into the fiery abyss. He will establish a new Jerusalem in place of the old, where righteous Israelites will live and be acknowledged by the nations. The 'white bull' or messiah will then appear, 'entreated . . . continually' (90:37) by the Gentiles. But, as even this brief outline shows, although his presence is certain, the actual role of the anointed one is fairly minimal. Certainly, God himself does the judging and sets up the new Jerusalem before the advent of the messianic figure.

As hinted earlier, the sectarian Dead Sea Scrolls present us with several layers of evidence which are difficult to harmonize, probably because the community's messianic ideas developed over time. If so, an early strand might be that which envisages the coming of a priest-messiah only, based on the priestly character of the founder of the sect himself, the Teacher of Righteousness (see 4QpPs 3:15; CD 6:11). Such an expectation is entirely understandable, given the scriptural promises made to the priesthood and the fact that the Hebrew term *mashiach*, 'anointed (one)', could evoke the anointing of the High Priest as much as the anointing of the Davidic king. Nevertheless, possibly in view of the stress on the latter in some quarters, those responsible for the Scrolls seem to have added Davidic characteristics to their priestly messiah, as can be seen in CD 20:1, with its reference to the 'coming of the messiah out of Aaron and Israel'. A further stage in the development of messianic ideas would have been to imagine the arrival of two separate figures – a priest-messiah or 'messiah of Aaron' and a Davidic messiah or 'messiah of Israel', with the latter subordinate to the former. This scenario is described in 1QS 9:11, with the expectation of 'the messiahs of Aaron and Israel', and especially in 1QSa.[32] Again, ample scriptural warrant exists for this combination, especially in the post-exilic books of Haggai and Zechariah 1–8.[33] Staying with 1QS 9:11, it also refers to the advent of 'the prophet', whom some scholars understand as a third messianic figure. In sum, therefore, it seems that the sect's various formulations of messianic hope reflect the fact that in the Bible three persons can undergo anointing: the High Priest, the Davidic king and, occasionally, prophets.

As stated earlier, the Psalms of Solomon were written not long after Pompey had brought Jerusalem and Judaea under Roman rule in 63 BCE. Of all the texts we have surveyed, they come closest to expressing what many assume was the common messianic expectation among Jews of the time, for, while the author had not been a supporter of the Hasmoneans, neither did he relish Gentile dominion. Instead, he looks forward to a time when God will raise up a new Davidic king who will rid Jerusalem of the Gentiles and purify the Jewish nation. Indeed, Psalm of Solomon 17:21–5 reads:

> Behold, O Lord, and raise up for them their king, the son of David,
> For the time which thou didst foresee, O God, that he may reign over Israel thy servant.
> And gird him with strength, that he may shatter unrighteous rulers;
> And purify Jerusalem of the nations which trample her down in destruction.
> In wisdom, in righteousness, may he expel sinners from the inheritance:
> May he smash the sinner's arrogance like a potter's vessel.
> With a rod of iron may he break in pieces all their substance:
> May he destroy the lawless nations by the word of his mouth,
> So that, at his rebuke, nations flee before him;
> And may he reprove sinners by the word of their own hearts.

The messianic figure himself will be strong and righteous, free from sin and endowed with miraculous powers. However, despite these characteristics beyond the ordinary, it is clear that a real this-worldly king is promised, not some supernatural divine or semi-divine being. Indeed, the kingship of God is viewed as paramount and in no way compromised by the role of this idealized messianic warrior figure.

In 4 Ezra it is predicted that the messiah, or 'son of God' (7:28–9), will appear after a time of tribulation and famine. He will be attacked by the nations, whom he will defeat by the word of the Torah. Afterwards, a new Jerusalem will descend from heaven and the ten lost tribes will be restored to the land of Israel. There, the people will live blessed lives under God's anointed for 400 years, after which they will all die, including the messiah himself. Following a seven-day primordial silence, the old corrupt order will vanish and a new age will dawn. God will then sit in judgement for seven years, rewarding or punishing people according to their deserts; fiery torment will be the lot of the wicked, while joyful blessedness will be in store for the faithful. As this summary makes clear, the role of God's anointed is important but limited, for his death shows the messianic era to be a mere prelude to the final age of blessing and judgement which shall follow, during which reward and punishment are to be implemented by God himself.

Against the background of our preceding general description of hopes for the future in the second half of the Second Temple period, our reconsideration of the messianic motif in these four works has again highlighted the extent of diversity in Second Temple Jewish thought.[34] A similar variety is evident in the precise shape taken by other items in Schürer's list, whether the presence or otherwise of an Elijah figure, for instance, or belief in a resurrection of the dead.[35] An examination of other texts would have highlighted this diversity even more.[36] As we have already remarked, the varied nature of such speculation may in large measure be put down to the fluidity of belief that characterized the Judaism of the period. This is a factor that many writing from a later, especially Christian, perspective are apt to forget.

5 Conclusion

The main emphasis of this study has been the diversity of Judaism in Second Temple times, evident in a range of texts that have come down to us from the last two centuries BCE and the first century CE. It appears that the only basic requirement within the Judaism of the period was adherence to the belief that God had revealed the Torah to Israel. All Jews were required to obey that Law, therefore, even though some disagreed over its interpretation to the point of schism, as in the case of the Qumran sect responsible for the sectarian Dead Sea Scrolls.

Other beliefs, including expectations about the future, were more fluid and open-ended. Indeed, even if we have observed that the circumstances of an author often had a major impact on his view of the future, we have also seen that it is by no means predictable just what form such hopes might take in a given context. This much is evident from a comparison of 1 Maccabees, for instance, with the sectarian Dead Sea Scrolls.

Moreover, from our preceding survey of specific texts, it is clear that the expectation of a messianic figure or figures was only one among a number of elements that might go into a particular writer's beliefs about the future. The anointed one might be a thoroughly this-worldly man (1 Maccabees), on the one hand, or a supernatural transcendent figure who would descend from heaven in apocalyptic fashion, on the other (4 Ezra). And, of course, positions in between these two extremes were also possible (Psalms of Solomon). Alternatively, a messiah might be excluded altogether from the future scenario, with his functions either absent or attributed directly to God himself. In practice, such matters were presumably determined by the particular religious preferences of the author and his community, or by a desire to emulate or diverge from rival religious groups or parties.

Further still, it must also be remembered that the Hebrew word *mashiach*, 'anointed one', carried no clear-cut meaning in Second Temple times. The term could designate almost any figure thought to have a special role, whether apocalyptic or otherwise, in God's plan for the world. This covers an expected successor to the line of King David, as presented in a this-worldly fashion in Sirach or, more dramatically, in the Psalms of Solomon. But it also includes a future priestly figure or 'messiah of Aaron', as described in some sectarian Dead Sea Scrolls. Or again, it might entail a combination of both of these aspects. Certainly, we should not think that the Jews of our period *en masse* awaited the advent of a universally expected or clearly defined saviour figure. Only in later times did 'the Messiah' come to designate such a fixed identity, as both Judaism and Christianity developed in the period after the destruction of the Temple.

Notes

[1] BCE and CE are used here in preference to BC and AD, but refer to the same blocks of time. In a similar way, 'Hebrew Scriptures' and 'Bible' will be employed in what follows as more or less equivalent to 'Old Testament'.

[2] For a short outline of the history of this period, see the relevant chapters in A. R. C. Leaney, *The Jewish and Christian World 200 BC to AD 200* (Cambridge, Cambridge University Press, 1984), or in H. Shanks (ed.), *Ancient Israel: A Short History from Abraham to the Roman Destruction of the Temple* (London, SPCK, 1989). More detailed analysis is available in J. H. Hayes and J. M. Miller, *Israelite and Judaean History* (London, SCM, 1990), or H. Jagersma, *A History of Israel from Alexander the Great to Bar Kokhba* (London, SCM, 1987).

[3] Discussion of these terms, more detailed than what follows, can be found under the appropriate entries in D. N. Freedman, (ed.), *The Anchor Bible Dictionary*, i–vi (New York, Doubleday, 1992).

[4] Thus, works like 1 Enoch or the Psalms of Solomon are among what scholars call the 'Pseudepigrapha', namely, works of this type which, unlike Daniel or the Wisdom of Solomon, were not later included in the Bible or Apocrypha. Translations of the main Pseudepigrapha, with introductory comments, can be found in H. D. F. Sparks, *The Apocryphal Old Testament* (Oxford, Oxford University Press, 1986), or R. H. Charlesworth, *Old Testament Pseudepigrapha*, i–ii (London, Darton, Longman & Todd, 1983–5).

[5] For a recent introductory outline of academic study of the Hebrew Scriptures, see R. J. Coggins, *Introducing the Old Testament* (Oxford, Oxford University Press, 1990).

[6] Introductory descriptions of individual books of the Bible, including the Wisdom literature, can be found in A. J. Soggin, *Introduction to the Old Testament* (London, SCM, 1989).

[7] Further consideration of both of these important biblical motifs can be found under appropriate entries in *The Anchor Bible Dictionary*, i–vi, as well as in H. Ringgren, *Israelite Religion* (London, SPCK, 1966), or W. H. Schmidt, *The Faith of the Old Testament* (Oxford, SCM, 1983).

[8] A clear and concise introduction to biblical prophecy is available in J. F. A. Sawyer, *Prophecy and the Biblical Prophets* (Oxford, Oxford University Press, 1993).

[9] This citation is taken from the New Revised Standard Version (New York, 1989) of the Bible, as are all quotations from the Hebrew Scriptures or Apocrypha.

[10] For details on these books, see Soggin, *Introduction*, 379–85, 386–92, 393–7, 401–4, 490–7, respectively. On Zechariah 9–14, which may stem from as late as the third or second century BCE, see Soggin, ibid., 405–9.

[11] The question of the formation of the canon is a complex one. See Soggin, ibid., 15–18, for a brief discussion of the issue.

[12] See G. W. E. Nickelsburg, *Jewish Literature Between the Bible and the Mishnah* (London, SCM, 1981), for a thorough survey of Jewish writings from the Second Temple period against their historical backgrounds.

[13] For details on this period of turmoil, consult the books listed above in n. 1. On the Maccabees and the Hasmonean dynasty, see Jagersma, *History of Israel*, 44–67.

[14] The stimulus for speculation about the figure of Enoch is the brief description of his unusual assumption into heaven without dying in Genesis 5:24. A translation of 1 Enoch from the Ethiopic, with a brief introduction, can be found in Sparks, *Apocryphal OT*, 169–319. For further details on the work, see the relevant portions of Nickelsburg, *Jewish Literature*. It seems likely that the fifth book, the Parables of Enoch in 1 Enoch 37–71, dates to the end of the first century CE; see below, n. 28.

[15] Hence, see the '70 generations' of 1 Enoch 10:12, the Animal Vision of 1 Enoch 85–90, and the Apocalypse of Weeks comprising both 1 Enoch 91:11–17 and 93:1–10.

[16] For details on the book of Daniel, see Soggin, *Introduction*, 473–82. Jubilees, although concerned in the main with correct observance of the Law, contains two passages with some apocalyptic schematization of history. See Sparks, *Apocryphal OT*, 1–139, for a short introduction and a translation, as well as Nickelsburg, *Jewish Literature*, 73–9.

[17] For two other works, Tobit and Baruch, which are rather more difficult to date but could be considered here, see Soggin, *Introduction*, 501–7 and 532–4.

[18] The Maccabee brothers – Judas, Jonathan, Simon – were succeeded by the latter's son and his descendants, usually referred to collectively as the Hasmonean dynasty after the name of Judas' great-great-grandfather.

[19] Ostensibly, 2 Maccabees, written about the same time, has the same subject-matter. However, while the Maccabees themselves are praised, there is implicit criticism of the Hasmoneans. As a result, the author looks ahead to a renewed glory for the Temple, while those martyred under Antiochus IV will share in the nation's ultimate blessing through resurrection.

[20] For the language here, compare 1 Kings 4:25 and Micah 4:4.

[21] For an introductory overview of the significance of the Dead Sea Scrolls, see the author's *Deciphering the Dead Sea Scrolls* (London, Fontana, 1996). A more advanced introduction and translation can be found in G. Vermes, *The Complete Dead Sea Scrolls in English* (London, Penguin, 1997).

[22] Readers may be unfamiliar with the names of the following sectarian Dead Sea Scrolls and associated abbreviations:

CD	Damascus Document	1QM	War Rule
1QS	Community Rule	4Qp Ps	Psalms Commentary
1QSa	Messianic Rule	4Q521	Messianic Apocalypse
1QpHab	Habakkuk Commentary	11QT	Temple Scroll

[23] E. P. Sanders, *Judaism: Practice and Belief 63 BCE–66 CE* (London, SCM, 1992), 302.

[24] See Sparks, *Apocryphal OT*, 649–82, for a translation prefaced by a brief introduction. Further discussion can be found in Nickelsburg, *Jewish Literature*, 203–12.

[25] On this book, which appears in all editions of the Apocrypha, see ibid., 175–85. A similar mix of the Greek and Jewish can be found in the writings of the first-century CE Jewish philosopher Philo, also from Egypt; see Leaney, *Jewish and Christian World*, 140, in the first instance, or R. Williamson, *Jews in the Hellenistic World: Philo* (Cambridge, Cambridge University Press, 1989) for greater detail.

[26] The Jewish core of the work was later supplemented by a Christian hand which added two opening chapters (1–2) and two concluding ones (14–15). This fuller Christian edition is found in many modern Bibles with an Apocrypha and usually goes under the title 2 Esdras. For further details, see Nickelsburg, *Jewish Literature*, 287–94.

[27] Although less precise in the formulation of its concerns, 2 Baruch deals with similar questions from the same historical perspective. See Sparks, *Apocryphal OT*, 835–95, for a translation and introduction.

[28] The Parables of Enoch in 1 Enoch 37–71 were probably composed at about the same time, although other dates have been proposed. Interpreting the imagery of Daniel 7:13–14, they depict a pre-existent and superhuman messianic figure, or 'son of man', whose role, especially that of judge, is revealed to Enoch.

[29] See E. Schürer *et al.*, *The History of the Jewish People in the Age of Jesus Christ*, iii/1 (Edinburgh, T. & T. Clark, 1979), 514–47.

[30] See Sanders, *Judaism*, 279–303.

[31] These dates are set by the Roman conquest of Palestine by Pompey in 63 BCE and the beginning of the revolt against Roman rule that commenced in 66 CE.

[32] This work looks ahead to the messianic future and pictures a messianic banquet attended first and foremost by a priestly messiah, but also by his subordinate, the messiah of Israel.

[33] A similar combination is to be found in parts of the Testament of the Twelve Patriarchs, another pseudepigraphical work from the Second

Temple period, the precise date of which is difficult to determine in view of later Christian interpolations. A translation of the book can be found in Sparks, *Apocryphal OT*, 505–600.

[34] However, we have encountered no sign of belief in a messianic figure whose sufferings would atone for others. On this question, see Schürer, *History*, ii. 547–9.

[35] For further details on these motifs, see Schürer, *History*, iii/1, 515f. and 539–44.

[36] In particular, we have not looked at the writings of the first-century CE Jewish historian Josephus, especially regarding the role of popular eschatological hope in support for the revolt against Rome in 66 CE. But see Sanders, *Judaism*, 280–9, for a brief discussion of a range of attitudes towards the taking up of arms in the struggle for independence from foreign domination. On the life and work of Josephus himself, see first Leaney, *Jewish and Christian World*, 76–7, and, for more detail, J. R. Bartlett, *Jews in the Hellenistic World: Josephus, Aristeas, The Sibylline Oracles, Eupolemus* (Cambridge, Cambridge University Press, 1985), 72–191.

6
Eschatological hope in the early Christian community – New Testament perspectives

D. P. DAVIES

'Are you the one who is to come, or are we to expect someone else?'.[1] This question addressed to Jesus of Nazareth by the messengers of John the Baptist according to the common tradition of Matthew and Luke[2] may be taken as typical of the attitudes of Jewish people living under Roman rule. They were looking for deliverance, if not a deliverer, to rid them of foreign oppression, but the form of deliverance and the kind of deliverer expected varied enormously from one group of Jews to another.[3] Some expected God to act directly in a supernatural, miraculous way; others expected a supernatural agent to intervene on God's behalf, while others again saw a human deliverer acting out this role. Similarly, the kind of deliverance looked for varied from nationalistic expectations of political liberation to salvation from sin and death in some new order either on earth or beyond space and time in some kind of heaven or new paradisal age.

The contemporary evidence does not point to a single clear-cut expectation. Consequently, in examining the kind of expectation found in the early Christian community in the years following Jesus' death as reflected in the various books of the New Testament we have little alternative but to start at the end and work backwards. In other words, we need to establish the kind of eschatological expectation that typified the Christian community in the second half of the first century of the Christian era, since this is what the New Testament represents; we can then work back from that to the expectation of Jesus himself and his immediate followers and seek to relate this expectation to its context in the Judaism contemporary with Jesus.

First, however, we might note that the answer given to the question, with which we started, in the Matthew-Luke tradition[4] says this: 'The blind receive their sight, the lame walk, lepers are made clean, the deaf hear, the dead are raised to life, the poor are brought the good news'. This answer reflects the conviction of Jesus' followers, maybe not at the time but after his death, that he had brought deliverance, and that if so he was the deliverer. Indeed, the words echo a prophetic text[5] that envisaged a time when physical deliverance – in this case from physical sickness, disease and disability – would be achieved through the power of YHWH, God of Israel. What is significant here is that something the prophet looked for in the *future* was believed by his followers *already* to have been achieved by Jesus of Nazareth in his ministry.

This, in fact, turns out to be the fundamental difference between the eschatological beliefs of the early Christians and those of the Jewish community from which they sprung: what the Jews expected in the *future*, Christians believed had in a sense *already* been realized. The other point worth noting in this passage is that deliverance from political oppression is not the main thrust. Certainly the deliverance is physical; certainly it entails the establishment of justice for the poor, but it does not explicitly involve political liberation. As we move to other parts of the New Testament, we shall see the emphasis shift even further away from any concern for political liberation and move in the direction of some kind of 'spiritual' salvation, often linked with the ultimate destiny of humanity beyond the grave and of the whole created order beyond the present space-time order. We shall also see more attention focused on Jesus as the deliverer and on his person, and not simply on the kind of deliverance he accomplished.

In the New Testament, then, we find evidence of a community which believed that its hope had in a sense already been fulfilled, though there was something still to be realized. There is therefore a tension between hope and reality, between hope fulfilled and expectation unfulfilled. The identity of the deliverer has, however, been established. He is Jesus of Nazareth, though the writers of the New Testament are much exercised not only as to his precise status but also as to his nature. Is he natural or supernatural? Is he man or is he in some sense to be identified with God? At some points Jesus is no more than God's agent (as prophet or Messiah or Son of man), but at others he seems to be presented as actually sharing God's status and even God's nature (as Son of God or Lord). On the other hand, whatever the ambiguity in its attitude to the status of the deliverer, the New Testament is absolutely clear that the salvation or deliverance, by whatever agency, human or divine, it is achieved, is ultimately God's deliverance.

In tracing the development of these beliefs our starting point will be the earliest written evidence found in the New Testament, the letters of Paul[6] (or Saul) of Tarsus to a number of early Christian communities, many of which he had himself founded. This evidence comes in the main from the fifties of the first century of the Christian era, some twenty to thirty years after the death of Jesus of Nazareth.

1 The letters of Paul

We may begin where Paul's own career as a follower of Jesus Christ begins – at his conversion. In Galatians 1:15–16 Paul himself describes this as a revelation. God chose to reveal to him something related to the end-time, in the same way as the so-called apocalyptic writers claimed to have received from God revelations about what would happen hereafter. As a Pharisee Paul is likely to have been influenced by these 'apocalyptic' ideas; he would have regarded our present existence as 'this age' and looked forward to 'the age to come', something that would be brought about by an act of God, a supernatural occurrence that would create a cosmic upheaval and usher in the revelation of the glory of God in all its fullness. What was revealed to Paul, however, as he tells us in Galatians 1:15–16 as well as in 1 Corinthians 15:8–9 and repeatedly elsewhere, was that God had raised Jesus of Nazareth, the crucified one, from the dead. Since belief in resurrection, whether of all humanity or of an elect, was one of the standard features of apocalyptic eschatology,[7] Paul's conversion to a conviction that Jesus had been raised would have led him to conclude that the sequence of events that would usher in the end-time, of which resurrection was one, had already begun and that all that remained was for the programme to be brought to completion.

In 1 Corinthians 15 Paul works this out in detail as he seeks to convince the Corinthians that accepting the resurrection of Jesus has a number of further implications for what will happen to them and indeed to the whole of humanity and the created order. The risen Jesus is the 'firstfruits' of a harvest that will consist of his followers at least, including Paul himself and the Corinthians. Each will come in his own order, and the process has already begun since Christ (=Jesus) has been raised. Jesus' resurrection has set in motion a process that will culminate in the transformation of the present world order, and since that process is already under way it is only a matter of time, and a short time at that, before the whole thing will be completed. This conviction that the end-time has already begun probably accounts for the impression Paul gives[8] that the process has already reached its climax, that Christians have already been raised and that they have already entered the new age. This is what is called 'realized' eschatology and it is often contrasted with 'future' eschatology. In the case of Paul this is a false dichotomy since even in passages such as those cited there is still a future dimension and orientation. Furthermore, he is elsewhere concerned to correct those who think that they are already so completely living in the new age that they have ceased to be part of the present age.

Paul nowhere gives us a systematic and detailed exposition of the full scheme of eschatological expectation, so we must beware of imposing such a scheme on him. None the less, his lengthy treatment of the subject in 1 Corinthians 15, 1 Thessalonians 4–5 and 2 Thessalonians 1–2 enables us to identify a number of features of Paul's expectation, which seem to constitute a sequence of future events, even if the precise sequence is not always clear.

The final state of those who are accepted at the judgement and saved from the wrath of God and the punishment of their sin is sometimes referred to as the 'kingdom' (of God, or even Christ),[9] the terminology favoured by Jesus according to the synoptic tradition, but more often Paul describes this state as 'glory'[10] or 'life',[11] and this corresponds to the condition of the risen Jesus.[12] Conversely, those who are condemned at the judgement will be deprived of glory[13] and destined to destruction. They will have no share in eternal life.[14]

This is the end of the process; the first event in the sequence following the resurrection of Jesus seems to be the coming of Jesus in glory, the so-called parousia.[15] Some see this as an expectation that Paul modified or even abandoned after writing the two Thessalonian letters and 1 Corinthians, but such an interpretation does not stand up to an analysis of the other letters, since similar views are found in Philippians and even in Colossians and Romans, if references to the 'day of the Lord' are references to the parousia under another name. This means that parousia expectation is still present in the last of Paul's genuine letters to have survived. It is, however, true to say that most of the detail relating to what Paul expected to happen at the parousia is found in the two Thessalonian letters and 1 Corinthians. Much of this is probably part of Paul's inheritance from apocalyptic Judaism. The prevailing impression is that the time before the parousia is very short; it may even happen in Paul's own lifetime. The parousia (coming) will be a supernatural event, involving cosmic upheaval. It will mark the end of the present order and therefore the defeat of death (the last enemy) and the end of the rule of evil (supernatural and natural) powers.

According to 1 Corinthians 15 and 1 Thessalonians 4 this will be a signal for the resurrection of the Christian dead. Other passages[16] hint at a general resurrection. This is the necessary preliminary for judgement, whether the exclusive judgement of Christians or the general judgement of all humanity.[17] Nor is it clear who precisely will be the agent of judgement, even if it is indisputably the judgement of God. Judgement then sorts out those who are destined for 'life' or 'glory' from those who are doomed to destruction and who therefore have to bear the 'wrath' of God, which is so prominent a theme of the letter to the Romans.

All this lies in the future. It will affect the whole body of Christians, and indeed the whole of humanity, even the whole of creation. It can therefore be spoken of as a 'new creation'.[18] This recalls a prominent feature of Jewish apocalyptic eschatology that the end-time will correspond to the paradisal state that preceded the fall of humanity, *Endzeit wird Urzeit*. Protology – what was believed about the conditions that prevailed at the creation before the fall – is therefore a governing influence on Paul's eschatology. The last state of humanity corresponds to its first.[19] And Christ, as the last Adam, has succeeded in reversing the consequences of the disobedience (sin) of the first Adam. Paradise is to be restored. That is a measure of the achievement of the coming deliverer, who has in a sense already come, in defeating sin, evil and death in his resurrection (by God) from the dead. For Paul, therefore, deliverance or salvation lies beyond death and beyond the present space-time order, though the ultimate condition of redeemed humanity will be life in the glory of a transformed and new creation.

So much for the deliverance, but what of the deliverer? Paul is absolutely clear that the deliverer is Jesus of Nazareth. His conversion experience has convinced him of this. The resurrection of Jesus, though it is constantly referred to as an act of God, establishes Jesus' status as God's agent in bringing about deliverance. Jesus is thereby confirmed as having a special role to play in the final drama of the end-time when he will come 'again'. Paul then moves back from the resurrection to reconsider his attitude to Jesus' death which he had previously regarded as a sign of God's rejection of Jesus' messianic claims. He now sees this as an act of God, a saving act: 'God was *in Christ* reconciling . . .'[20] Jesus is still God's agent, and his death shows that his work as agent has already begun; it does not have to wait until his coming again. And between the past achievement (the cross) and the future promise (the parousia) Jesus, by virtue of his resurrection, is now exalted 'at God's right hand', which again confers a special status upon him.

We can almost see the gradual and perhaps painful progression in Paul's thinking about Jesus. As last Adam, Jesus is one with humanity; he has to be fully human to reverse Adam's disobedience 'in the flesh'. But his resurrection shows that God confers a special status upon him. This is described in the famous Philippian hymn[21] as giving him 'the name above all names', a name at which 'every knee shall bow'; that name is the name of God, the title *Kyrios*, which in the Greek version of the Hebrew Scriptures represents the tetragrammaton YHWH, the name of the God of Israel. Jesus therefore not only achieves the deliverance of humanity from the sin that alienates humanity from God; he also achieves the reunification of humanity with the God in whose image humanity was created. Not only is paradise restored, so also is 'the divine nature which was his from the first'.[22]

2 The fourth gospel

We turn from Paul's letters, the earliest of the New Testament writings, to the fourth gospel,[23] which is almost certainly the latest of the gospels and among the latest books in the New Testament. It was probably published just before the beginning of the second century of the Christian era, even if it is based on traditions which were significantly earlier. If Paul had to work his way towards identifying Jesus with God, the author of the fourth gospel begins his work by asserting the identity of Jesus and God explicitly and unambiguously: 'In the beginning was the Word [= Jesus] and the Word was with God, and the Word was God'.[24] The one who achieves the deliverance of God is one with God, a unity usually expounded in terms of the analogy of father and son, though in the Prologue to the gospel the deliverer is introduced as the Word (of God). The Word of God articulates and reveals God's will and God's nature. That much is familiar from the Hebrew Scriptures. What goes beyond the Hebrew Scriptures is the affirmation at the climax of the Prologue that 'the Word became flesh'. This adds a new dimension to the role of the deliverer. The Word not only reveals God; the Word now incarnates (gives flesh to) God in the person of Jesus of Nazareth. Furthermore, the second part of the same verse makes an astonishing eschatological claim in the words: 'We beheld his glory, glory as of the only son from the Father'.[25] The significance of this is that the glory of God, which for Paul was still to be revealed, has for this writer already been revealed in the incarnate Word, Jesus of Nazareth.

As we read the rest of the gospel, we find that this claim is consistent with other eschatological pronouncements found usually on the lips of Jesus: for example, '*Now* is the judgement of this world',[26] or 'This is eternal life, to know thee the only true God, and Jesus Christ whom thou *hast* sent'.[27] This seems to suggest that a future parousia such as Paul envisaged, with its general resurrection followed by judgement and subsequent salvation and destruction, is ruled out. Has the author of this gospel then rejected the eschatological beliefs which he inherited and substituted for them what we call 'realized' eschatology? Conversely, does he reflect the original teaching of Jesus? Is it Paul who reintroduces elements of future apocalyptic eschatology?

In seeking to answer these questions we must first note that this gospel does in fact contain passages which reflect the traditional apocalyptic scheme. The parousia is alluded to,[28] the general resurrection is mentioned,[29] as is the gathering in of the elect.[30] Judgement is a common theme, and though it is usually described as a present reality, there is a reference to future judgement.[31] There are a number of references to future salvation in chapters 6[32] and 16,[33] and even a reference to the fires of eternal hell.[34] These and other references make it clear that the author is familiar with future apocalyptic eschatology; he talks of the Son of man, of resurrection, of the last day, of judgement, of eternal life as a future blessing and of the wrath of God and fire.

Nevertheless, the author is a long way from the sort of eschatological expectation found in Paul or in Mark 13 or the book of Revelation. Instead of seeing judgement as a future event, he more often links it with the past. Rather than proclaim salvation as something promised for the end-time, he points to the reality of eternal life here and now. For one reason or another his whole perspective has changed dramatically from that of Paul and Paul's contemporaries. It is even different from that of an author associated with the same Johannine circle, John the 'divine', author of the book of Revelation. It could, of course, be argued that this change was to some extent anticipated by Paul, with his emphasis on the salvation already achieved by the death of Christ on the cross and confirmed by God in the resurrection of Jesus from the dead, but since the fourth evangelist's approach to this adjustment in eschatological thinking is quite different from that of Paul it is profitable to look at how he achieves it in a little more detail.

First, and most importantly for our present purposes, our author presents a series of christological claims for the Jesus of history which imply that he is already the deliverer. He does not have to wait until the parousia to act as deliverer. Even at the beginning of the ministry Jesus is proclaimed as the Lamb of God who takes away the sins of the world,[35] the Messiah[36] and Son of God.[37] He is the saviour of the world,[38] the prophet,[39] the bread of life.[40] He has already conquered the world.[41] At the end of his earthly life he can say that the work of salvation is accomplished.[42] The need for a future act of salvation is eliminated. All that needs to be done has been done; all that is to be revealed has been revealed. The change in attitude to christology has resulted in a changed attitude to eschatology.

Then, secondly, there is a specific concentration on the death of Jesus as the consummation of the revelation of God's glory and the exaltation of Jesus as Son of man. There is a conscious build-up throughout the gospel in anticipation of this. We are repeatedly told in the first half of the gospel that Jesus' hour has *not yet* come[43] and this is then picked up with references to the hour having come in the passion narrative.[44] In other words, the author seems to be talking parousia-type language, which speaks of the 'hour of the coming of the Son of man',[45] meaning the parousia, and applying it to the cross as the glorification and exaltation of the Son of man.

The evangelist's third way of changing direction is to proclaim that judgement has already happened and that, consequently, eternal life is already available to those who are vindicated at the judgement on the strength of their belief in Jesus as the Christ, the Son of God.[46] Belief now becomes the chief criterion for entry into eternal life (a phrase the author prefers to the traditional language of 'new age' or 'kingdom of God'). Most references to judgement speak of it as a present reality.[47] Judgement is already taking place in the ministry and death of Jesus; it does not have to wait until the last day. Similarly, eternal life is available here and now to those who believe,[48] just as those who do not believe are condemned already.[49]

Judgement extends not only to Jesus' contemporaries, but to the author's contemporaries and, indeed, to future generations yet unborn. They too will be judged, but not by Jesus. Their judge will be the paraclete (the spirit). This is the author's fourth way of eliminating future eschatology since the coming of the paraclete is presented as a parousia.[50] The paraclete exercises the functions of the Son of man at the parousia, and so the abiding presence of the paraclete eliminates the need for a parousia and for judgement at the end-time.

If the teaching of Jesus himself was based on expectation of a future fulfilment of the eschatological hope, then Paul represents a half-way house between the teaching of the Jesus of history and the wholly realized eschatology of the Johannine community. If, on the other hand, Jesus saw his own ministry and intended his own death as a means of realizing what for his contemporaries was a future expectation, then the fourth evangelist has either preserved or recovered an interpretation which Paul was in danger of setting on one side by reintroducing the eschatology of Jewish apocalyptic. Where then did Jesus himself stand? Did he see the future hope as realized in his own ministry? If so, did he see himself as the coming deliverer? To answer these questions we turn finally to the synoptic tradition.

3 The synoptic gospels

In considering the evidence for the history of Jesus found in the synoptic gospels[51] we must acknowledge at the outset that this evidence cannot always be taken at its face value. This is because the three gospels concerned (Matthew, Mark and Luke) were not produced until the second half of the first century of the Christian era. Indeed, it is likely that the earliest (probably Mark) was not published until the late sixties or early seventies, that is not until after Paul's death. The other two gospels probably come from the eighties. Consequently, the authors are not unaware of and almost certainly open to the influence of the attitudes, beliefs and needs of their contemporaries. Furthermore, the material at their disposal was undoubtedly subject to modification in the course of its transmission to suit the needs of different communities at different points in time. Having said all that, scholars are now increasingly confident that certain historical questions about Jesus can be answered on the basis of the evidence of the synoptic tradition, sensibly and cautiously handled.[52] Nor can we discount the evidence of the fourth gospel, though as we have seen this gospel is less reliable historically when it deals with the two issues which concern us here, namely christology and eschatology.

An example of the confidence of contemporary scholars in making historical judgements about the teaching of Jesus is the virtual consensus among scholars that the principal theme of that teaching was 'the kingdom of God'. Moreover, it is now widely agreed that this concept, which Jesus assumed as part of his Jewish heritage, is probably to be interpreted along the lines of Jewish apocalyptic. That it is central to Jesus' teaching may quickly be established. For example, in one way or another it is the basic theme of most of the clauses in the so-called Lord's Prayer,[53] where it is referred to explicitly in the petition, 'Thy kingdom come', a petition which implies that during the time of his ministry Jesus did not believe that the kingdom had come. This conclusion is supported by a saying of Jesus found in the Last Supper narrative: 'I shall not drink again of the fruit of the vine until the day when I drink it new in the kingdom of God'.[54] This suggests strongly that even at the end of his life Jesus still saw the coming of the kingdom as a future event.

One of the most characteristic teaching methods used by Jesus in seeking to put his message across was the parable.[55] Here again the principal emphasis is the coming of the kingdom, again seen as a future event. This is seen clearly in the parables based on the image of harvest or those which are set in the context of a meal, symbolizing the so-called messianic banquet, or those which focus on the image of a wedding.[56] All of these were images in common use as symbols for the kingdom of God (or heaven) in Jewish circles. Not surprisingly, therefore, Jesus again betrays the influence of his upbringing.

As the Lord's Prayer implies, the kingdom or rule of God will be a time when all humanity (all creation even) will freely acknowledge God as king or ruler, when God's name will be universally honoured as holy and God's will obeyed. At this point paradise will have been restored 'on earth', but almost certainly a transformed earth, to quote the Lord's Prayer again. In this respect Paul is true to the teaching of Jesus, though both reflect the strong influence of Jewish apocalyptic.

In the passage known as the 'little apocalypse' found in Mark 13 and largely reproduced by Matthew and Luke, Jesus speaks at length about the end-time. Some of this material has been coloured by subsequent events, such as the threat to Jerusalem and, at least as far as Matthew and Luke are concerned, its final destruction in 70 CE. None the less, there is enough authentic material here to confirm that, notwithstanding the arguments of C. H. Dodd,[57] for Jesus the final coming of the kingdom lay in the future, possibly the immediate future. The kingdom involves a complete reversal of everything present and earthly.[58] Its coming is miraculous; it involves a cosmic upheaval.[59] In Mark 13 this is the prelude to the coming of the supernatural Son of man as judge. Jesus refuses to set a timetable for these events, and even disclaims any knowledge of such a timetable, since this is known only to God. This is interesting since the admission seems to put a distance between Jesus and God. Nor is it by any means certain that the historical Jesus identified himself with the coming Son of man predicted here, though it is clear from the gospel tradition that his followers undoubtedly did.

For Jesus then the kingdom lies in the future, but its coming is so certain and so imminent that its benefits may be anticipated and many of its characteristic features put into effect in advance of the end-time. This explains Jesus' willingness to declare the forgiveness of sins and to act out the consequences in sharing table fellowship with sinners. It also accounts for Jesus' claim to victory over evil powers in his exorcisms and his triumph over disease and disability in his mighty works of healing. Though the final realization of the kingdom lay in the future, Jesus and his followers lived *as if* it had already come. In that sense the fourth gospel is a legitimate development of Jesus' eschatological teaching.

But what of Jesus' own role in all this? And what of his death? Did he see himself as deliverer and his death as an act of deliverance? Whatever the scholarly consensus on the centrality of the theme of the kingdom in the teaching of Jesus, there is little evidence of consensus on the issue of Jesus' understanding of his own role in relation to the kingdom.[60] On the question of Messiah, for example, three quite contradictory positions are adopted: first, that Jesus aspired to fulfil the role as it was popularly understood among his contemporaries, as a national leader expected to lead the Jewish people to victory over their enemies; secondly, that Jesus accepted the title, but reinterpreted it in such a way that it became a way of referring to the saviour who redeems his people through suffering – this by and large is the position adopted by Paul and other New Testament writers, though this does not of course mean that Jesus himself necessarily saw things in this way; thirdly, that Jesus rejected the title and everything it represented as a demonic temptation.

It is difficult to establish conclusively that any one of these positions represents the historical truth about Jesus of Nazareth. One historical fact that cannot be gainsaid, however, is that Jesus was crucified. If so, he must have been tried and condemned as a political subversive. This much is confirmed by the *titulus* at the head of the cross: 'Jesus of Nazareth, King of the Jews', that is Jesus the Messiah. There must have been enough evidence to persuade the Romans that Jesus was a political threat. Some at least of his contemporaries must have seen him as a political as well as a spiritual leader, but it is virtually impossible to determine whether or not Jesus himself interpreted his mission in this way. Certainly in terms of achievement or lack of it, his death on the cross would have indicated complete and utter failure. A crucified Messiah could hardly free his fellow countrymen of foreign oppression.

Again, the scholarly debate about 'Son of man' is inconclusive. Geza Vermes,[61] for instance, doubts if 'Son of man' is a title at all, and sees the apocalyptic passages as subsequent Christian interpretations based on Daniel 7. More promising is Jesus' consistent practice of referring to God as *Abba* (=father) in prayer.[62] This may indicate a claim to a special relationship with God, or at any rate an awareness of a close intimacy between himself and God. This too is something Paul develops, particularly in Galatians and Romans.[63]

Perhaps, in the final analysis, the role of charismatic prophet and teacher is the one which most closely corresponds to the ministry exercised by the Jesus of history.[64] This would account for the content and the method of his teaching, for his fondness for symbolic acts and gestures, such as eating with sinners, and for his mighty works of exorcism and healing. All this fulfilled the role of the prophet, and a revival of prophecy was expected to mark the coming of the end-time and the dawn of the new age. It is not impossible that Jesus interpreted his death as a supreme act of prophetic symbolism, an act that not only acted out the message, but one which in some mysterious way helped bring about its fulfilment. This seems to be the intention of the words of interpretation over the bread and wine at the Last Supper Jesus shared with his disciples on the night before his death, though again we cannot be certain to what extent this reflects subsequent Christian interpretation of Jesus' death as opposed to Jesus' own understanding.

Whatever may be the truth about Jesus' own understanding, what cannot be denied is that the New Testament bears witness to the world-shattering impact Jesus' ministry, life and death had on his followers and how their conviction that Jesus had been vindicated by God, in an act they described in imagery derived from Jewish apocalyptic as resurrection from the dead, led to an unshakeable belief that far from being an ignominious failure Jesus' death was an act of deliverance which fulfilled all their hopes of salvation. If so, they reasoned that Jesus must therefore be the deliverer. Since he had already lived, worked and died among them he could hardly be 'the coming deliverer'. He had already come; he had already achieved deliverance on their behalf. On the other hand, their awareness that they were not yet living in a perfect world led some to project paradise onto some other plane of existence (heaven) which they were destined to enjoy with Christ after death and others, like Paul, to look for his coming again in glory to secure the final defeat of evil, sin and death and to establish the unchallenged rule of God over a transformed humanity in a new and perfect age.

Notes

[1] Matthew 11:3 (all biblical references are to the Revised English Bible).

[2] This tradition is sometimes referred to as Q (probably from the German Quelle = source). At one time Q was thought to be a single written source used independently by the authors of Matthew and Luke, but not by Mark. In contemporary discussion Q refers simply to the various traditions, mainly oral, but some perhaps written, available to the authors of Matthew and Luke and maybe the author of Mark as well. Some of these traditions are no doubt very old and may go back to the time of Jesus himself.

[3] See, for example, J. Neusner *et al.*, *Judaisms and their Messiahs at the Turn of the Christian Era* (Cambridge, Cambridge University Press, 1987); James H. Charlesworth (ed.), *The Messiah: Developments in Early Judaism and Christianity* (Philadelphia, Fortress Press, 1992); articles by Richard Horsley and Seán Freyne in *Concilium*, 1993/1 (Wim Beuken, Seán Freyne and Anton Weiler (eds.), *Messianism Through History*) and the chapter by my colleague, Dr Jonathan Campbell, in the present volume.

[4] Matthew 11:5, Luke 7:22.

[5] Isaiah 35:5–6.

[6] For the theology of Paul and its Jewish background see particularly W. D. Davies, *Paul and Rabbinic Judaism* (London, SPCK, 2nd edn., 1955); E. P. Sanders, *Paul and Palestinian Judaism* (London, SCM, 1977); H. Ridderbos, *Paul: An Outline of his Theology* (London, SPCK, 1977); J. A. Ziesler, *Pauline Christianity* (Oxford, University Press, rev. edn., 1990); M. Hengel, *The Pre-Christian Paul* (London, SCM, 1991).

[7] See D. S. Russell, *The Method and Message of Jewish Apocalyptic* (London, SCM, 1964), pp.353ff; M. Hengel, *Judaism and Hellenism*, i (Philadelphia, Fortress Press, 1974), 196ff.

[8] In passages like 2 Corinthians 5:17, 6:2 and Colossians 3:1–4.

9 See 1 Corinthians 4:8, 15:12ff.; 1 Thessalonians 2:12; 2 Thessalonians 1:5; Colossians 1:15ff.

10 Romans 5:2, 8:17–25; 1 Corinthians 5:12ff.; 2 Corinthians 3:18, 4:3ff., 14ff.; Philippians 3:20f.; 1 Thessalonians 2:12; 2 Thessalonians 1:7ff.; Colossians 1:26, 3:1ff.

11 Romans 2:5–10, 6:8, 22f.; 1 Corinthians 9:25, 13:12, 15:12; 2 Corinthians 5:1ff.; Galatians 6:7ff.; Philippians 1:21ff.; 1 Thessalonians 4:13ff.; Colossians 1:5, 3:1ff.

12 See Romans 8:17–25; Philippians 3:20f.; 2 Corinthians 4.

13 2 Thessalonians 1:7ff.

14 Galatians 6:7–9; 2 Thessalonians 2:1–12.

15 1 Corinthians 4:5, 11:26, 15:12ff., 16:22; 1 Thessalonians 1:10, 2:19f., 3:13, 4:13ff., 5:23; 2 Thessalonians 1:7ff., 2:1ff.

16 For example, Romans 2:5–10; Galatians 6:7f.

17 2 Corinthians 5:1ff. implies that only Christians will be judged, but 2 Thessalonians 1 suggests that the whole of humanity will be judged.

18 For example, 2 Corinthians 5:17.

19 See especially 1 Corinthians 15; 2 Corinthians 4–5.

20 2 Corinthians 5:19.

21 Philippians 2:6–11.

22 Philippians 2:6.

23 On the theology of the fourth gospel see J. Ashton (ed.), *The Interpretation of God* (London, SPCK, 1986); J. Ashton, *Understanding the Fourth Gospel* (Oxford, Oxford University Press, 1991); D. Moody Smith, *Johannine Christianity* (Edinburgh, T. & T. Clark, 1987); D. Moody Smith, *The Theology of the Gospel of John* (Cambridge, Cambridge University Press, 1994); S. Smalley, *John: Evangelist and Interpreter* (Exeter, Paternoster, 1978).

24 John 1:1.

25 John 1:14.

26 John 12:31.

27 John 17:3.

28 For example, in John 14:18, 16:16, 22 and 21:23.

29 John 5:25, 28–9, 6:40, 54, 11:24.

30 John 11:52.

31 John 16:8–11.

32 John 6:27, 40, 54, 56–7, 58.

33 John 16:20–2.

34 John 15:6.

35 John 1:29.

36 John 1:41.

37 John 1:49.

38 John 4:42.

[39] John 6:14.

[40] John 6:35.

[41] John 16:33.

[42] John 19:30.

[43] John 2:4, 7:6, 8, 30, 39, 8:20.

[44] John 12:23, 31–2, 13:1, 31, 19:28, 30.

[45] For example, Mark 13:32.

[46] John 20:31.

[47] John 3:18–21, 5:21–4, 30, 9:34, 12:31.

[48] John 1:12, 3:16, 36, 6:47, 50–1, 8:51, 10:28, 17:3, 20:31.

[49] John 3:18–21, 36.

[50] John 14:16–18, 28, 15:26, 16:7–11, 16.

[51] The 'synoptic' gospels are the first three in the New Testament (Matthew, Mark and Luke) and are so called because they can be 'viewed together' in a *synopsis* (Gk., 'viewing together') on account of the substantial amount of material they have in common. For an outline of various explanations advanced as solutions to the 'sypnotic problem' (i.e. the literary interrelationship of the three gospels) see R. P. Martin, *New Testament Foundations*, i (Exeter, Paternoster, 1975); H. H. Stoldt, *History and Criticism of the Markan Hypothesis* (Edinburgh, T. & T. Clark, 1977).

[52] For a discussion of the problem and the issues involved, with particular reference to the teaching of Jesus on the future, especially in terms of the kingdom of God, see Norman Perrin, *Rediscovering the Teaching of Jesus* (London, SCM, 1967); J. Jeremias, *New Testament Theology: the Proclamation of Jesus* (London, SCM, 1971); John Riches, *Jesus and the Transformation of Judaism* (London, Darton, Longman & Todd, 1980); E. P. Sanders, *Jesus and Judaism* (London, SCM, 1985); G. R. Beasley-Murray, *Jesus and the Kingdom of God* (Exeter, Paternoster, 1986); Bruce D. Chilton, *God in Strength: Jesus' Announcement of the Kingdom* (Sheffield, Sheffield Academic Press, 1987); D. L. Tiede, *Jesus and the Future* (Cambridge, Cambridge University Press, 1991).

[53] Matthew 6:9–13, Luke 11:2–4.

[54] Mark 14:25, Matthew 26:29.

[55] See C. H. Dodd, *The Parables of the Kingdom* (London, Fontana, Collins, rev. edn., 1961); J. Jeremias, *The Parables of Jesus* (London, SCM, rev. edn., 1963); Eta Linnemann, *The Parables of Jesus* (London, SPCK, 1966); C. Westermann, *The Parables of Jesus* (Edinburgh, T. & T. Clark, 1990).

[56] For example, the parable of the ten virgins (Matthew 25:1–13).

[57] See Dodd, *Parables of the Kingdom, passim.*

[58] Cf. the Beatitudes in the Sermon on the Mount (Matthew 5:3–10).

59 Mark 13:24–5.

60 On this issue, see the various contributions to E. Bammel and C. F. D. Moule (eds.), *Jesus and the Politics of his day* (Cambridge, Cambridge University Press, 1984).

61 See *Jesus the Jew* (London, Collins, 1973), excursus ii, 188–91.

62 See J. Jeremias, *New Testament Theology*, 61–8. Jeremias's conclusions are, however, challenged by Vermes, *Jesus the Jew*, 210–13.

63 Galatians 4:6–7; Romans 8:14–17.

64 See Vermes, *Jesus the Jew*; M. Hengel, *The Charismatic Leader and His Followers* (Edinburgh, T. & T. Clark, 1981).

7

Beware the trumpet of judgement!: John Nelson Darby and the nineteenth-century Brethren

KENT EATON

1 An introduction to the Brethren dispensational thought

Among the nineteenth-century Nonconformists in the United Kingdom, the dissenting group that most emphasized the Christian doctrine of eschatology (the 'doctrine of the last things') in terms of anticipating a literal, proximate coming of Jesus Christ were the Plymouth Brethren. While the Brethren certainly shared the widespread interest of nineteenth-century evangelicals in the second advent of Jesus Christ, following primarily the teachings of John Nelson Darby (1800–82), their insistence on a literal interpretation of all scripture, especially the prophetic portions, led the majority of them to a distinctive interpretation scheme called 'dispensationalism'. Dispensationalism is basically a hermeneutical system which divides biblical history into distinctive periods of time in which God's specific demands on people are believed to differ. As a way of attempting to understand the interrelation and progressive development of both the Old and New Testaments, it continues to be closely aligned with many fundamental and evangelical groups to this day. In comparison with other nineteenth-century British millenarian groups, perhaps only the Irvingites or the Catholic Apostolic Church under the leadership of Edward Irving (1792–1834) and Henry Drummond[1] (1786–1860) placed the same degree of emphasis on Christ's return as an imminent event as did the Brethren. The striking difference between the two contemporary movements is that the Brethren did not share the charismatic focus of the Irvingites, who were in many ways the modern precursor of the Pentecostal Movement with their stress on the charismata such as speaking in tongues and prophecy.

As to a general summary of the Brethren view of the end times, Jesus Christ was more than just their anchor of hope in the present moment and their soon-to-be Saviour throughout eternity. Following the lead of Darby, the majority opinion of this group was that Christ currently reigned literally in heaven as he had been doing since his ascension mentioned in the New Testament book of Acts. Furthermore, he would soon be manifest as the promised coming deliverer who would prove to be the protagonist of the end times scenario. As head of the universal church he would, first of all, deliver the real church through the rapture of all true Christians.[2] The rapture was believed to be the moment when Christ meets his church in the air to take them up to heaven. To understand Brethren and dispensational doctrine, it is most important to understand that they held that Christ would come first for his church at the time of the rapture which would be prior to his second advent. This position is referred to as premillennialism. The universal church, which was soon to be raptured, was said to consist of all true believers who were scattered throughout the world and, to some extent, held captive by the visible church in its various denominational forms. The Brethren are not, then, exclusivists in thinking that they alone are numbered among the elect, as is the case with some marginal Christian sects that are millenarian in their theology, such as the Watchtower Bible and Tract Society (Jehovah's Witnesses) and the Church of Jesus Christ of the Latter Day Saints (Mormons).

Returning to the Brethren view of the work of the messianic king, following his rescue of the church, his primary responsibility was believed to be that of overcoming his enemies in order to initiate his personal rule upon the earth for a literal period of one thousand years. During this time all God's Old Testament covenant promises given to Abraham and his descendants would be literally fulfilled, and the Davidic royal line would once again be established in Jerusalem through the reign of Jesus Christ, the descendant of the ancient Hebrew King David. Old Testament prophecy then was, and is, believed to pertain only to ethnic Israel which is held to be radically distinct from the church. After this millennium, all existing corruption and depravity, as personified in the fallen archangel, Satan – the primary cause of all evil – would come to an end as Satan would be freed to deceive the human race for a brief period before he was finally condemned to eternal punishment so as never again to lead human beings astray from the perfect will of God. The coming deliverer's role is understood first of all in terms of rescuing his people from the deceiver and, secondly, as the one who would securely establish his people under his literal government. Following the commencement of the eternal punishment of Satan in the 'lake of fire' mentioned in the New Testament book of Revelation 20:10, Christ would subsequently lead both his kingdom of Christians still in heaven (the raptured Church) and the members of the restored Jewish nation or the millennial kingdom on earth into the eternal state as the temporal messianic kingdom gave way to everlasting, endless bliss.

That the Plymouth Brethren, known also today as the Christian or Open Brethren, would make any doctrinal contribution to the historical development of theology in terms of their eschatology is interesting in itself. As a movement of dissent, the Plymouth Brethren are much more characterized by their puritanical approach to personal piety and evangelistic zeal than by their theological genius or innovation. As one recent Brethren author has pointed out, simplicity of lifestyle, a willingness to sacrifice and 'exceptional personal piety' were characteristic traits of the Brethren from the first, as 'they were known for their sacrificial lifestyle which became embedded in the soul of the Brethren renewal movement'.[3] In regard to the evangelistic zeal just mentioned, in order to understand the mind set of the Brethren, one must observe that a critical part of the experience of the primitive church which the Brethren sought to restore was its missionary and evangelistic thrust. It is not possible, according to Brethren thought, radically to separate ecclesiology, the doctrine of the church, and evangelism and missions, for the latter is the logical outcome of 'biblical ecclesiology' when it is rightly understood and put into practice. Without missionary vision there is no church based upon the New Testament model.[4]

When comparing the Brethren with other Nonconformists, perhaps the most interesting conclusion is that the Brethren are somewhat anachronistic, that is to say, historically out of place. They may well have more in common with the movements of Old Dissent, that is those of the seventeenth century, than with those of the eighteenth century, or the New Dissent. For example, like the earlier Presbyterians and Particular Baptists (Calvinists), Darby and most Brethren were overwhelmingly in agreement with Calvinist theology. Like all Baptists, they jealously guarded the absolute autonomy of the local congregation, rejecting any or all superior ecclesiastical structures or authority, and eventually settled on the practice of believers' baptism. Furthermore, their primary worship service which involved the celebration of the eucharist or communion, referred to as the 'breaking of the bread', is strikingly similar to the worship of the Society of Friends or Quakers. According to the understanding of both groups, silence is observed until the time at which God's Spirit is believed to move or empower the Christian to 'share' or teach what he or she understood the Spirit desired be communicated to the entire group. This Brethren-Quaker similarity may be more than just coincidental due to the fact that many of the first Brethren Assemblies benefited numerically and in terms of leadership from the involvement of many former Quakers. Therefore, that there exists the same common stress on mutual edification apart from the planned intervention of ordained clergy in worship is not surprising.

In terms of the Brethren and the so-called New Dissent, many Brethren followed the lead of fellow evangelicals in terms of dedicating themselves wholeheartedly to social action, and like the Wesleyans, even more radically underscored the importance and practice of lay ministry. Yet, at the same time, the differences are also dramatic: the Brethren overwhelmingly rejected involvement in the political arena on theological grounds while their fellow dissenters jockeyed for political clout; they resisted the pressure to organize themselves denominationally, and refused to form a formal missionary society as other 'denominations' had done. In this way the Brethren certainly swam against the prevailing tides as there was indeed a tendency, if not a movement, among other Nonconformists in the first half of the nineteenth century to band together so that doctrinal distinctiveness might be defined, giving the group both identity and doctrinal moorings. For example, the Baptists formed an association or union in 1813 and the Congregationalists had in place a national union by 1831.[5] In contrast, to this day the Plymouth Brethren still do not have in place any denominational structure or hierarchy. They do, however, co-operate with one another for the purposes of 'Bible Conferences' not unlike the Keswick Conventions and in order to support Brethren missionaries throughout the world, primarily through the Echoes of Service organization located in Bath, England.

With the exception of dispensational theology and the absolute rejection of ordained clergy, there is one other group which closely parallels the Brethren. This is the movement popularly referred to as the 'Campbellites' which eventually led to the formation of denominations such as the Disciples of Christ and the Church of Christ. The Campbellite dissenting groups under the direction of both Alexander and Thomas Campbell, immigrants to North America from Ireland, instigated their movement at approximately the same time as the early Brethren. They, too, believed that the scriptures were, and are, to be seen as the exclusive rule for all questions of faith and practice. Also like the Brethren, the early Campbellites insisted upon a rejection of all forms of Christian practices that were not thought to be in use among early Christians such as creeds, confessions, non-scriptural words, and any theological speculation. The absolute independence of each church under the care of elders and deacons was also a cornerstone of both groups' understanding of the nature of the church. In addition to these similarities, other commonly held views were the emphasis given to the organic unity of the church, leading to strong ecumenical ideals, open acceptance of somewhat widely divergent views, adult believers' baptism by immersion, weekly open communion understood as the climax of a simple order of worship, membership confined to baptized believers and a rigidly puritanical social ethic.[6] Also like the Brethren, the initial leaders of the Campbellites were strong missionary advocates. The main areas of difference between the Brethren and the Campbellites are found in those two places in which the Brethren carry out unique theological innovations. These represent two major breaks with Protestantism in general and are in Brethren ecclesiology ('doctrine of the church'), especially in doing away with a professional clergy caste, and the development of dispensationalism as a new theological system.

Here, then, is the greatest difference between the Brethren and the New Dissent – the former's total rejection of a caste of professional clergy, which also serves as the explanation for the eventual distancing of the Brethren from other dissenting groups. It was, and is, believed that God would, and will, direct the members of the assembly in the selection of a plurality of elders to exercise spiritual authority and pastoral responsibility over the members of their congregations. These men held absolute authority over the 'assembly', the preferred term to 'church', which was thought to reek of denominationalism and was, therefore, shunned. The classic word used to denote their places of worship is exactly the term 'assembly' or, at times, 'Gospel Hall'. There does exist, however, a modern tendency to abandon the word 'assembly' and to use the word 'chapel' instead. The word 'men' just used is a deliberate sexist reference, as women were progressively restricted in terms of their participation in all levels of the movement, with the one exception being foreign missionaries. The closed doors in Victorian Britain are directly inversely proportionate to the female presence in exotic lands enjoying ministry roles exclusive to men back home in Great Britain!

Given the desire of the Brethren to recreate the purity of the New Testament church, it is not surprising to see that as a general rule theology was viewed as static rather than dynamic. In fact, for the Brethren, any theological development beyond the apostolic age was suspect and viewed as evidence of the worldly and decadent state of the church. Nevertheless, in the beginning of the movement one encounters a rather unique ecumenical spirit, as opposed to an overemphasis on doctrinal uniformity. The primary catalyst behind the formation of the movement was almost exclusively the desire for visible unity within the Protestant church and not necessarily doctrinal unity.[7] However, when John Nelson Darby's (1800–82) literal hermeneutical approach to the scriptures led him to declare that the visible church, particularly in the form of any given state church, lay in ruins without any hope whatsoever for revival, doctrinal and eschatological issues moved to the forefront. Darby's criticism of the church was directed towards Protestant churches and, to an even larger degree, the Roman Catholic Church. Brethren theology began to sound a definite apocalyptic note for all to hear. Due to the profound impact of Darby's thought, the Brethren, more than any other group of British millenarians, looked for a soon-to-be-established period of messianic rule and blessings. Yet, in contrast to many other millennarians, according to Darby, the earthly bliss of the millennial kingdom was not to be the immediate experience of true believing Christians but was reserved solely for the restored nation of Israel. The church was destined to be an entirely heavenly institution as Christians would remain in heaven for the duration of the earthly kingdom. Furthermore, the essentially pessimistic position of Darby must be emphasized, as his initial expectation was a solemn one. He believed that spiritual order in the world would only be brought about through the chaos of judgement, and that blessing would only come as a result of the intense fire of God's judgement. There was no hope for revival of the church as an institution. The church had failed miserably in its divine commission. As a spiritually bankrupt institution, it had come to the point where its only possible future experience was that of God's judgement for having been unsuccessful in accomplishing its divine calling, as had all of God's chosen people during each and every one of the preceding dispensations.[8] The following remarks of Darby illustrate the sobriety and gloominess of his position:

> instead of permitting ourselves to hope for continued progress of good, we must expect a progress of evil; and that the hope of the earth being filled with the knowledge of the Lord before the exercise of His judgment, and the consummation of this judgment on the earth, is delusive. We are to expect evil, until it becomes so flagrant that it will be necessary for the Lord to judge it.[9]

It should not surprise us, then, that as a composer of hymns, Darby's emphasis on the present decadent state of the world and the church should find expression as it did in the following hymn:

> This world is a wilderness wide:
> I have nothing to seek or to choose,
> I have no thought in the waste to abide,
> I've nought to regret nor to lose . . .[10]

We do well to note that Darby's view is as passive as it is negative. It is the perfect theology for the person who feels the need to retreat and be, as the saying goes, 'so other worldly that they are no worldly good'. Even the two recognized ordinances of the church age could be interpreted in such a way as to reinforce both the need to withdraw from active involvement in society and enclose oneself in this kind of Protestant semi-monastic community. One late nineteenth-century Brethren writer said that baptism 'shews forth our separation from the world' and that the communion service was the 'expression of fellowship one with another'. He then defines 'fellowship' exclusively in terms of what it prohibits: for example 'the child of God ought to be in no society, association, or fellowship, but the Church of God', for 'God has ordained the fellowship of saints, and with this fellowship we ought to be content'. Baptism is, then, summarized as the 'outward badge of . . . separation from the world' and the 'Lord's Supper' as the 'outward badge of fellowship' of true believers as they awaited the coming of Jesus who would 'deliver them from the wrath to come'.[11] This resignation and passivity, combined with the view that the last days would be marked by an ever-increasing wickedness and apostasy, lead one to the conclusion that nothing can be done to impede the satanic onslaught. If one expects all things to get worse, any new negative experience is interpreted as further confirmation of the theological presupposition and leads to further passivity. The only viable option was to retreat as much as possible into the community of like-minded saints. However, the purpose of the withdrawal was not to regroup to attack the evil world, but to nurse one another's wounds and keep the enemy outside the fortress walls. This millenarianism, then, stands in sharp contrast to the militant forms currently resurging in many of the major religions, for it is grounded in resignation.

With the exception of their novel eschatology, throughout the history of the movement relatively little attention has been given to questions of doctrinal uniformity and a systematic explanation of their theological positions. While they are not given to systematic theology, this observation needs to be balanced with the fact that the movement has produced a good number of excellent biblicists and teachers of the scriptures. Referring to the question of theological latitude among the Brethren, the late Emeritus Professor F. F. Bruce of the University of Manchester, himself a second-generation, lifelong practising Brethren, once addressed the theological diversity of the church, remarking that 'the Brethren are a diverse lot, and I suppose no two of us would give exactly the same account of ourselves'.[12] This statement points to the simple truth that the Brethren have evolved to the point today that there hardly exist any clear-cut theological distinctions that are true of all the flock. In fact, for all of the nineteenth century and most of the twentieth, the movement can be classified almost as anti-theological in nature apart from its view of the church and the end times. This is especially true when it is compared with other dissenting ecclesiological traditions which hold to standard theological systems as summarized in their doctrinal statements.

Instead of a doctrinal emphasis, what is stressed above all else in the Brethren camp is pietism, that is the personal and intimate experience of the Christian with the God of the Bible. One of the more important first-generation Brethren figures and the first Brethren missionary, Anthony Norris Groves, said the following concerning the basis of Brethren unity and the existing theological latitude:

> The basis of our fellowship is life in the Christ of Scripture rather than light on the teaching of the Scriptures. Those who have part with Christ have part with us. Because our communion is one of life and love more than one of doctrine and opinion, we seek to show that the oneness in the life of God through Jesus Christ is a stronger bond than that of being one of us – whether organizationally or denominationally . . . We do not consider an act of fellowship to be indicative of total agreement; indeed we sometimes find it a needed expression of love to submit to others in matters where we do not fully agree, rather than to prevent some greater good from being brought about . . . We feel it biblical never to pressure anyone to act in uniformity farther than they feel in uniformity; we use our fellowship in the Spirit as an opportunity to discuss our differences and find this to be the most effective way of leading others – or being led by them – into the light of the Word.[13]

Given this ecumenical spirit, one might very well wonder how the Brethren ever solidified into a dissenting movement! To understand how the group eventually began to cohere around some distinctive set of beliefs or practices in order to achieve a sense of calling and/or personal identity, it is crucial to observe that the nature of its objections to standard positions then held by both the Anglican and Nonconformist churches were not strictly theological, but related more to questions of the practice of the Christian faith. Therefore, while within the Brethren there is a general theological appreciation for the moments of revival throughout history, previous reform movements were thought not to have succeeded in what God had called them to do: re-establish the purity of faith and practice of the New Testament church. This was also thought to have been the case for the Protestant Reformation. All of the Protestant groups, even the more radical Anabaptists who were more often than not millenarianists like the Brethren, had stopped short of the necessary goal of actually recreating the primitive church. This was particularly true regarding the universal priesthood of all believers. This doctrinal position, often associated with Luther, affirms the dignity and calling of every Christian, ordained or laity, to directly enter into the symbolic presence of God and to exercise ministry in the lives of the community of faith. This crucial issue, according to Brethren thought, would become, as early as the 1830s, one of the primary reasons for their eventual break with the Church of England and other Protestant denominations. While 'universal priesthood' remained simply a 'slogan' with most of Christendom, for the Brethren, as biblical literalists, this cornerstone doctrine had to be converted into a living reality in order to model the New Testament church. Among the Brethren there would be no ordained clergy caste.[14]

The second reason why the Brethren were not able to assimilate their message of reform into other denominational entities is the subject of this chapter – the Brethren millennial expectation. As a movement, they saw themselves returning to the understanding of the primitive church of the first century regarding messianic prophecy. However, it should be stated that the eschatological emphasis was not necessarily the most important reason for the eventual formation of the Brethren as a separate 'church'. What was deemed to be most important was their desire to recreate the life and ministry of the apostolic New Testament church. For example, when the message of Darby is compared with that of the even more radical millenarian, William Miller (1782–1849), who was laying the foundation for a contemporary parallel movement in the United States, the Seventh Day Adventists, Darby was not so carried away with the imminence of the second coming of Christ as to be prone to

pronounce actual dates of the coming rapture.[15] Miller,
monotone in his apocalyptic message while stirring 'millennial
fear and fervor'[16] as he looked for a premillennial, personal and
imminent second advent, was much quicker to create a separate
movement than was Darby. Notwithstanding, Darby clearly
thought and taught that the church, particularly the Church of
England from which the majority of the early Brethren
proceeded, had failed miserably in the present age. The church
had not carried out God's command in its divine commission to
remain faithful to the Bible and to evangelize the entire world. He
referred to all people's 'continual failing in the service of the
Church'.[17] The Brethren message as propagated by Darby was to
abandon this sinking ship, the visible church, in its many forms
and prepare as many faithful souls as possible for the impending
divine judgement. A true remnant had to be called out from the
contexts of the existing visible churches. The coming deliverer
was, first of all, the coming judge and executioner. A heightened
sense of urgency abounded which Peter Cousins, Brethren
apologist, summarized in the following way:

> Christians thought the time was near when Jesus would return to
> judge the world and set it to rights. There had been a great deal of
> upheaval, caused by the French Revolution and a series of European
> wars. Such upheavals were thought to be signs of the 'Second
> Coming'. If Christ were to return, he would judge unfaithful
> Christians first of all (1 Peter 4:17). There was not much time left,
> they thought, to set things right.[18]

Because of the stress laid upon the imminent return of Christ,
who would establish his earthly kingdom, the initial ecumenical
spirit and the rejection of strict doctrinal conformity waned as,
with time, the name Plymouth Brethren became closely aligned
with dispensationalism as a developing theological system. From
Darby onwards, dispensational theorists would formulate the
most elaborate explanation up until that time of just what God
was doing in the outworking of human history. The truth is that,
even to this day, much of John Nelson Darby's theological
thought still holds great influence for many Brethren, as well as
other fundamentalist circles and even in some evangelical groups,
particularly outside of the British Isles. In fact, Darby would

appear to have a growing number of followers as we approach the close of the second millennium. How many other nineteenth-century theologians have ninety-four of their works, both books and tracts, under current publication in 1996?[19] What other figures of church history contemporary with Darby already have their complete works published on CD-ROM?[20] Darby is even present on the Internet, with at least two World-Wide-Web sites![21] From September 1995 to December 1995, I daily monitored the international discussion group operated by the Brethren located at sender pb-list-owner@cs.dal.ca. During this time period, the name of Darby was mentioned weekly and the version of the Bible most often quoted by far was the translation by Darby referred to as the Darby Version. In addition to his English translation, Darby also translated the scriptures into German and French. Of particular interest was the week of 12–18 November 1995 in which the primary subject which was debated was the 'Relevance of Darby's Writing'. No negative opinions whatsoever were expressed except for some passing references to the somewhat archaic vocabulary and sentence structure characteristically employed by Darby. One avid Darby fan who has also translated several of his works into Spanish stated his position in this way: 'The fact that Darby lived during the last century does in no way minimize his contribution as a Bible expositor and apologist. In fact, many of the issues now confronting Christianity were dealt by him in a most helpful way.'[22] Who is this millenarian theologian who appears to be making such a comeback?

2 The life of Darby: the discontented minister

Darby was born at Westminster, England, on 18 November 1800 into the home of a wealthy merchant and as the godson of Lord Nelson. Prior to taking orders as a priest in the Church of Ireland in 1826 and serving a parish in the county of Wicklow, Darby graduated from Trinity College, Dublin, having studied for the bar to which he was admitted in 1822.[23] Shortly thereafter, Darby underwent some kind of personal spiritual crisis which led to his decision to seek ordination. However, his years of service as an Anglican priest would be short-lived as he soon broke ranks. History was to repeat itself and Darby's life can be understood as a series of three breaks with existing ecclesiastical bodies. Following the move out of the Anglican Church, Darby would also separate with all other Nonconformists and, even more surprisingly, he would eventually sever the ties with his own rank and file, the other Brethren. It is important to understand this threefold dissolution because it helps to explain why Darby was so extremely negative with regard to his own ecclesiology. His own religious and church experience must at least to some extent have helped to solidify his theological convictions and conclusions as to the decadent state of the church.

Darby's move towards breaking with the state church can be tied to two primary factors. In the first place, around 1827–8, he began to meet together with an ecumenically minded group of men for the purpose of worship and fellowship. The issues which were important for Darby and these men were not so much theological as to do with the understanding of the practice of the Christian faith. As noted earlier in this chapter, this phenomenon would also later be characteristic of the entire Brethren movement. Their meetings consisted of Bible readings and the simple celebration of the Christian communion service, or 'the breaking of bread'. In addition to Darby, the other key figures present in the Dublin meetings were Anthony Norris Groves and J. B. Bellet, who both shared an Anglican background with Darby. Groves had left behind a successful career as a dentist in Exeter to train at Trinity College, Dublin, for missionary service. When Groves presented himself to the Church Missionary Society as a candidate and was told that he would not be allowed to celebrate the Lord's Supper without the presence of an ordained minister, his faith in the Anglican doctrinal system was shattered. He interpreted this position as an attack upon the priestly duties open to, and required of, all true Christians. In his view, the church was actually shackling itself both in theory and in practice by its overemphasis on the ministry of ordained clergymen. Hence, it is important to notice both the historic emphasis given to the priesthood of all believers and the centrality of the Lord's Supper as the climax of weekly Christian worship from the very beginning of the movement. Darby, too, gravitated towards a rejection of ordained ministers in spite of his own ordination.

It was that I was looking for the body of Christ (which was not there, but perhaps in all the parish not one converted person); and collaterally, because I believe in a divinely appointed ministry. If Paul had come, he could not have preached (he had never been ordained); if a wicked ordained man, he had his title and must be recognized as a minister; the truest minister of Christ unordained could not. It was a system contrary to what I found in Scripture.[24]

It is also important to note that what Darby objected to was not the idea of full-time ministry, but the requirement of ordination, be it episcopal or congregational in origin. His view was that a minister should not be 'appointed by the king or chosen by the people . . . but [by] God'. In fact he deemed full-time ministry 'to be as essential to the dispensation, as the fact of Christ's coming'. Given what we have seen already of Darby's emphasis on the second advent, he could not stress the point more! Ordination to the ministry was simply a 'perversion' as it in all likelihood represented merely 'the mere will of king or people' and their interference 'with a holy thing'. He summarized his position by saying:

I read that when Christ ascended up on high, 'He gave some apostles, and some prophets; and some, evangelists; and some, pastors and teachers'. This is the only source of ministry, not the appointment of a king, nor the choice of a people . . . Christ gives when and how He pleases – woe be to them who do not own it![25]

Quite early in the movement other clergymen, both Anglican and Nonconformists, were attracted to the Brethren understanding of the practice of the Christian faith. Some examples from the Church of England included the Reverend J. L. Harris who threw in his lot with the Brethren as early as 1832, and the Reverend Henry Borlas, a gràduate of Trinity College, Cambridge, who had held the curacy of St Keyne, Cornwall. Borlas was instrumental in bringing about a degree of cohesion to the movement as the first editor of the *Christian Witness*, the first Brethren magazine, which began publication in 1834.[26] Also joining the Brethren and abandoning the Church of England were Benjamin Wills Newton and Percy Hall. In the former case, like Darby, one encounters a brilliant academic career as Newton had prepared himself at Oxford for the Anglican ministry. Hall's ties to the Anglican Church were also very strong as his father had been Dean of Christ Church and Regius Professor of Divinity.[27] Examples of dissenters who would minister within the ranks of the Brethren include Henry Craik who studied at St Andrews with the idea of ministering in the Church of Scotland before opting for service in the Baptist Church, then subsequently the Brethren. Likewise, George Müller, before his pilgrimage into the Brethren fold, found himself in Bristol in the Baptist ministry after having studied at the University of Halle in Germany with a view to entering the Lutheran ministry. Müller would become most famous due to his founding of orphanages, such as 'Ashley Down'. Equally important was his understanding of the principle of faith as total dependence upon God for every need, be it spiritual or material, which has permeated Brethren thought.

Due to the Brethren's radically different position on the interpretation of the practice of the Lord's Supper and their absolute rejection of ordained clergy, the fact that they could not incorporate their reform movement into any existing dissenting movement is logical. The Brethren simply understood themselves to be more in line with the continuation of the primitive, apostolic church as seen in the book of Acts and the Pauline Epistles. One Brethren author even acknowledged that 'the Brethren believe that their story goes back more than nineteen hundred years'.[28] This, then, is the second separation of Darby and the Brethren. As was explained earlier in this chapter, these theological characterisics made assimilation into the Baptist, Methodist, Congregationalist or any other then existing denomination totally impossible. As Harold Rowdon has observed, the Brethren 'were also nonconformists who deplored certain features of nonconformity in their day'.[29]

Darby's third break was not long in coming. In the year 1850 the Brethren movement became, in the word of Coad, 'irremediably divided',[30] with the schism between the Open Brethren and the Darbyites, or Exclusive Brethren. It is important to recognize this distinction because of the radically different historical evolution of the two groups, with the Plymouth Brethren gravitating toward middle-of-the-road evangelicalism, and the Exclusives, as the term suggests, towards separation from others. In the words of one Open or Plymouth Brethren, the Exclusive Brethren are known as such 'because they excluded from Christian fellowship members of churches they disapproved of'.[31] Unlike the Open Assemblies, the Exclusive Brethren, of which there are a large variety of groups, do not co-operate with other churches and are centrally controlled. Perhaps the most well-known Exclusive group is the Taylor party or the Taylorites. In contrast, and as noted earlier, the Open Brethren practise absolute congregational independence.

The division has often been referred to as the 'division of Bethesda' because of its origin in that assembly. The root problem, aside from personality clashes among the leaders, centred on the Open position regarding participation in the Lord's Supper. Should those who did not share all the rapidly developing Brethren dogma, of which Darby was the principal source, be allowed to participate in the most important Brethren worship event? That this should have become an issue is most ironic given the fact that the celebration of the Lord's Supper was from the very beginning an ecumenical celebration for the Brethren, which all true believers (that is, those who were evangelical in their theological orientation) were invited to attend. A group of Plymouth Brethren from the United Kingdom and Spain, reflecting nostalgically on the early ecumenical desires of the first Brethren, explained the importance of the Lord's Supper in this way:

> It was a very 'denominational' time in evangelical circles in Great Britain, and various ministers from different groups along with believers from different professions, got to know one another and arrived at the idea of making manifest their communion in Christ – above all denominational barriers – by 'breaking the bread' . . . all together in a private house. This experience brought them great joy and renewal so that very soon they arrived at the conclusion that meetings such as these of 'two or three in the name of Christ' (Matt. 18:20) should not be just an appendix to their previous church life but rather the very centre of their Christian life in the collective sense.[32]

This quotation is significant not only for showing in a pronounced way the disdain of denominational barriers that marked the movement from the very beginning but also for highlighting the centrality of the celebration of the Lord's Supper in church life. For the Brethren, the worship service is when they come together to break bread. Unfortunately for the future unity of the movement, Darby moved dramatically toward a closed, dogmatic position. His break with Brethren ecumenism regarding the ordinance of communion, together with his rejection of all other eschatologies but his own as false, sealed the fate of the Brethren division permanently. B. W. Newton, a prominent leader of the Brethren in Plymouth, differed with Darby in his views regarding the second coming of Christ. The fact that both were strong personalities did little to ease their differences. As Darby travelled widely preaching and teaching, he eventually announced that both he and all other churches holding his same interpretations would not associate or have fellowship with the members of the assembly located at Plymouth. This action by Darby split the Brethren into two groups, according to whether or not they accepted Darby's positions. As Cousins pointed out,

> the group led by J. N. Darby believed that their most important duty was to separate themselves from any local church which tolerated practices or beliefs that were disapproved by Darby. It was not long before they disagreed among themselves into many small groups, often known by the name of the man leading each group.[33]

In the years following the division, the Plymouth Brethren, known also as the Open or Christian Brethren, became by far the most important group numerically. Their influence has been especially important in terms of Brethren missionary work around the world as their missionary effort, in terms of willing workers and percentage of church funds dedicated, has been most impressive and their very heartbeat and lifeblood. The growth of the Brethren Assemblies is particularly impressive in the nations that are, or were, a part of the British Commonwealth.

In spite of the division, the figure of Darby, even though he is the patriarch of the Exclusive or Closed Brethren, is almost omnipresent, in the theology of the Open Brethren, as his importance as a theologian transcends the self-imposed ecclesiastical barriers among the Brethren. His systematic theology became the standard for most, but not all, Brethren, even after the division of

Bethesda in 1850. The schism explains why J. N. Darby and his theological thought is not an entirely pleasant subject to most Plymouth Brethren to this day. Darby was a polemical figure and even an embarrassment to a movement built upon the foundation of evangelical ecumenical unity among dissenters. He was the black sheep who should largely be excluded from the collective consciousness of the group identity. From 1850 onward he was relegated to being, as one early twentieth-century Plymouth Brethren writer put it, the primary figure of 'the sad history of the Exclusive party, now divided by personal and doctrinal quarrels'.[34] Darby would remain a reactionary historical figure who caused a good degree of uneasiness and whose skeleton the Plymouth Brethren preferred to keep in the closet. In spite of his key role as the developer of dispensational theology, his name is more often than not avoided by dispensational theologians both within and outside of the Brethren camp.

Before returning to the question of the distinctive features of Darby's dispensational theology, we would do well to reflect upon the great influence that Darby's thought has had upon Christian fundamentalism and the more conservative elements of evangelicalism. Darby's pessimistic message of coming doom and the need to withdraw from the church, and, to some extent, society, has provided – at least in part – the theological justification for the defensive 'siege' mentality that is often characteristic of fundamentalism. Darby and dispensational theology are far from popular topics for European students of theology, but his impact has been felt to an infinitely larger degree on the North American theological scene.[35]

Darby travelled extensively and was personally involved in beginning and shepherding many Brethren groups in Switzerland and France, and even travelled to New Zealand, Canada and the United States.[36] In terms of finding numerous converts, Darby enjoyed much more success outside Europe. Great inroads into the North American religious scene were made by Darby and his team of itinerant evangelists, and then popularized by prophetic Bible conferences. It is, then, in the United States that, as Stephen H. Travis notes, 'Dispensationalism has been very influential during the last hundred years among evangelicals . . .'.[37] As observed by John Marsden, historian of North American fundamentalism, in the USA few would 'separate from their churches. John Nelson Darby was puzzled by this when he first brought his teaching to America. Many Americans were interested in his approach to prophetic studies, yet few took seriously the Brethren teaching of the "ruin of the church".'[38] This, then, led to the major difference between European and American dispensationalism: on the European Continent, the system would be largely confined to Brethren circles and not even representative of all of its church leaders and members. In contrast, in the nineteenth and early twentieth centuries in the United States, the five most key figures in the dissemination of dispensationalism come from an incredibly wide variety of denominational backgrounds. James Brooks (1830–97) and Lewis Sperry Chafer (1871–1952) were Presbyterians, William E. Blackstone (1841–1935) and Arno C. Gaebelein (1861–1945) were Methodists, and C. I. Scofield's (1843–1921) denominational background was that of the Congregational Church.[39] What served to consolidate dispensationalism as a permanent fixture in the spectrum of American theology was the establishment of schools that would give form to its theological development. As Hudson notes, like the European Brethren, these first American 'converts' displayed 'little concern for denominational peculiarities' and, quickly, 'the proponents of this prophetic understanding of the Scriptures made inroads in practically all the Protestant denominations'.[40] In his frequent travels to the United States, while Darby was extremely successful in winning many converts to his dispensational thought, very few took the second step of leaving their denominations to form Brethren Assemblies. As Marsden points out, Darby especially found an open ear with the Calvinists:

Darby spent a great deal of his time proselytizing in North America. He found relatively little interest there in the new Brethren sect, but remarkable willingness to accept his views and methods of prophetic interpretation. This enthusiasm came largely from clergymen with strong Calvinistic views, principally Presbyterians and Baptists in the northern United States. The evident basis for this affinity was that in most respects Darby was himself an unrelenting Calvinist. His interpretation of the Bible and of history rested firmly on the massive pillar of divine sovereignty, placing as little value as possible on human ability.[41]

Darby was helped by the popularity of the Scofield Reference Bible, which imposed a rigid schematization on the complex biblical materials by relating each part of scripture to a timetable of dispensations which was to culminate in the return of Christ to glory.[42] Many of the first leaders of this US brand of 'Darbyanism' were associated with Moody Bible Institute and had also been influenced by the Keswick Conventions in England.[43] From Moody Bible Institute, dispensational theology would soon prove to be the driving force behind the formation of new conservative theological colleges and seminaries in the United States as the debate heated up in the Fundamentalist-Modernist controversy. Schools such as the Bible Institute of Los Angeles, known today as Biola University and Talbot Seminary, along with Dallas Theological Seminary, would soon join the ranks of Moody Bible Institute in grounding several generations of North American fundamentalists and evangelicals in dispensational thought made in the image of Darby. These same institutions would also be a potent force in the preparation of generations of Protestant missionaries to carry the distinctive views of Darby's dispensationalism around the world to a degree that he certainly never dreamed of as being possible. That Darby's dispensationalism has impacted upon the conservative North American theological scene can be seen from the number of papers dealing with dispensational theology that were presented at the fall 1995 annual meeting of the Evangelical Theological Society.[44] This group is composed primarily of North American theologians.

Marsden suggests two reasons for the acceptance of the thought of Darby in the USA:

> Two factors . . . seem to have converged. One was a set of intellectual predispositions – characteristic of one type of nineteenth-century thought – to interpret Scripture in a literal way and to develop a distinctive view of history. The other was the secularization of the culture. With the rapid process of secularization throughout the nineteenth century, inevitably some people questioned the continued close identification of the church with the culture.[45]

What, then, was Darby's teaching concerning eschatology and, in particular, his view of Jesus Christ as the soon to come millennial king?

3 Millenarianism as taught in Darby's dispensational theology

Darby's eschatology and ecclesiology are understandably inter-dependent and inseparable in his dispensational scheme. This is observed both in the fact that the church was born through the Jewish rejection of the Messiah and by the fact that the church only reaches its completeness once it is raptured from the earth to heaven. Bruce noted this when he wrote that,

> Darby's eschatology and ecclesiology were interdependent elements in a carefully constructed system – not surprising, since in the New Testament itself eschatology and ecclesiology are interdependent. One cannot logically retain Darby's eschatology and reject his ecclesiology, as some schools of thought in our own day attempted to do. (I have never known anyone who accepted his ecclesiology without at the same time accepting his eschatology.)[46]

This is due to the fact that had the Jewish nation not rejected Jesus Christ as their present deliverer, the millennial kingdom, Jewish in nature, would have been established in place of the New Testament church. The church would never have come into existence for it is understood to be a parenthesis between the past and future manifestations of the kingdom. Yet, in order to understand his view of the church and the millennium, one must start with the concept of 'dispensation'. Darby was of course neither the first to use the word 'dispensation', nor the first to emphasize the coming of a literal thousand-year period of messianic rule.[47] Indeed, modern-day dispensationalists are prone to see traces of dispensational thought early on in the history of the church. Charles C. Ryrie, who, along with Cyrus Ingerson Scofield and Lewis Sperry Chafer, has to be considered as one of the most prominent dispensational theologians since Darby, points to Justin Martyr (100–65), Irenaeus (130–200), Clement of Alexandria (150–215), and Augustine (354–430) as evidences of dispensational thought early on in the historical development of theology.[48] In defence of this position it is indeed quite possible that Justin's literalistic interpretation of the eschatology of the New Testament led him to the 'millenarian belief in an earthly reign of the saints with Christ'. The same can be said for Irenaeus and Tertullian regarding their literalistic view of the reign of the saints.[49] Such ancient allusions to a literal thousand-year rule of Christ are important to dispensationalists as they are often charged with recency, that is, holding a non-apostolic position. In all probability, these most ancient millenarians were not able to establish a following largely due to the negative association of millenarianism with Montanism.[50]

Likewise, in the context of the Reformation, both Roman Catholics and the newly formed Protestant Churches were quick to condemn millenarianism due to its association with the radical wing of the Reformation such as the Anabaptists. Only in post-Reformation thought does Christian millenarianism begin to overcome the prejudices against it from within the church. Modern dispensationalists look to theologians such as Pierre Poiret (*L'Œconomie Divine*, 1687), John Edwards (*A Compleat History or Survey of All the Dispensations*, 1699) and Isaac Watts (*The Harmony of all the Religions which God ever Prescribed to Men and all his Dispensations towards them*) as theologians who set forth dispensational understandings of scripture.[51] Notwithstanding these prior examples, even modern dispensationalists recognize that Darby is singular in his contribution: 'it was the ministry and writings of John Nelson Darby . . . that systematized the concept' and 'was the foundation for later dispensationalists'.[52] As one of the principal modern historians of American fundamentalism, George Marsden, could rightly affirm that Darby is the 'immediate progenitor' of dispensational premillennialism,[53] and popular North American evangelical theologian Millard J. Erickson could truthfully call Darby the 'developer of dispensationalism'.[54]

4 The dispensational system

As an attempt to systematize biblical revelation, Darby and subsequent dispensationalists distinguish different stages, dispensations or economies through which God has sovereignly worked in terms of his progressive revelation and his ways of relating to human beings. Darby divided the biblical revelation into seven distinct stages:

    I.   Paradisiacal state to the Flood
    II.   Noah

Darby stated his own understanding of dispensational theology in the following way:

> This however we have to learn in its detail, in the various dispensations which led to or have followed the revelations of the incarnate Son in whom all the fullness was pleased to dwell . . . The detail of the history connected with these dispensations brings out many most interesting displays, both of the principles and patience of God's dealing with the evil and failure of man; and of the workings by which He formed faith on His own thus developed perfections. But the dispensations themselves all declare some leading principle or interference of God, some condition in which He has placed man, principles which in themselves are everlastingly sanctioned of God, but in the course of those dispensations placed responsibility in the hands of man for the display and discovery of what he was, and the bringing in their infallible establishment in Him to whom the glory of them all rightly belonged . . . in every instance, there was total and immediate failure as regarded man, however the patience of God might tolerate and carry on by grace the dispensation in which man has thus failed in the outset; and further, that there is no instance of the restoration of a dispensation afforded us, though there might be partial revivals of it through faith.[56]

One can see that Darby highlights at least four distinctive features of each dispensational stage that lead us to a definition of the term 'dispensation'. First, each dispensation is a new period of God's interaction with humans based upon a particular divine revelation that must be understood as sequentially dependent upon the previous revelation and interpreted from the vantage point of the New Testament. Darby's scheme is christological in its focus as well as evolutionary: the Bible is, above all, understood as the progressive outworking of God's plan of salvation.

God does not change or evolve, yet his way of relating to humankind does. The Old Testament dispensations look forward to the salvation offered through Christ, and the dispensations following his earthly ministry look forward to seeing him establish the earthly millennium and then reigning throughout eternity. Another commentary by Darby which serves to illustrate the importance of interpreting salvation history from the point of view of the church is the following:

> Every dispensation has its character, from the manner in which Christ is manifested and introduced in it; and its order from Him under whom it takes its rise as to ministration. God, not yet known to the Church in covenant, but the same God revealed as Almighty, was the dispensation to Abraham called out to trust in Him, and gave its character to the path in which he had to walk in hope.[57]

Secondly, there is a specific test or 'condition' associated with each dispensation which ends up illustrating the 'total and immediate failure' of all people in terms of their obedience to the test. From Adam and Eve onward, none have passed their spiritual test. This failure on the part of humans, which is the third distinctive feature, then logically results, it is believed, in a likewise specific divine judgement. The judgement is the fourth element common to all dispensations. One critic of dispensational theology succinctly summarized the chief characteristics of each dispensation in this way and underscored the basic negativism of the system as it concerns the development of human history:

> each is characterized by (a) a divinely-imposed testing, (b) man's sinful response to the same, and (c) God's judgement accordingly upon man's sin. The seventh dispensation only appears not to fall into this pattern. In each of the other periods God demands man's obedience to the test imposed, man fails to measure up to the divine demand, and receives accordingly the divine condemnation or judgment – a dismal picture, indeed![58]

The present age is the 'Dispensation of the Spirit' and was also thought to correspond to the period of history beginning with the church of the book of Acts. According to dispensational thought, we are obviously still in this dispensation because the coming deliverer has not yet arrived to establish his earthly rule. This period is significant for both Jews and Christians because of the fact that this dispensation signals the Jewish nation's final absolute rejection of Jesus as the Messiah. According to Darby:

> The glory of God, His real visible presence, was once at Jerusalem, His throne was over the cherubim; but ever since the Babylonish [*sic*] captivity His presence abandoned Jerusalem, and His glory as well as His presence were no more in the temple in the midst of the people. And though His great patience endured long, until Christ was rejected, yet God cut them off as regards that covenant. The remnant became Christians, but all the system was terminated by judgement. Such will be the issue of the christian [*sic*] system, if it continue not in the goodness of God. But it has not continued in God's goodness.[59]

Now that God has established his church, for the present moment he has ceased to work through Israel. Crucial, then, to Darby's dispensationalism is its differentiation between God's programme for Israel in the Old Testament and his programme for the church in the New Testament. According to Darby, the church does not continue the work begun with Israel. In fact, the church did not begin in the Old Testament but on the day of Pentecost when God instituted the beginning of a new 'administration' or 'plan' in his unfolding historical drama of redemption. Bass noted that it is at this point where Darby differed radically with past understandings of the nature of the development of salvation history:

> It is not that exegetes prior to his time did not see a covenant between God and Israel, or a future relation of Israel to the millennial reign, but they always viewed the church as a continuation of God's single program of redemption begun in Israel. It is dispensationalism's rigid insistence on a distinct cleavage between Israel and the church, and its belief in a later unconditional fulfilment of the Abrahamic covenant, that sets it off from the historic faith of the church.[60]

The church is a radically new institution, but the dispensation of the church age is likewise interpreted as a historic parenthesis until the messianic kingdom is established. As to Darby's basic understanding of the church as encountered in the first chapter of the book of Acts, he defines it as 'those connected with Christ in the flesh, who had seen Him in the resurrection, and derived their authority from Him in earthly association, though endued with power from on high'.[61]

From the very beginning, the church's other-worldliness is stressed in the thought of Darby, for the primitive church's lifeblood was its messianic expectation. The church's primary hope in the beginning was to see the repentance of the Jewish community so that 'He might return' and that the 'kingdom might be restored to Israel'.[62] According to Darby, following the Jewish 'rejection of the apostolic word and power', the church ceased its witness to the Jew and turned its attention to the Gentile. There was now no national hope as to the establishment of the earthly millennium. Salvation was now interpreted primarily as an individual experience, for, according to Darby, 'Individuals might be converted and doubtless were; but the order of Jewish ministry ceased'. In Darby's thought any hope for the establishment of the messianic kingdom was completely shattered after the stoning of Stephen in Acts 7. Until that time, Christ was said to have been, 'Christ risen, still a Jewish hope, the securer of the sure mercies of David', who was rejected by the Jews 'in spite of the testimony of the Holy Ghost sent down from heaven'.[63]

Certainly there exists a degree of tension on the level of salvation history and in terms of the practical implications of the nature of the church as seen by Darby. His conclusion that the calling of the church into existence was logically a second-best option seems impossible to escape. Given the negativism found at the beginning of the church age, as the church was brought about by Israel's rejection of the Messiah, it should not be surprising to see Darby being so negative in his concept of the church in ruin. However, Darby seemed to be aware of the reasonableness of conclusion that the church was a second, and less than perfect, option that God brought into existence:

> Looked at as an earthly dispensation, it [the church] merely fills up, in detail exercise of grace, the gap in the regular earthly order of God's counsel, made by the rejection of the Jews on the covenant of legal prescribed righteousness, in the refusal of the Messiah, till their reception again under the new covenant in the way of grace on their repentance: but, though making a most instructive parenthesis, it forms no part of the regular order of God's earthly plans, but is merely an interruption of them to give a fuller character and meaning to them.[64]

Yet, in spite of being a 'parenthesis' and 'interruption' that merely fills a gap, Darby would somehow argue that the church was not just a second-best solution for God. The church was thought to represent the maximum development of the people of God until the beginning of the end of this age. Darby defined the nature of the church in two ways: 'it is the formation of the children of God into one body united to Christ Jesus ascended to heaven, the glorified man', and 'it is the house or habitation of God by the Spirit'.[65] Characteristic of Darby, the importance of the church was not seen in relation to its calling or function on earth but rather to its relationship with the Trinity.

Darby attempted to deal with the inherent tension of his position by playing down the church's earthly purpose and radically emphasizing its heavenly existence. The future of the church lay in heaven while for Israel, the restored nation, its glorious future was to be found in the millennial kingdom. Darby 'accomplished' this by explaining his unique view of the new covenant as presented in the New Testament. Christ's new covenant was offered only to Israel and not to the church. It was the basis of the promise of the establishment of the restoration of Israel as a nation in the millennial kingdom. All Old Testament promises made to Israel regarding a complete national restoration in the messianic kingdom would be literally fulfilled. On the other hand, all promises made in the New Testament regarding the church were interpreted as being fulfilled in heaven and would not be related to the period of the one thousand-year rule of Christ. The following two separate quotes by Darby show how he interpreted the new covenant as strictly pertaining to the Jews:

This covenant of the letter is made with Israel, not with us; but we get the benefit of it . . . Israel not accepting the blessing, God brought out the church, and the Mediator of the covenant went on high. We are associated with the Mediator, it will be made good to Israel by-and-by.[66]

The Gospel is not a covenant but the revelation of the salvation of God. It proclaims the great salvation. We enjoy indeed all the essential privileges of the new covenant, its foundation being laid on God's part in the blood of Christ, but we do so in spirit, not according to the letter . . . The new covenant will be established formally with Israel in the millennium.[67]

One other doctrine taught by Darby must be explained in order to demonstrate the extent to which he believed the church was unrelated to the present world order. The ascension of Christ into the heavens signals for Darby not only the first step toward the formation of the church, but also the beginning of the kingdom of heaven. This kingdom is explained as a parallel dispensation taking place in heaven as the church exists on earth. Darby explained the relation of the two simultaneous dispensations in this way:

> The kingdom of heaven we have as a state of things during the period when the Son is sitting on the Father's throne. During this period the children are in the Son's, but heirs of the Father's kingdom – a period during which the world is not ordered according to the righteous judicial power of the Son of man's kingdom – the interval between the rejection of the Son of man upon earth and His reigning upon earth, in which the saints are sustained by the Spirit, in the midst of the world, but the Spirit sent of the Son by the Father, the witness of His exaltation there.[68]

The words of Darby when he speaks of being 'sustained by the Spirit, in the midst of the world' do not offer any proximate hope to true believers in terms of the future of the church. In the midst of rampant apostasy, one could only hope to be 'sustained'. Darby would readily affirm that the church is a glorious creation and had its moments of splendour in the opening chapters of the book of Acts as the Body of Christ, yet it was also doomed to failure, as Israel had been in the previous dispensation.

Darby personally understood that the church at large stood at the end of the Dispensation of the Spirit, as God continued in the outworking of his total programme. As in every single one of the previous dispensations, the church had failed miserably in carrying out its divine mandate. The church lay in ruin and was without hope.

> But the point which is proved in this is not merely that it is in a bad state now, but that like all others it broke down in the commencement – no sooner fully established than it proved a failure . . . Thus, whatever grace and power from Him that was glorified might effect, this dispensation as well as any other *failed and broke off in the very* outset; and in point of fact the gospel has never been preached in all

the world, nor all nations discipled to this day, but the church which was gathered has departed from the faith of the gospel, and gone away backward, so as to be as bad or worse than the heathen.[69]

Given this tremendous, all-encompassing pessimism, the only activity open to the true church in the present dispensation, which was to continue until the time of actual judgement, was to participate with God who had been actively calling out the true spiritual Christian church from among the Jews and the Gentiles to form the heavenly people of Christ. Darby's call was to retreat, for the battle had been lost. To escape the generalized apostasy, one had to join in the 'informal gathering of Christians in Brethren fashion', which was the only way deemed to be 'compatible with the heavenly nature of the church'.[70] In this way Darby was able positively to spiritualize his theology of passivity and non-involvement in the world. Notice how the following words of Darby are utterly void of any optimism and emphasize the heavenly existence of the church while completely minimizing any understanding of it as God's people who possess a sense of high calling or divine mandate:

Such was the Church [of the New Testament]: how is it now and where does it exist? It will be perfect in heaven. Granted: but where is it found now on earth? The members of Christ's body are now dispersed; many hidden in the world, others in the midst of religious corruption; some in one sect, some in another, in rivalry one with another to gain over the saved . . . The Church – once beautiful, united, heavenly – has lost its character, is hidden in the world; and the Christians themselves – worldly, covetous, eager for riches, honour, power – like the children of the age. It is an epistle in which one cannot read a single word of Christ. The greatest part of what bears the name of Christian is the seat of the enemy or infidel; and the true Christians are lost in the midst of the multitude . . . We ought to be profoundly grieved at such a state of the Church in the world, because it no way answers to the heart and love of Christ.[71]

While the visible church was largely apostate, Rowdon is correct in noting that 'Darby's method of interpretation doomed any attempt to give the Christian Church earthly status or power'.[72] Darby's position on the church condemned his followers to retreat into a kind of monastic or ghetto mentality. There was no chance for singing 'Onward Christian Soldiers' within the thought of Darby. The following lyrics penned by Brethren composer Emma Frances Bevan (1827–1909) reflect this idea that the only Christian option is to passively abide until rescued by the coming deliverer:

> Midst the darkness, storm and sorrow,
> One bright gleam I see;
> Well I know the blessed morrow
> Christ will come for me.
> Midst the light and peace and glory
> Of the Father's home,
> Christ for me is watching, waiting -
> Waiting till I come.[73]

Instead of hoping for and working towards the manifestation of God's justice, righteousness and kingdom principles on earth, here and now, for the betterment of the church and society, the only logically possible option was to retreat and wait to be called out as a faithful remnant. The overriding feeling is one of utter helplessness given the condition of the visible church and the past failure of all previous dispensations. The following words of Darby demonstrate the sharp dichotomy between the true heavenly church and the current world order:

> But the Church is not of this world, even as Christ is not of this world. And how is Christ not of this world? Surely in spirit and in character He is not of it, as it is an evil world, unholy, opposite to God . . . It was the secret of God hidden from ages and generations, and formed an extraordinary break in the dispensations, to the rejection, for their unbelief, of the proper earthly people of God; a forming out of the earth, but not for it, a body for Christ – a heavenly people associated with Him in the glory in which He should reign when the full time was come, over the earth, in those times of restitution which should come from the presence of the Lord; a system forming no part of the earthly system, though carried on through the death of Christ in the forming of its members in it, but that, when all things are gathered together in one in Christ, in the dispensation of the fullness of time, these should be associates of His glory, in whom it and the riches of His grace should be shewn, given them in Christ Jesus before the world began, according to the gift of the Father . . . The Church has sought to settle itself here; but it has no place on the earth. It may shew forth heavenly glory here according to that given to it; but it has

no place here, but in glory with Christ in heavenly places at His appearing. We, through the Spirit, wait for the hope of righteousness by faith . . . The moment there is a minding of earthly things, there is enmity to the cross of Christ; for 'our conversation is in heaven; from whence also we look for the Saviour, the Lord Jesus Christ: who shall change our vile body that it may be fashioned like unto his glorious body . . .'[74]

Darby's position was firm: 'there cannot be a more solemn consideration for God's children – the failure from the outset, through man's folly and evil, of the economy of the Church in the world'.[75]

Darby's understanding of the church's role in the present age is crucial and based largely on his interpretation of the parable of the weeds or tares (Matthew 13:24–9). Darby used this parable to show that the 'New Testament constantly presents to us evil as going on increasing until the end, and that Satan will urge it on until the Lord destroys his power.'[76] In the following quotation it is important to note that Darby's interpretation of this parable provides him with the biblical-theological justification for radically underscoring the helplessness of the church in terms of any positive future evolution:

Christ sowed the good seed of the kingdom in the world; and the devil, with craft, sowed tares there amongst it, while men slept, 'perverse men . . . ordained to this condemnation.' The power of extermination was not given . . . to the Church, the servants of the householder: they must 'both grow together until the harvest.' It was no service to Christ, then, to kill a heretic: the rude hand of a servant might destroy a saint, in attempting the purity of the crop, by that which was reserved for other hands. The ripening of both was the present process, ripened together in the world. The Church would never become a system to purify or set right the world. The providential power of God in the ministration of the Son by his angels, would clear out of His kingdom in bundles, into the field, in the worked, the tares to be burned; and thereupon the righteous would shine forth as the sun, not in the kingdom of the Son, not in the kingdom of the Son of man, but in the kingdom of the Father. In a word, we have the clearing of the world, the field, by providential interposition, by a judicial process in the hands of the Son of man, sending His angels. The righteous of the kingdom, i.e., those who had been righteous while the world was evil, shall be as the sun. We know who 'the Sun [*sic*] of Righteousness' is, and 'when he shall appear we shall be like him, for we shall see as he is'; but it is in the kingdom of the Son of man we know not hence, only that he gathered all that offend out of it, and that the earthly 'kingdom of our Lord and his Christ was come' . . . and the kingdom of the Son of man now purged judicially, the earthly kingdom being now brought in . . .[77]

According to Darby, Christians should not 'judge' the world (that is, actively engage in its affairs), nor should they concern themselves with 'taking away evil' because evil will 'remain until the day of judgement'. Tares have always existed and will continue to be among and within the visible church until this dispensation is 'closed by the coming of Christ'. Tares may be defined as 'heresy' or 'corruption of the truth in whatever way, or to whatever extent'. The one common denominator is that all tares are satanic in origin.[78]

Given the decadent and fragmented state of Christianity, the only hope for the church was Jesus Christ's imminent and temporary quick return to the earth in order to rapture his true church, which was scattered around the world as the faithful remnant within the visible church. With the church finally in its true heavenly home, Christ could proceed to establish his earthly kingdom as he moved apocalyptically towards the restoration of Israel.[79] Darby's eschatological scheme can be summarized as taking place in two very distinct stages. The first coming is for his church and the second is to the Jews. First, as to his work as the coming deliverer of the true church, Darby taught that Christ will appear to the earth, yet only on the atmospheric level of the clouds. He was thought to be coming for his church rather than to the earth. This rapture was believed to be imminent, as is still the case with most dispensational theorists. Dispensational use of the term 'imminent rapture' simply means that there are no future conditions which must be met nor are there any apocalyptic signs that must take place prior to the moment of the rapture of the church. As a literal interpretation of 1 Thessalonians 4:13–18 reads, the Brethren held that those who were the believing Christian dead would meet him first in the clouds, and secondly, those who were alive would also be caught up in the air, or raptured, to be forever with Christ from that moment onward. At this instant both groups would find that their bodies had been transformed into a heavenly, glorified body which is thought to be immortal and like that of Christ's following his resurrection. Darby wrote:

> Those who believe in the rapture of the Church before the appearing of Christ hold that the Church has a special and peculiar character and connection with Christ . . . The Church's joining Christ has nothing to do with Christ's appearing or coming to earth. Her place is elsewhere. She sits in Him already in heavenly places. She has to be brought there as to bodily presence . . . The thing she has to expect for herself is not . . . Christ's appearing, but her being taken up where He is . . . It is this conviction, that the Church is properly heavenly, in its calling and relationship with Christ, forming no part of the course of events of the earth, which makes the rapture so simple and clear: and on the other hand, it shows how the denial of the rapture brings down the Church to an earthly position, and destroys its whole spiritual character and position.[80]

Those who are raptured and with Christ in heaven will be judged as to their faithfulness in God's service while on earth. Yet, this judgement does not determine the issue of eternal salvation. The fact of any person being raptured was already proof of his or her election as a true child of God. This judgement will determine one's degree of heavenly rewards.

Parallel to the heavenly joy as the church finally arrives at its proper, long awaited, eternal home, judgement associated with the seven years of tribulation is now ready to take place upon the earth as the rapture of the church also signals the beginning of the tribulation. As the apostasy of Christendom is totally complete, the Antichrist is free to work his diabolical will. In effect, he becomes an instrument of divine judgement as he extends his evil kingdom throughout the world now composed only of unbelievers. Darby explained that the Antichrist will be the maximum historical expression of evil as he brings together 'in his person the characters of wickedness which have appeared from the beginning'.[81] The beginning of the seven years of tribulation is also the beginning of the Day of the Lord spoken of by both the prophets of the Old and New Testaments. This day begins with the tribulation but also includes the period of the Messiah's rule when God will once again turn his attention to Israel and literally complete all the Old Testament prophecies regarding the Jewish nation, the city of Jerusalem, and the land itself. This soon-to-be established kingdom has nothing to do with the church! As Darby explained,

> Prophecy applies itself properly to the earth; its object is not heaven. It was about things that were to happen on the earth; and the not seeing this has misled the Church. We have thought that we ourselves had within us the accomplishment of these earthly blessings, whereas we are called to enjoy heavenly blessings. The privilege of the Church is to have its portion in the heavenly places; and later blessings will be shed forth upon the earthly people. The Church is something altogether apart – a kind of heavenly economy . . .[82]

Darby believed and taught that the church, once taken to heaven in the rapture, would not participate directly in the millennial kingdom by ruling with Christ. It would enjoy a simultaneous heavenly existence as the heavenly Jerusalem while the earthly Jerusalem was the centre of the Messiah's earthly reign. Darby's thought along these lines is unique:

> The glorified Church – witness for all, even by its state, of the extent of the love of the Father, who has fulfilled all His promises, and has been better to our weak hearts than even their hopes – will fill the heavenly places with its own joy; and in its service will constitute the happiness of the world, towards which it will be the instrument of the grace which it shall be richly enjoying. Behold the heavenly Jerusalem, witness in glory of the grace which has placed her so high! In the midst of her shall flow the river of water of life, where grows the tree of life, whose leaves are for the healing of the Gentiles: for even in the glory shall be preserved to her this sweet character of grace. Meanwhile, upon the earth, is the earthly Jerusalem, the centre of the government, and of the reign of the righteousness of Jehovah her God . . . she will be the place of His throne . . . For in that state of terrestrial glory . . . she may be witness of the character of Jehovah, as the Church is that of the Father.[83]

The seven years of tribulation climax with Christ's second coming to the earth. The first step towards the establishment of his kingdom is punishing his enemies as he appears in glory to defeat the enemy nations in the battle of Armageddon. As noted by Darby, 'He had a vesture dipped in blood. He came as the avenger. He tramples now the wine-press of God's wrath. It is not in the lowliness of humiliation . . . He comes to tread down in power.'[84] Following this victory his literal earthly kingdom is established and his glory becomes manifest in all the earth. The kingdom is, then, a restoration of the Jewish kingdom which was offered to Israel by Christ but which was rejected in his first advent. The peace and prosperity promised by so many Old Testament prophets becomes a reality. The Antichrist, now defeated by the heavenly army, is punished and the one whom he had served, Satan, would be bound throughout the thousand-year period. Thus, in the words of Darby, 'the source, and all the forms of evil, of corruption and violence, idolatry and apostasy, were swept away'.[85] Those nations which hopelessly participated in the revolt led by the Antichrist in his foolish attempt to oppose the restoration of the kingdom of the Messiah would be judged as Jesus Christ, the Messiah, had delivered Israel. He who was, seven years earlier, the present deliverer of the church, is now the present deliverer of Israel, and both the Abrahamic and Davidic covenants become literally fulfilled. Christ reigns on earth along with 'two classes . . . who might have seemed otherwise not to have had their place there – the witnesses slain for the testimony, and those who would neither worship the beast nor own him'.[86]

At the close of the one thousand years, Satan would be released once more to deceive those living during the millennium. Then, following the final triumph of Christ over Satan and the resurrection of the unbelieving dead, Satan and the unbelieving are condemned to eternal punishment. On the positive side, this complete and final judgement of evil initiates the transformation of the millennial kingdom into the eternal state of heaven. Once this new order is established, all of God's eternal purposes for human beings and the rest of creation will be brought about as the redeemed people, both Jew and Gentile, both those of the messianic kingdom and those of the church, will enjoy spiritual, moral and intellectual perfection as they dwell with God forever. Given what has been said about Darby's eschatology, surely the millennium can be understood in three ways as noted by Ernest Trenchard:

1. As the completion of many promises made to Israel that Jerusalem would become the centre of all earth as it radiated

forth a universal reign of peace, prosperity and blessing on all people.

2. As the last test of the human race, given that, having lived under the optimum governmental conditions and prosperity during one thousand years, with all this, when Satan is let loose to tempt them again, a great part of mankind will once again fall.

3. As a picture anticipating the New Creation in the eternal state as the prophetic vision passes on to the New Earth and the New Heavens, that must replace the old creation which is so very stained by sin both prior to the Millennial kingdom and then again at the close of the same.[87]

As the Brethren approached the end of the nineteenth century, the sense of expectation and urgency regarding the moment when Christ would separate the 'wheat from the tares' increased dramatically. The observation, of course, holds true for most groups holding a premillennial theology. One popular Brethren periodical expressed the idea in 1890 in the following way:

> *A Happy New Year!* Such is the language on all hands. How frequently has the wish been expressed. How comparatively seldom has it been fulfilled – Never thoroughly! nor [*sic*] ever can be until He whose right it is to reign, shall Himself take the sceptre . . . the coming of the Lord draweth nigh . . . It may be that bright anticipations are thrown to the ground, the ranks of valiant ones seemed thinned, and the stream of earth's tears is swollen to overflowing. Where shall we look for comfort – as one has said, that if we look around we are dismayed, if we look within we are discouraged, but if we look up we are made happy. Torrents of iniquity threaten the very foundation of society. Error, like a noisy rushing torrent, seeks to sweep everything before it. We would not under-estimate the difficulties, neither would we constantly be occupied with them, but rather in the face of all, cling tenaciously to the blessed promise 'I come quickly'– Even so, come, Lord Jesus![88]

At the close of the first thousand years David B. Barrett noted that 'millennial fever gripped Christendom . . . [and] vast numbers of medieval millenarian movements had arisen, involving millions of desperate rebel, radicals, and rootless poor seeking hope in a newer world'.[89] Certainly, as the calendar moves to the close of the second millennium, we can expect that millennial expectation will once again be heightened as it was with the close of the first. 'Prophets' among us already denounce above mentioned 'torrents of iniquity' which 'threaten the very foundation of society'. While Barrett acknowledges that many Christian groups are not interested in the attraction of the millennial year, he also speaks of those Christians who are 'attracted to the AD 2000 date'. In fact, the year attracts them 'like a huge electromagnet or stellar magnetic field' as they formulate 'large numbers of plans to evangelize the world by the end of the century'.[90] Dispensationalism such as that expounded by Darby provides an adequate theological framework for 'millennial fever', with its unparalleled emphasis on the establishment of a literal messianic millennial kingdom. Yet, in sharp contrast to the type of militant millenarianism held by the Branch Davidians in Waco, Texas, the views propagated by Darby lead only to passive resignation. His invitation is one to retreat within because of the simple fact that we are hopeless until the manifestation of the Messiah. Therefore, Darby's thought is very likely to continue to appeal to other Christian groups in Western society such as those who are tired of the relentless rate of change in the modern world. A return to the position of Darby is attractive to such people for it offers the chance to disengage and retreat from active involvement in the world. Darby's thought also provides the theological framework for those Christians who are overwhelmed and feel that it is useless to work towards the implementation of God's kingdom principles in the present historical moment, given the magnitude of global problems such as nuclear proliferation and global environmental crises. Whether due to 'millennial fever' or to one of the other just mentioned conditions, in this moment in history where fundamentalism is a present reality in the major religions of the world, one can easily see that Darby's thought, instead of being a relic of nineteenth-century Nonconformist thought, may well once again become relevant. As recent electronic editions of his works and presence on the Internet might suggest, he is speaking to a growing number of the tired, disillusioned and/or displaced among us whose only apparent option is to wait for the coming deliverer.

Notes

[1] The Henry Drummond referred to here, who was ordained in this

same church as the 'angel of Scotland' in 1834 and active in the sect until his death, should not be confused with the Scottish evangelical theologian and revivalist (1851–97) involved in the revival campaigns conducted in the British Isles by Dwight L. Moody and Ira D. Sankey.

2 'Rapture', from the Latin *rapto*, is often used in millennial thought with reference to the Greek verb ἁρπαζω (*harpazo*) found in 1 Thessalonians 4:17. This verb is most often translated 'caught up' (see RSV and AV).

3 Nathan DeLynn Smith, *Roots, Renewal and the Brethren* (Pasadena, CA, Hope Publishing House, 1986), 7.

4 One Brethren historian said of the movement: 'Brethren churches have played a unique part in modern missions. The concept of the "faith" mission was born within the movement. Brethren pioneered the idea of the local church as both the sending agency and also the goal of mission. Today, eighty eight hundredths of one per cent of members (estimated figure) are in missionary service, compared with sixty one hundredths of one per cent of Baptist and thirty six hundredths of one per cent of Pentecostals. And – contrary to what is sometimes suggested – interest in mission is increasing among English-speaking Brethren.' Harold H. Rowdon (ed.), 'Into all the world', in *Christian Brethren Review*, 40 (1989), cover of journal.

5 Ian Sellers, *Nineteenth-Century Nonconformity* (London, Edward Arnold, 1977), 3–6.

6 David Christie-Murray, *A History of Heresy* (Oxford, Oxford University Press, 1989), 201.

7 This desire to foster unity was not just characteristic of the Brethren in their infancy stage but was a widespread concern among evangelicals of Great Britain throughout most of the nineteenth century. As to examples one can point to the formation of interdenominational missionary societies such as the London Missionary Society in 1795, which was initially supported by Congregationalists, Anglicans, Presbyterians, and Wesleyans, and the British and Foreign Bible Society begun in 1804 by members of several denominations. Another attempt at unity was the Evangelical Alliance constituted in 1846.

8 At the start of this chapter, dispensationalism was defined as a hermeneutical system which divides biblical history into distinctive periods of time in which God's specific demands on people differ. The concept of 'dispensation' in the thought of Darby will be defined below. C. C. Ryrie, a modern dispensational theologian, defined the term in the following way: 'The world is seen as a household administered by God in connection with several stages of revelation that mark off the different economies in the outworking of his total program. These economies are the dispensation in dispensationalism.

Thus from God's viewpoint a dispensation is an economy; from man's it is a responsibility to the particular revelation given at the time. In relation to progressive revelation, a dispensation is a stage within it. Thus a dispensation may be defined as a distinguishable economy in the outworking of God's program'. 'Dispensation', in Walter A. Elwell (ed.), *Evangelical Dictionary of Theology* (Grand Rapids, MI, Baker Book House, 1984), 322. This definition is in agreement with the theology of Darby.

9 John Nelson Darby, *The Collected Writings of J. N. Darby*, ed. William Kelly, 32 vols. (London, G. Moorish, n.d.), i, 471, 'Prophetic'.

10 Quoted in 'Brethren Hymnology' by John S. Andrews, *Evangelical Quarterly*, 28 (1956), 217.

11 'Book Notice. What Mean Ye by this Service?', *The Eleventh Hour* (October 1886), 8.

12 F. F. Bruce in the foreword to Peter Cousins, *The Brethren* (Exeter, A. Wheaton, 1982), v.

13 Anthony Norris Groves, quoted in Nathan DeLynn Smith, *Roots, Renewal and the Brethren*, 10.

14 See Harold Ellison, *Household Church* (Exeter, Paternoster Press, 1963),13.

15 There is, however, some evidence to suggest that at least early on in the ministry of Darby he predicted that Christ would come for his church in the year 1842. (See F. Roy Coad, *A History of the Brethren Movement* (Grand Rapids, MI, Eerdmans Publishing Co, 1968), 118.)

16 Sydney E. Ahlstrom, *A Religious History of the American People*, 2 vols. (Garden City, NY, Image Books, 1975), i. 580.

17 Darby, *Collected Writings*, ed. Kelly, *Ecclesiastical*, i. 141.

18 Cousins, *The Brethren*, 23.

19 'Catalog 1996' (Addison, IL, Bible Truth Publishers, 1996).

20 *The Collected Works of J. N. Darby* (Kent, STEM Publishing, 1995). This edition was helpful in the preparation of this chapter.

21 See http://ccel.wheaton.edu/darby/synopsis and http://www.c.s.pitt.edu/~planting/book:/darby.

22 'The Relevance of Darby's Writings', 19 November 1995.

23 Harold H. Rowdon, *The Origin of the Brethren 1825–1850* (London, Pickering & Inglis Ltd., 1967), 1, 43.

24 W. G. Turner, *John Nelson Darby* (London, C. A. Hammond, 1944), 18, quoted in C. C. Ryrie, *Dispensationalism Today* (Chicago, Moody Press, 1965), 156.

25 Darby, *Collected Writings*, ed. Kelly, i. 128, 'Prophetic', 'Three Considerations'.

26 Rowdon, *Origin of the Brethren*, 77.

27 Ibid., 1.

28 Cousins, *Brethren*, 22.

29 Harold Rowdon, quoted in *Eerdman's Handbook to the History of Christianity*, ed. Tim Dowley (Berkhamsted, Herts, Lion Publishing, 1977), 520.

30 Coad, *History of the Brethren Movement*, 164.

31 Cousins, *Brethren*, 26.

32 *Contestaciones*, Madrid, 3. (This paper reflects a group effort on the part of British Brethren missionaries and Spanish Brethren to respond to a series of questions by Spanish Catholics about the Brethren's history and beliefs. It appears to have been written in the late 1960s. The translation is by the author of this chapter.)

33 Cousins, *Brethren*, 26.

34 A Younger Brother (pseud.), *The Principles of Christians called 'Open Brethren'* (Glasgow, Pickering & Inglis, 1913), 94. The real name of the author is unknown.

35 Probably the best analysis of the direct influence of Darby over the thought of North American fundamentalists and evangelicals is the work of Clarence B. Bass, *Backgrounds to Dispensationalism: Its Historical Genesis and Ecclesiastical Implication* (Grand Rapids, MI, Eerdmans Publishing Co., 1960), pp. 13–21 are especially helpful.

36 Ibid., 204, 213–14 and W. A. Hoffecker, 'Darby, John Nelson' in Elwell (ed.), *Evangelical Dictionary of Theology*, 292–3.

37 Stephen H. Travis, *Christian Hope and the Future* (Downers Grove, IL, InterVarsity Press, 1980), 64.

38 George Marsden, *Fundamentalism and American Culture* (Oxford, Oxford University Press, 1982), 70.

39 Robert G. Walton, *Chronological and Background Charts of Church History* (Grand Rapids, MI, Zondervan Publishing House, 1986), 64. As to Gaebelein and his high esteem for Darby, he once wrote of him in the context of the Lord's coming in this way: 'What a meeting it will be! All the saints will be there . . . No one will claim a denominational name or boast in a Cephas, a Paul, an Apollos, a Luther or in the four Johns: John Calvin, John Knox, John Wesley or John Darby'. A. C. Gaebelein, *Half a Century* (New York, Publications Office of Our Hope, 1939), 85, quoted in Bass's *Backgrounds to Dispensationalism*, 18.

40 Winthrop S. Hudson, *Religion in America* (New York, Charles Scribner's Son, 3rd edn., 1982), 284

41 Marsden, *Fundamentalism*, 46.

42 Hudson, *Religion in America*, 284.

43 Ibid., 284–5.

44 The 'Post Conference Audio Cassette Tape Order Form' of the Evangelical Theological Society 47th Annual Meeting, 16–18

November 1995 in Philadelphia, PA, mentions five specific papers presented on dispensationalism and the existence of the 'Dispensational Study Group' at the meeting.

45 Ibid., 54.

46 F. F. Bruce, in Rowdon (ed.), *Origin of the Brethren*, xi–xii.

47 As to examples of those contemporary with Darby using the word 'dispensation' in their eschatology, see Henry Gipps's *A Treatise on the First Resurrection and the Thousand Years* (London, J. Nisbet, Berners Street, 1831). The Reverend Gipps, Vicar of Saint Peter's, Hereford, used the term in his explanation of his postmillennial interpretation of the New Testament book of Revelation. His system is composed of two dispensations roughly equivalent to the Old Testament and the New Testament. Also see Patrick Fairbairn, *The Revelation of Law in Scripture* (Edinburgh, T. & T. Clark, 1869). Darby wrote a critique of the thought of Fairbairn which was included in his collected works.

48 *Dispensationalism Today*, 65–70.

49 Hubert Cunliffe-Jones (ed.), *A History of Christian Doctrine* (Philadelphia, PA, Fortress Press, 1984), 39, 50, 62.

50 Ibid., 62. (The leader of this charismatic group, Montanus, prophesied in the second century that a heavenly Jerusalem would soon descend near Pepuza in Phrygia. See 'Montanism' in the *Oxford Dictionary of the Christian Church*, 934.)

51 *Dispensationalism Today*, 65–70.

52 Charles C. Ryrie, 'Dispensation, Dispensationalism' in Elwell (ed.), *Evangelical Dictionary of Theology*, 321–3.

53 *Fundamentalism*, 46.

54 Millard J. Erickson, *Christian Theology* (Grand Rapids, MI, Baker Book House, 1988), 1162.

55 This summary of Darby's system is found in Ryrie's *Dispensationalism Today*, 75, 84.

56 Darby, *Collected Writings*, ed. Kelly, i. 192–3, quoted in Ryrie, *Dispensationalism Today*, 76.

57 Darby, *Collected Writings*, ed. Kelly, 'Ecclesiastical' i. 149–50.

58 John W. Bowman, 'Bible and Modern Religion: II Dispensationalism', *Interpretation*, 10 (1956), 174.

59 Darby, *Collected Writings*, ed. Kelly, 'Ecclesiastical', iii. 131.

60 Bass, *Backgrounds to Dispensationalism*, 27.

61 Darby, *Collected Writings*, ed. Kelly, 'Ecclesiastical', i. 146.

62 Ibid.

63 Ibid., 147–50.

64 Ibid., 144.

65 Ibid., iii. 115.

66 Ibid., xxvii. 565–6, cited in J. Dwight Pentecost, *Things to Come*

(Grand Rapids, MI, Zondervan Publishing House, 1982), 121. This work by Pentecost has been the standard reference work for dispensational eschatology during the last generation. Its impact has been felt worldwide. For example, in a recent friendly conversation regarding the nature of the Christian hope with a Spanish Brethren elder, the closest position to that of pastor within the 'denomination', the gentleman kindly reminded me that, 'The issue in question had been settled long ago by Dr. Pentecost!' Apparently, it could be argued that for post-Second World War dispensationalists, *Things to Come* represents dogma.

[67] Darby, *Synopsis of the Books of the Bible*, v. 286, cited in *Things to Come*, 122.

[68] Darby, *Collected Writings*, ed. Kelly, 'Prophetic', i. 95–6.

[69] J. N. Darby, *The Darby Disk: The Apostasy of the Successive Dispensation* (Ramsgate, STEM Publishing, 1995), 128. Emphasis added.

[70] Rowdon, *Origins*, 208.

[71] Darby, *Collected Writings*, ed. Kelly, 'Ecclesiastical', iii. 128–30.

[72] Rowdon, *Origins*, 208.

[73] Quoted in John S. Andrews, 'Brethren Hymnology', *Evangelical Quarterly*, 28 (1956), 226.

[74] Darby, *Collected Writings*, ed. Kelly, 'Ecclesiastical', i. 142–4.

[75] Ibid., 187.

[76] Ibid., 'Prophetic', i. 471.

[77] Ibid., 92–4.

[78] Ibid., 472.

[79] A good nineteenth-century summary of Brethren dispensational eschatology is that of John Ritchie found in 'The Return of the Lord', *The Eleventh Hour* (March 1888), 47–8. Ritchie was well-known for having published several religious tracts.

[80] J. N. Darby, 'The Rapture of the Saints', 180, 233, 237. Quoted in Bass's *Backgrounds to Dispensationalism*, 39.

[81] Darby, *Collected Writings*, ed. Kelly, 'Prophetic', i. 477.

[82] Ibid., 572.

[83] Ibid.,580–1.

[84] Ibid., 'Expository', II, 594.

[85] Ibid., 597.

[86] Ibid.

[87] Ernest Trenchard, *Bosquejos de Doctrina Fundamental* (Madrid, Literature Biblica, 1972), 133–4.

[88] '1890', *The Eleventh Hour* (January 1890), 1.

[89] David B. Barrett, 'Annual Statistical Table on Global Missions: 1990', *International Bulletin of Missionary Research*, 14 (1990), 26.

[90] Ibid.

Further reading

Ahlstrom, Sydney E., *A Religious History of the American People*, 2 vols. (Garden City, NY, Image Books, 1975).

Andrews, John S., 'Brethren Hymnology', *Evangelical Quarterly*, 28 (1956), 208–29.

Barrett, David B., 'Annual Statistical Table on Global Missions: 1990', *International Bulletin of Missionary Research*, 14 (1990), 26–30.

Bass, Clarence B., *Backgrounds to Dispensationalism: Its Historical Genesis and Ecclesiastical Implication* (Grand Rapids, MI, Eerdmans Publishing Co., 1960).

Bowman, John W., 'Bible and Modern Religion: II Dispensationalism', *Interpretation,* 10 (1956), 170–87.

Christie-Murray, David, *A History of Heresy* (Oxford, Oxford University Press, 1989).

Coad, F. Roy, *A History of the Brethren Movement* (Grand Rapids, MI, Eerdmans Publishing Co., 1968).

Cousins, Peter, *The Brethren* (Exeter, A. Wheaton & Co. Ltd., 1982).

Cunliffe-Jones, Hubert (ed.), *A History of Christian Doctrine* (Philadelphia, PA, Fortress Press, 1984).

Darby, John Nelson, *Collected Works of J. N. Darby*, CD-ROM edn. (Ramsgate, STEM Publishing, 1995).

——, *Collected Writings of J. N. Darby*, 32 vols, ed. William Kelly (London, G. Moorish, n.d).

Ellison, Harold, *Household Church* (Exeter, Paternoster Press, 1963).

Elwell, Walter A. (ed.), *Evangelical Dictionary of Theology* (Grand Rapids, MI, Baker, Book House, 1984).

Fairbairn, Patrick, *The Revelation of Law in Scripture* (Edinburgh, T. & T. Clark, 1869).

Gipps, Henry, *A Treatise on the First Resurrection and the Thousand Years* (London, J. Nisbet, Berners Street, 1831).

Hudson, Winthrop S., *Religion in America* (New York, Charles Scribner's Son, 3rd edn., 1982).

Marsden, George, *Fundamentalism and American Culture* (Oxford, Oxford University Press, 1982).

Pentecost, Dwight, *Things to Come* (Grand Rapids, MI, Zondervan Publishing House, 1982).

Rowdon, Harold H., *The Origin of the Brethren, 1825–1850* (London, Pickering & Inglis Ltd., 1967).

——, 'The Brethren', in Tim Dowley (ed.), *Eerdman's Handbook to the History of Christianity* (Berkhamsted, Herts., Lion Publishing, 1977), 519–20.

Ryrie, Charles C., *Dispensationalism Today* (Chicago, Moody Press, 1965).

Sellers Ian, *Nineteenth-Century Nonconformity* (London, Edward Arnold, 1977).

Smith, Nathan DeLynn, *Roots, Renewal and the Brethren* (Pasadena, CA, Hope Publishing House, 1986).

Travis, Stephen H., *Christian Hope and the Future* (Downers Grove, IL, InterVarsity Press, 1980).

Trenchard, Ernest, *Bosquejos de Doctrina Fundamental* (Madrid, Literature Biblica, 1972).

Turner, W. G., *John Nelson Darby* (London, C. A. Hammond, 1944).

Walton, Robert G., *Chronological and Background Charts of Church History* (Grand Rapids, MI, Zondervan Publishing House, 1986).

8

'Take one, it's FREE!': the story behind the Worldwide Church of God and The Plain Truth magazine

NEIL O'CONNOR

1 Introduction

George Bradford Caird once suggested that the book of Revelation has been subverted over the centuries to articulate the peculiar beliefs and practices of many sectarians:

> From the time of the Millenarian Papias to the present day it has been the paradise of fanatics and sectarians, each using it to justify his own peculiar doctrine and so adding to the misgivings of the orthodox. And in modern times scores of commentaries have been written on it so diverse as to make the reader wonder whether they are discussing the same book.[1]

There are other books in the Bible upon which the millenarian has based his apocalyptic conclusions, but the book of Revelation is by far the most significant in that its theme is a chronicle of the future course of history, through the ecstatic visions of John, a pastor of the apostolic church who was deported to the island of Patmos for being a Christian proselytizer. His message is to the seven churches of Asia, and his visions culminate with a picture of the end of time and the ushering in of the millennium – the thousand-year reign of Jesus Christ with his saints, and the establishment of the kingdom of God on earth.

The word *millennium* comes from the two Latin words, *mille*, a thousand, and *annum*, a year. It is used to refer to Revelation 20:5 – 'They came to life and reigned with Christ for a thousand years.' Much controversy surrounds the interpretation of the idea of millennialism, and since the early Christian period there has been a great difference of opinion concerning what exactly the millennium means, and whether the passages in Revelation and other scriptures about this coming kingdom can be taken literally. There are some who believe that Christ will reign on earth for one thousand years after his second coming, a view known as premillennialism or *chiliasm* (from the Greek word *chiliad*, a thousand). This holds that the second coming of Christ will be *before* his thousand-year reign. On the other hand there are those who deny a *literal* reign of Christ on the earth, and hold that the present age between the first and second comings is the fulfilment of the millennium, that is, we are currently living in the millennium. This view is known as amillennialism. There is much disagreement among the many proponents of this view regarding the prophetic passages and how they might be fulfilled, and regarding even the second coming itself – whether it will be an actual bodily manifestation, or whether it will be merely a 'spiritual presence' of Christ among the blessed. Still others argue that the scriptures point to a period of great spiritual revitalization of the world towards the end of the age as a result of the benefits of worldwide evangelism. This view holds that the whole world will be converted to a belief in Christ *before* his second coming, but *after* this millennial period of great blessing. This belief is thus referred to as postmillennialism, a view not commonly held today. The main argument regarding millenarian ideas, then, lies between those who believe in a literal interpretation of the prophetic passages of Revelation and other scriptures, and those who consider that these are symbolic, or at least, can be *spiritualized* so that they are not to be taken literally. Most, though not all, of the NRMs who espouse millenararian teachings opt for the premillennial view.

If one looks at the development of millenarian ideas over the centuries, one might be tempted to conclude that Caird's thesis, outlined above, may not be far from the mark. Not only have there been many who claimed special prophetic insight into the second coming and the millennium, but there have been messianic pretenders who claimed that they themselves in one way or another were personally involved in the establishing of the millennial kingdom and the salvation of mankind.[2] Despite the failure of the second coming in the years after the death of the original Apostles, millenarian ideas and millennial movements arose and disappeared on different occasions. In many cases these reflected the social, political, religious or economic upheavals of the times, when the affairs of men seemed bleak and hopeless, and the end seemed imminent. With the coming of religious pluralism in the post-Reformation centuries, a greater tolerance of differing beliefs, greater freedoms of expression, and progress in and widened interest in biblical studies, the eschatological debate has been enlarged to the extent that many respected scholars and 'orthodox' commentators (rather than alleged fringe fanatics) have become involved in attempting to tease out the millennial enigma. As the eighteenth century progressed changes in society and political structures fuelled this debate, and from that time a spate of pamphlets and sermons by Church of England clergy and orthodox American ministers widened the issue of millennialism for the ordinary person. Millennialism came to be widely espoused by leading scholars and divines, such as Timothy Dwight (President of Yale), John H. Livingstone (President of Rutgers) and Joseph Priestly, in America: in Britain George Stanley Faber, Edward King and Edward Irving.[3] By the late eighteenth century the 1,260 days mentioned in Revelation 12:6 came to be interpreted as 1,260 years and there was general agreement that this period had now ended.[4] An alternative theory which became increasingly popular after 1800 emphasized the importance of the 2,300-year period of Daniel 8:14 and the 'cleansing of the sanctuary' which was calculated to fall due some time in the 1840s. The fulfilment of the time prophecies meant that humankind was living in the last days, that the 'midnight cry' might soon be heard, and that the coming of the Messiah might be expected shortly. Such beliefs had an influence far beyond the members of the explicitly adventist sects. They were part and parcel of everyday evangelical religion.[5] Professor Harrison (after Edward Lee Tuveson) distinguishes between what he terms 'the intellectually sophisticated millennialists', and the 'popular, largely self-educated adventist millenarians', and submits that these latter are the people condemned by the opulent classes as fanatics and imposters, and by the historians as cranks and the lunatic fringe.[6] Many of the NRMs emerging out of the eighteenth and nineteenth centuries were begun by individuals from this group who emphasized the importance of personal divine revelation in its founders but who did not set a very high regard on reason or intellectualism among its followers. 'Mother'

Ann Lee, for example, strongly discouraged formal education among her 'Shaker' followers, emphasizing instead the efficacy of manual labour and self-reliance. Joseph Smith, the founder of the Mormons, was derided by his critics for his ignorance and illiteracy, and anti-intellectualism in Mormonism has been commented on in the literature (though this charge is not true of later Mormonism). Similarly, the Millennial Dawnists, followers of Charles Taze Russell (later to be called Jehovah's Witnesses) were discouraged from entering university or similar institutions and instead were advised to concentrate on door-to-door proselytizing since Armageddon was considered to be just around the corner. Indeed the entire development of the Second Advent movement of the period is firmly rooted in a fragmentation of the original theories of William Miller, a Baptist layman who was converted to Christianity in 1816,[7] and whose self-study of the scriptures convinced him that the second coming was imminent: 'I was thus brought, in 1818, at the close of my two years' study of the Scriptures, to the solemn conclusion, that in about twenty-five years from that time all the affairs of our present state would be wound up.'[8]

By 1831 Miller began to present his findings publicly. Basing his calculations on Daniel 8–9, he counted 2,300 years from the time Ezra was told he could return to Jerusalem to rebuild the temple. The date of this event was calculated to be 457 BCE. Thus Miller concluded that 1843 would be the date of Christ's return.[9] As the predicted year grew closer, Miller, in a letter dated 4 February to his close friend Joshua Himes, confirmed his belief of over twenty-three years that 'Jesus Christ will come again to this earth, to cleanse, purify, and take possession of the same, with all his saints, some time between March 21st 1843, and March 21st 1844'.[10] However, when these dates passed without any event taking place Miller wrote to his followers on 2 May 1844:

TO SECOND ADVENT BELIEVERS
Were I to live my life over again, with the same evidence that I then had, to be honest with God and man I should have to do as I have done . . . I *confess my error* and acknowledge *my disappointment*; yet I still believe that the day of the Lord is near, even at the door . . .[11]

Then in a letter dated 11 October 1844 Miller expressed the

opinion that Christ would return 'in the seventh month'[12] (of the Jewish year) and a revised date of 22 October 1844 was set. Failure of this event has come to be known as 'the Great Disappointment'. Miller again acknowledged his error but remained confident in the imminence of the second coming. He refused to become involved in further attempts to set dates, and gradually retired from active leadership in the movement as his health failed.

A general confusion arose among the adventists in the aftermath of the Great Disappointment. This continued for several years with one adventist group after another forming in an effort to save the message of millennial adventism. An attempt was made to explain why Christ had not returned, and a theory was put forward that he had begun to cleanse the heavenly 'sanctuary' as a prelude to returning to earth in judgment. Between 29 April and 1 May 1845 a conference of all Millerite followers was called in Albany, New York. This was an attempt to restore order to the confused Millerite movement. However, there seemed to be no effective bond among those who attended, and indeed, a number of key figures in the movement did not turn up at all. The result was a fragmentation and the inevitable spawning of a number of NRMs, each with its own brand of millenarian ideas.[13]

By 1858 the dominant body, who had become known as the 'evangelical Adventists', were distinguished by their adherence to the doctrines of consciousness in death and an eternally burning hell. They steadily declined in numbers and influence, especially after Joshua Himes deserted them. Shortly after this, other groups arose who disagreed with such doctrines, postulating instead the notions of conditional immortality and the annihilation of the wicked.[14] John T. Walsh, for example, taught that the wicked dead would never be raised again – that their first death was their last, and that the millennium was in the past. George Storrs, in his *Bible Examiner*, preached the notions of conditionalism and 'soul-sleep' – that immortality is not an inherent attribute of mankind, but is conditional on their having faith in Christ and keeping the law. This, of course, logically led to the denunciation of the doctrine of eternal punishment, since if one did not fulfil the conditions necessary for salvation, one simply ceased to exist. 'Soul-sleep' is the notion that the dead are in an unconscious state in the grave, and will not be conscious until the resurrection. Prominent also in this group was Jonathan Cummings, who believed that Miller was in error by ten years in his calculations and that Christ would return in 1854. He started *The World's Crisis* and went on to form the Advent Christian Church. This movement became the predominant body among the first-day adventists. After a time Storrs left this group and formed the Life and Advent Union.

A group led by Jonas Wendell, John H. Paton and Nelson H. Barbour which was not directly connected with the Millerites, but which nevertheless used Miller's dating system, began to suggest 1873 as the new date for the second coming, and subsequently 1874. When these dates failed to produce a personal, visible return of Christ, a theory based on a new Greek-English translation of the New Testament by Benjamin Wilson[15] was put forward. This translation rendered the Greek word often connected with Christ's prophesied return – parousia (Matthew 24:3) – as 'presence' instead of the usual word 'coming'. Barbour concluded from this that Christ's return might be invisible, rather than visible, as popularly believed. It was accepted by the group that Christ *had* in fact returned in 1874, but unobserved by human eyes. Shortly afterwards (1876) Charles Taze Russell, then a young haberdasher, came in contact with Barbour and accepted the latter's chronology and the 1874 date. Russell formed a Bible-study group in the city of Allegheny and for a time joined with Barbour's group. When they parted in 1879 over a doctrinal dispute, Russell called his group the International Bible Students (also known as the Millennial Dawn Bible Students) and began to publish *Zion's Watchtower and Herald of Christ's Presence*. This group came to be called Jehovah's Witnesses under Russell's successor, Judge Joseph Rutherford. Russell taught a 'ransom for all' doctrine, that Christ's death allows *all* persons who have ever lived an opportunity for everlasting life, whether during one's earthly life, or upon a resurrection from the dead. This 'second chance' would be offered during the millennium, which, according to Russell, would begin in 1914 after the Battle of Armageddon. He believed that the human family is destined to be returned to the perfect fleshly state that Adam and Eve once enjoyed, in an earthly paradise. Only the 144,000 (Revelation 7:4–9) would receive the ultimate reward of being 'priests and kings' in heaven (a belief currently held by the Jehovah's Witnesses). Russell acknowledged that Jesus was the Son of God, but not God. After his death in 1916 the movement split into a number of groups (see Appendix I).

A third group emerged from the Great Disappointment to form the Sabbath Adventist movement.[16] A number of adventists including Ellen G. White and her husband James, Hiram Edson, Joseph Bates and others began to meet in Washington, New Hampshire. Mrs White, in a trance, claimed she saw adventists going straight to heaven, and was soon accepted as a prophetess by many in the movement. In a vision she claimed she saw Jesus indicating on tablets of stone that the seventh day should be kept holy, which prompted the beginning of the Sabbath Adventist Movement. Edson claimed to have had a vision picturing Christ entering the heavenly Holy of Holies to cleanse the heavenly temple and to open a period of investigating those who claimed to be God's people. Edson proposed that Miller's 1844 date was correct, but that Christ came not to cleanse the earthly sanctuary, but the heavenly. Christ's cleansing work was supposed to cover the past sins of his followers, but they would have to keep God's laws during a period of probation here on earth. This doctrine came to be known as the 'investigative judgment' of Christ. After the probationary period was over, Christ would lay the sins of the people (adventists) on Azazel (Satan) and their sins would then be blotted out. The second coming would then take place. The adventists believed that they were the remnant Church of God, and that salvation was conditional on their keeping the law (including Old Testament food laws) and a belief in Jesus Christ. They held also that the Saturday Sabbath was the mark of the remnant of God and the only true church. In 1858 the Review and Herald Publishing Association was established at Battle Creek, Michigan, and a periodical, the *Review and Herald*, was begun. In 1860 the name Seventh Day Adventist Church was adopted.

As time went on a number of spin-off movements developed (see flow-chart in Appendix I). One of these was through Victor Houteff who founded the Davidian Seventh Day Adventist Church, with headquarters at the Mount Carmel compound, near Waco in Texas. Houteff considered himself to be a divinely inspired messenger of God with the task of gathering in the 144,000 of Revelation 14, after which they would move to Palestine to establish the Davidic kingdom under a theocratic rulership, and direct the closing work of the gospel before the second coming of Christ. When Houteff died in 1955 his wife Florence took over for a time, but was forced to disband the movement after the failure of her prediction that Christ would return and the Davidic kingdom be set up in Palestine in 1959. A new and separate movement called the Branch Davidians was then founded by Benjamin Roden, a west Texan businessman, one of Houteff's former followers. Roden had purchased land in Israel and was able to convince some of the Davidians that he was a prophet. The Branch Davidians not only kept the seventh-day Sabbath, but also the Jewish Old Testament feasts of Passover, Tabernacles, Atonement, and so on. When Roden died in 1978 his wife Lois took over the group. Then, in 1981 Vernon Howell, also known as David Koresh, joined the group. Obsessed with the book of Revelation and Old Testament end-time prophecies, he soon exercised a major influence on the group and took control of the movement after a gun battle with Roden's son, in 1987, taking over the property at Waco into which the Rodens had moved after the Davidian SDAs had disbanded. Koresh claimed to be the Lamb of Revelation, a prophet of God, and to hold the priesthood or office of Christ. Matters remained relatively quiet at the compound until early 1993 when the group came under FBI investigation for arms stockpiling and other alleged offences. After a long standoff, the compound was set ablaze on 19 April 1993 – allegedly by Koresh and his followers, though some claim that FBI bullets triggered the fire in the building which was packed with high explosives and barrels of kerosine. All but nine perished in the blaze, and many of the dead were children.

Another spin-off from the Sabbath Adventist movement was the Church of God (Seventh-day) with headquarters at Stanberry, Missouri.[17] Andrew N. Duggar, an elder in this group, led a division in 1933 and moved the headquarters to Salem, West Virginia. He taught the keeping of the Jewish festivals, Sabbatarianism, Anglo-Israelism and a rejection of the Trinity. Herbert W. Armstrong fellowshipped with both these groups between 1927 and 1937, and for a time was a salaried minister of the Church of God. However, due to doctrinal disputes and personality clashes Armstrong left the movement in the 1930s to form his own Radio Church of God, later to be incorporated in 1968 as the Worldwide Church of God.

2 A profile of the Worldwide Church of God

> *DIED*: Herbert W. Armstrong, 93, autocratic founder – leader of the 75,000-member Worldwide Church of God; in Pasadena Calif. Forsaking an advertising career in 1934 to become a radio preacher and self-proclaimed 'Chosen Apostle' of God, Armstrong taught that Christians should shun medical care (though he used it as his own health deteriorated) and that remarried members should divorce their second spouses and rejoin their first (a dictum he repealed in 1976 before marrying a divorcee). Loyal members, many of them poor, nevertheless tithed to his church as much as $75 million a year.[18]

This entry in the 'Milestones' section of *Time* magazine closed the final door on the career of a man who had used the mass media with consummate skill to promote his religious movement. Throughout much of his time as leader of the Worldwide Church of God his name was frequently in the world's press, not always as an object of adulation and reverence, but as a focus of controversy and discord. To his detractors almost as equally as to his supporters, Herbert W. Armstrong was indeed a most remarkable man. Born on 31 July 1892 in Des Moines, Iowa, he states in his *Autobiography* that his ancestors had emigrated from England to Pennsylvania with William Penn, and through his paternal great-grandfather claims to be related to Edward I, king of England,[19] and says that his ancestry had been traced back to King David of Israel through the British Royal Genealogy. Hence, he was born 'of the House of David'.[20] He relates that he dropped out of high school early in life, and entered the business world in the field of advertising. It was his natural flair in the art of creating interesting and eye-catching advertisements that contributed to his later success in the field of religion. He established a number of business ventures, but due to the vagaries of the market-place in the period before the Depression, his businesses failed three times. As a result he was on the edge of penury and destitution, being forced 'to buy beans and such food as would provide maximum bulk and nourishment on minimum cost'.[21] Coming from 'solid Quaker stock', he says at that time of his life he had no active interest in religion, and 'had drifted away from church about age 18'.[22] Due to his many reverses he felt that God had abandoned him. He had tried so hard but had failed. He ended up homeless, depending on his in-laws for basic sustenance.

It was around this time in his life that his wife's beliefs began to have a major impact on his life. In his *Autobiography* he describes his wife's great religious 'discovery': 'In the autumn of 1926 my wife said she had found, in the Bible, that Christianity was intended to be a WAY OF LIFE . . .'[23] and said that she had found 'she was keeping the wrong *day* as the Sabbath'.[24] (She had been a life-long Methodist.) This 'discovery' and other religious ideas were in fact revealed to his wife Loma by a next-door neighbour called Mrs Ora Runcorn, who was a member of the Church of God, Seventh Day. Armstrong did not take very kindly at first to his wife's new beliefs and practices. To him, then, it was 'religious fanaticism'. He wondered if she had really lost her mind, deciding to 'keep Saturday for Sunday'. He prevailed on her to give up this new way of life, but to no avail. He even threatened divorce.

> I felt I could not tolerate such humiliation. *What would my friends say?* What would former business aquaintances think? Nothing had ever hit me where it hurt so much . . . right smack in the heart of all my pride and vanity and conceit! And this mortifying blow had to fall immediately on top of confidence crushing financial reverses.[25]

His wife's reaction was that if he could 'prove by the Bible that Christians are commanded to observe Sunday',[26] then she would change her course. Besides this threat to his religious beliefs came a challenge from a sister-in-law on the theory of evolution. She said that he was 'simply ignorant'[27] because he did not accept or believe the theory.

And so it was in the autumn of 1926 – crushed in spirit from business reverses, and humiliated by what he regarded as wifely religious fanaticism, that Armstrong entered into an in-depth study of the Bible for the first time in his life. This 'dual challenge' drove him into a determined night-and-day research, which lasted for six months before he found the answers he was looking for. 'All those churches can't be wrong',[28] he thought, and he attempted to prove that his wife was wrong in her new beliefs. After much study, especially of Seventh Day Adventist literature, he came to the conclusion that his wife had found the truth after all. It was for him 'the most bitter pill (he) had ever swallowed'.[29] The year was 1927. Armstrong and his wife became more interested in the Stanberry Church of God group and began to fellowship with their scattered and few members in Oregon, mainly in the Willamette Valley, between Salem and Eugene, Oregon. They were mostly farmers or truck gardeners, but they welcomed the fellowship of his wife and himself.

Through his studies Armstrong says he found that many of the teachings and practices of the Christian church were *not* based on the Bible, but had originated in paganism. The opening of his eyes to the truth, he says, brought him to the crossroads of his life. To accept it meant to throw in his lot with a class of humble and unpretentious people he had come to look upon as inferior. It meant being cut off from the high and mighty of this world whom he had aspired to join. In final desperation, he says, he threw himself on God's mercy.[30] If God could use his life he would give it to him 'as a living sacrifice to use as He willed',[31] for to him, 'it was worth nothing any longer',[32] he was only 'a worthless piece of human junk not worthy to be cast on the junk pile'.[33] Armstrong likened his conversion to that of the Apostle Paul:

> . . . the Gospel which (is) preached of me is not after man. For I neither received it of man, neither was I taught it, but by the revelation of Jesus Christ . . . but when it pleased God . . . to reveal His Son in me . . . immediately I conferred not with flesh and blood; neither went I to a theological seminary, but I was taught by Jesus Christ, the Word of God (in writing)[34]

He also considered himself to be a type of John the Baptist, and of the prophet Zerubbabel:

> God's TIME had come! His time for one, of whom John the Baptist was type and forerunner, to prepare the way for Christ's *second* coming. For one whom Zerubbabel, in building the *second* temple at Jerusalem, was type and forerunner, of one through whom Christ would build this era of God's CHURCH – the spiritual TEMPLE to which Christ will come the SECOND time to *rule* and RESTORE THE GOVERNMENT OF GOD.[35]

After his conversion, Armstrong appears to have entered into that peculiar mental state frequently manifested by cult figures, in which he saw God working directly only through him in the last days. During his initial six months in-depth study, he says, Christ made plain to him 'the NAME of the true Church'.[36] He revealed to him also the truth about the 'lost sheep' of the house of Israel – 'the modern identity of which is the KEY that unlocks the whole THIRD of the Bible, which is PROPHECY for now'.[37] (This is the theory of Anglo-Israelism – that the British and American peoples are the descendants of Ephraim and Manassah, and hence heirs to all the promises given to Abraham.) Christ revealed to him also, he says, the truth of the existence of angels under Lucifer. This was so important, because 'it opened his mind to the BACKGROUND, making clear God's PURPOSE in creating man on earth'.[38] Further, Christ revealed to him 'God's annual Holy Days, which depict His Master Plan'.[39] Thus, he claimed, 'Jesus Christ, Head of Christ's Church, started his servant out with the basic foundation to *understanding* Christ's Gospel, and *He revealed that Gospel which had not been proclaimed to the world for $18\frac{1}{2}$ centuries*',[40] to him.

Armstrong says that God, in using man, has dealt through *one man* at a time. He has not used committees or groups. At the beginning, one man, Peter, was the leader.'[41] During his own conversion process, he says, 'Jesus cleared his mind of earlier false assumptions – such as going to heaven or hell, the immortality of the soul, the false "Trinity" doctrine, and other fables of so-called "Christianity".'[42] Jesus 'was preparing one called and chosen by God, even against that one's will, for an important service *in restoring the law and government of God to earth*'.[43] He was preparing 'one whom He conquered and brought to repentance through faith, for this great *end-time* commission'.[44] Armstrong thus saw himself as the specially chosen Apostle who would spring from the House of David in the latter days:

God has said: 'The Lord also shall save the tents of Judah first (in the latter days – now just ahead of us), *that the glory of the house of David* and the glory of the inhabitants of Jerusalem do not magnify themselves against Judah. In that day (*now soon* to come) . . . he that is feeble among them shall be as David; and *the throne of David shall be as God*, as the angel (messenger) of the Lord before them . . . I will pour *upon the house of David* . . . the spirit of Grace.' Zech. 12 : 7–10.[45]

It has already been mentioned that Armstrong in his *Autobiography* claimed ancestry back to King David. He enlarges on this in a later work:

> Plainly the apostle (one sent forth – or messenger of God) God would use in these perilous last days would be of the HOUSE OF DAVID, The House of David is NOT one of the tribes – but those individuals descended from David . . . God has preserved my ancestry every generation from David, and I am OF THE HOUSE OF DAVID![46]

Having likened his conversion to St Paul's, and having compared his new mission in life to that of John the Baptist, Armstrong then saw a parallel between his new ministry and that of Jesus Christ:

> First Jesus Christ began His earthly ministry at about age 30. God took away my business, moved me from Chicago, started bringing me to repentance and conversion, preparatory to inducting me into His ministry *when I was 30!*
> Second, Jesus began the actual *teaching and training* of His original disciples for carrying His Gospel to the world in the year 27 AD. Precisely 100 time cycles later, in 1927 AD. He began my intensive study and training for carrying HIS SAME GOSPEL to all the nations of today's world.[47]

Armstrong saw further parallels:

> The actual ordination, or completing of the ordination and enduement [his term] of power for sending out the original disciples into the ministry occurred after $3\frac{1}{2}$ years of intensive instruction and experience. It was on the Day of Pentecost, and the year was 31 AD.
> Exactly 100 time-cycles later, after $3\frac{1}{2}$ years of intensive study and training, Christ ordained me to preach this *same* Gospel of the kingdom in all the world as a witness to all nations (Matt. 24:14). This ordination took place, at, or very near the Day of Pentecost, AD 1931.[48]

From the very outset Armstrong was an apocalyptist who claimed, in the words of Schmitals, 'to have irrefutable certainty that he stands at the end of time, will soon have history behind him, and will experience the great transformation . . .'[49] This certainty led him boldly into prophetic utterances during the decades which followed the establishment of the Radio Church of God, and played no small part in attracting large numbers into his movement. Evidence of this apparent awareness comes out again and again even in the earliest editions of *The Plain Truth*. In the very first issue (February, 1934), he wrote the leading article entitled: 'IS A WORLD DICTATOR ABOUT TO APPEAR?' In this article he writes:

> Will it be Mussolini, Stalin or Roosevelt? Everybody senses that something is *wrong* with the world . . . that some mighty event is about to occur. What is it? Bible prophecy tells! Here is a solemn warning . . . and it is the plain truth![50]

In the June–July issue of the same year Armstrong attempts to interpret the book of Revelation and to give 'a complete synopsis of impending events, placing each future prophesied event in its proper time order as revealed by the story flow of the book of Revelation'.[51] In the same issue, he expected that 'the year 1936 will see the END of the Times of the Gentiles . . .'[52] and 'quickly after that time, we may expect to see the heavenly signs of the sun and moon becoming dark, the stars falling . . . which shall be followed by the "Day of the Lord" '.[53] When this failed to take place a different scenario was substituted. In the March 1938 edition of *The Plain Truth* Armstrong stated that Mussolini would be the coming dictator of Europe and the Beast of Revelation. The Italians would force the British out of the Mediterranean, take over the Suez Canal and the Middle East, and in alliance with the Pope 'will hatch up an idea between them of setting up a world headquarters at JERUSALEM'.[54] At the time he was convinced that the Second World War would end with the coming of Christ:

> But this you may KNOW! This war will be ended with CHRIST'S RETURN! And war MAY start within SIX weeks! We are just *THAT NEAR* Christ's coming! [55]

As the war in Europe developed, it became clear that Mussolini would not, in fact, become the dictator, and Armstrong decided instead that Hitler would be the coming ruler of Europe and destroyer of Britain and America:

Plain Truth readers know world events, before they occur! . . . Bible prophecy does indicate that Hitler MUST BE THE VICTOR, in his present Russian invasion! . . . Hitler will emerge from his Russian campaign stronger than ever, free to turn the entire might of his forces against Britain and AMERICA.[56]

Until the very last days of the war Armstrong was convinced that Germany would be victorious, and he refused to believe that Hitler was dead for some time after the war, predicting that he would emerge from hiding in Argentina and rise to power again.

These failures in prophecy caused some problems for Armstrong and his church, but during those years the church was small, and the members were, for the most part, simple rural people who, considering the difficult times Europe and the world had been through, did not generally take as very serious the fact that Armstrong's predictions of the end-time were not on schedule. The troubles then for the church were small by way of comparison with those which emerged later from predictions made by him in a number of books published in the post-war era. In these he indicated that 1972 would be the end of the times of the Gentiles and the beginning of the Great Tribulation – before which, the members of the Worldwide Church of God would be miraculously taken to a 'place of safety' – and that 1975 would see the return of Jesus Christ to rule the world in power and glory for a thousand years.

The first of the books alluded to above was published in 1956 and was entitled *1975 in Prophecy*. Among the many tribulations prophesied, Armstrong predicted that a devastating drought would hit the United States. (The 'he' referred to in the quotation was then United States Assistant Weather Chief I. R. Tannahill.)

But the indications of prophecy are that this drought will be even *more* devastating than he foresees, and that it will strike *sooner* than 1975 – probably between 1965 and 1972!

This will be the very *beginning*, as Jesus said, of the Great Tribulation![57] (Matt. 24:7).

Armstrong said that Ezekiel's prophecy is even more specific. This prophecy indicates he said, that one third of the entire population of the United States will die in that famine and disease epidemic.[58] Then,

Once we are weakened by starvation and disease, and the resulting calamitous economic depression, the Ten Nation European Colossus will suddenly STRIKE with hydrogen bombs that shall DESTROY OUR CITIES and our centres of industrial and military production![59]

The survivors of the holocaust will be uprooted from their homes – transported like cattle as slaves to Europe, and there they will not only be forced under the lashes of cruel taskmasters to do the work of slaves, but they will be forced to give up whatever belief they may have in the Bible, and be forced to accept idolatrous pagan beliefs that masquerade as Christianity, and millions will be martyred.[60]

Yes, millions of lukewarm inactive professing Christians will suffer MARTYRDOM – and that *before* the anticipated push-button leisure year 1975 dawns upon us! You'll read of this martyrdom – the Great Tribulation – in Matthew, 24:9–10, 21–2.[61]

Not only was this scenario taught by the church ministers to the member congregations, but it was broadcast powerfully worldwide by Armstrong himself. This writer has in his library a recording of *The World Tomorrow* programme broadcast by Armstrong around 1955. A partial transcript (including errors in syntax) is as follows:

Israel means us today, and if you want to know more about that why don't you send for our book *United States in Prophecy.*

Israel's house and Judah's house had been faithless to God. They had be-lied the Eternal crying: '*he'll* do nothing, no harm can come to us, no suffering from war or famine.' Now we've come to the place that's what we think now.

Notice war OR famine. Now I want to tell you this, that all this weather disturbance means that a terrible famine is coming on the United States that is going to RUIN us as a nation inside of less than twenty years!

All right, I stuck my neck out there! You just wait twenty years and see whether I told you the truth.

God says, if a man tells you what is going to happen, wait and see; if it *doesn't* happen he was not speaking the word of God, he is speaking out of his own mind. If it happens, you know God sent him. You watch and see whether these things happen. You'll see who is speaking to you, my friends. The prophets, said the people, are but windbags.

That's what a lot of you are saying about me right now. All right, that's in the Word of God.[62]

In a publication released in 1962 Armstrong said that the Roman Empire would be resurrected by 1972.

And in the days of those kings . . . This, by connecting the prophecy with Daniel 7 and Revelation 13 and 17, is referring to the UNITED STATES OF EUROPE which is *now forming,* out of the European Common Market, before your very eyes! Revelation 17:12 makes plain the detail that it shall be a union of TEN KINGS or KINGDOMS which (Rev. 17:8) shall resurrect the old ROMAN EMPIRE.

So, mark carefully the time element! 'In the days of those kings' – in the days of these ten nations or groups of nations that shall, *within the decade,* now, IN OUR TIME, resurrect briefly the Roman Empire.[63]

Then, in 1967 Armstrong published a 226-page volume entitled *The United States and British Commonwealth in Prophecy.* Of this book, in the *Foreword,* he said:

Events of the next five years may prove this to be the most significant book of this century. People of the Western World would be STUNNED! – DUMBFOUNDED! – if they knew!

The government of the United States, Britain, Canada, Australasia, South Africa, would immediately institute drastic changes in foreign policy – would set in motion gigantic crash programs – IF THEY KNEW!

. . . The events prophesied to strike the American and British peoples in the next four to seven years are SURE![64]

Armstrong said that God had already broken the pride of US power, but other prophecies reveal that it was soon to have (probably in about four years) such drought and famine, that disease epidemics would follow taking millions of lives.[65] He went on to say that God 'is going to lay *much more* INTENSE punishment'[66] on the British and American people between 1972 and 1974. However, worse was to come.

God warns us through prophecy that our sins are fast increasing. And now the day of reckoning is here! . . . In this fearsome atomic age,

> World War III will *start* with nuclear devastation unleashed on London, Birmingham, Manchester, Liverpool, New York, Washington, Philadelphia, Detroit, Chicago, Pittsburg, without warning![67]

> The sevenfold more INTENSITY of punishment now soon to come upon American and British peoples is, simply the prophesied GREAT TRIBULATION! It will be the most frightfully intense PUNISHMENT, and time of TROUBLE ever suffered by any people![68]

> Yet YOU need not suffer in it.[69]

How could one avoid this terrible suffering? According to Armstrong, if one comes to repentance and makes an unconditional surrender to God Almighty through Jesus Christ, then one will be accounted worthy to escape all those frightful things and to stand before Christ at his return.[70]

> Those in the true Body of Christ shall be taken to a place of SAFETY, until the Tribulation be over (Rev. 3: 10–11 – applying to those faithful in God's Work now going to the world. Rev. 12:14; Isa. 26:20).
> But YOU must make your own decision – to NEGLECT doing so is to have made the WRONG decision![71]

Armstrong closes by saying that he has taught these prophecies on God's authority: 'By God's direction and authority, I have laid the TRUTH before you! To neglect it will be tragic beyond imagination!'[72]

The doctrine of a 'place of safety' had been taught by the church for many years, and the idea seemed very plausible to the membership. It was considered to be a vital part of the gospel of the 'soon-coming Kingdom of God', – the notion that Jesus promised protection to his own elect, that he promised they would survive the prophesied holocaust which would strike an unsuspecting world.[73] However, only those who were members of the church would have an absolute guarantee of safety.[74] How would the members of the Worldwide Church of God, scattered all over the globe, be brought to this 'place of safety'?

> . . . and the woman (the Church) was given two wings of a great eagle, that she might fly into the wilderness, into her place, where she is nourished for a time and times and half a time, from the face of the serpent. Rev. 12 : 14.[75]

This wilderness was to be Petra, an abandoned city carved out of the cliffs in an arid and barren valley south-east of Jerusalem in what is now Jordan. Armstrong, in his travels, had become very friendly with King Hussein of Jordan, and presumably, as a result of this, the church had found favour in his eyes:

> All the top ministers taught Petra. Some who understood how nations function, had Herbert Armstrong and King Hussein of Jordan becoming fast friends long before 1972. Herbert Armstrong himself wrote of this beginning to happen in 1967, shortly before the Arab-Jew war of that year. Many thought the arrangements were already far advanced. Ambassador College News Bureau articles also had the Jews in an advanced stage of preparation and planning for the rebuilding of the temple in Jerusalem.[76]

The notion of a 'Petra fund' was put forward. It was suggested that people should sell their homes and contribute the money to this fund so that Stanley Rader (then treasurer and church legal counsel) could make the necessary purchases of planes and supporting equipment. Those who refused to contribute to the fund, it was said, would go into the Laodicean church group and be consigned to the Great Tribulation.[77]

Not long after Armstrong's baptism, a division occurred in the Church of God (Seventh Day)' as the brethren he was fellow-shipping with wanted to organize a state conference, so that the tithes collected from the people could be kept locally and not sent to the headquarters at Stanberry. Hence, in 1931 'they incorp-orated themselves as the Oregon Conference of the Church of God'.[78] In June of that year Armstrong was ordained by that conference, and began his ministry with an evangelistic campaign in Eugene, Oregon. The Oregon Conference continued to remain affiliated with the General Conference headquarters at Stanberry. However, in time, Armstrong reports, ministers in the church hatched plots to discredit him and get him off the payroll of the Oregon Conference of the Church of God. As a result of disagreements over the approach to baptizing new converts, he wrote a letter to the conference refusing to accept any further wages from them, but he emphasized that he did not resign from the conference. Regarding this, he states in his *Autobiography*:

> My wife and I did not leave the Church. This was God's Church . . . They came closer to Biblical truth than any other. What actually was happening was that a *new era* was dawning in the history of the Church of God . . . this was the transition from the Sardis era (Rev.3:1–5) into the beginning of the Philadelphia era.
>
> Mrs Armstrong and I continued to fellowship with these brethren. I continued to work with them and with their ministers . . .[79]

So the time had come, he thought, for the Philadelphia era to begin, and this started a week later when he established a new local Church of God beginning with 19 members. This was in August 1933.[80] Armstrong said that it is to the Philadelphia era of God's church that Christ said he would open doors so that his gospel might go worldwide, 'into all nations in power'.[81] Shortly after this, on 9 October 1933, he preached for the first time over the radio station KORE in Eugene, Oregon, and by the New Year of 1934 his programme went out over the same station every Sunday. He called his new programme *The Radio Church of God*. At the same time as his radio broadcast, he began working on *The Plain Truth* magazine. This was produced on an old mimeograph machine. The first issue was published on 1 February 1934, and the 'press run' was about 250 copies. It was advertised on the broadcast and sent free to anyone requesting it.

Armstrong continued his affiliation with the Stanberry headquarters of the Church of God (Seventh Day) until 1933 when a split occurred. In that year approximately half of the church remained with the headquarters at Stanberry while the other half set up a new church claiming world headquarters at Jerusalem, Palestine, but with U.S. headquarters at Salem, West Virginia. This second group was controlled by an elder named A. N. Dugger. According to Dugger, the original twelve apostles were intended to form the top governing board of the church as Christ organized it. He called this board 'the Twelve'. Next, taking 'the Seventy' which Jesus appointed for a special mission (Luke 10), Dugger, with Elders Dodd and McMicken, set up a 'Board of Seventy' leading ministers. Armstrong accepted ministerial credentials from the Salem group, and was appointed to this board as 'one of the Seventy'.[81] He proved a difficult person to get on with, and after a time, 'being self-willed and reflecting continuous haughtiness, it was determined that his continuing membership with the Church's ministry was of negative value'.[82] Hence, in 1937 his credentials were revoked by the church. After this, the members of the Oregon conference severed connections with the Salem branch, who, according to Armstrong '. . . had proved themselves willing to serve Satan and their own personal greed, and *injure the very work of God'*.[83]

Armstrong then went out on his own, expanded his *Radio Church of God* broadcast, and continued to publish his 'magazine of understanding', *The Plain Truth.* In April 1942, the *Radio Church of God* programme was changed to *The World Tomorrow* because the former title 'did not reach a listening audience from non-churchgoers',[84] whom Armstrong wished primarily to reach. By this time the broadcasts were going out over a number of stations in the Pacific north-west, including KMTR in Hollywood, California, and his church continued to grow. Later, Armstrong found the establishment of an educational institution of higher learning to be imperative. It was needed, he said, 'to provide an educated ministry, and to educate people for the work of proclaiming the good news worldwide'.[85] Pasadena, California, was chosen as the location for the college. He named the new institution Ambassador College, and it was opened to students on 8 October 1947. It was separately incorporated in 1951. (In time two more campuses were opened, one at Bricket Wood, near London, the other at Big Sandy in east Texas.) Armstrong had moved the church headquarters from Eugene, Oregon, to Pasadena in April 1947, shortly before the opening of the college. From 1 January 1953, *The World Tomorrow* programme was broadcast on long wave all over Europe. The Radio Church of God was on its way to having worldwide media coverage. In 1968, the name Radio Church of God was changed to the Worldwide Church of God.

Unlike, for example, the Jehovah's Witnesses, the Worldwide Church of God is not a mass-recruitment movement. Their members do not go from door to door seeking new converts, but claim rather, that Christ's statement, 'No one can come to me unless the Father who sent me draws him' (John 6:44), applies to them. Besides *The Plain Truth* magazine, the church produces a television programme called *The World Tomorrow*, which is beamed worldwide by satellite, and is on cable in some countries. For many years this programme was broadcast on Radio Luxembourg (and later on pirate offshore stations) and beamed at the UK. It is still broadcast worldwide on various stations, although recently the church's policy seems to be to cut back on, or even abandon, this aspect of its ministry.

The Plain Truth, the telecast, and the broadcast may be viewed as 'shop windows', to introduce the movement to the public, the material featured in them being interesting and informative and never controversial. Until December, 1990, the church published also a magazine called *The Good News*, which contained articles on biblical themes and church doctrine. Originally for baptized members only, this policy was changed in 1974 when it was made available to 'co-workers' and other contributors. Between 1969 and 1972 the church published a magazine named *Tomorrow's World*, which was similar in style and content to *The Good News*, but was available to those of the general public who desired a more in-depth treatment of the religious themes which, during that period, *The Plain Truth* dealt with in a general way. A newsletter titled *The Worldwide News* is produced for members only, and another full-colour, high quality magazine, *Youth*, is published monthly especially for the members' teenage children, but is also made available to 'co-workers' and the general public on request. The magazine contains articles on education, study skills, life skills, sexuality and the benefits of a high moral lifestyle, and teen Bible-study lessons. It has a 'Yuppie' ambience. All publications are sent free, as the church claims to take seriously Christ's admonition to his followers: 'freely you have received, freely give' (Matthew 10:8). *The Plain Truth* at one time had a circulation of about 10 million and was printed in English, Spanish, French, German, Dutch, Norwegian and Italian, although recent budgetary cutbacks by the church have significantly reduced this figure, and the magazine is now available in English, Spanish, French and German versions only. The church offers a wide range of attractively produced literature to explain in more detail the themes and issues discussed in the magazine. No matter how long the reader continues to accept *The Plain Truth*, or how many pieces of literature he writes in for, he will never be asked for money, he will never be asked to join anything, and no one will ever call on him.

Armstrong saw his church as the 'firstfruits' of God's salvation, which would always be small in numbers.[86] Its members will be 'kings and priests' in the coming millennium, and will rule with Christ for a thousand years when he returns to the earth in power and glory.[87] It will be during this thousand years, he said, that God will be saving mankind as a whole. Right now, he is calling only those (members of the WCG) who will take part in 'the first resurrection'.[88] Later, all of humanity who have never heard of the true gospel will be given their first chance to accept or reject the message. This will take place after 'the second resurrection',[89] which will occur near the end of the millennium period, and such a testing period will last about a hundred years.[90] A third and final resurrection (Revelation 20:13–15) will be of the wicked, who will be raised and then annihilated forever by being cast into the lake of fire.[91]

The church's approach to the public is always low-key. *The World Tomorrow* broadcast puts its audience at ease, and guarantees that 'no one will call and there will be no follow-up'. Only when specifically requested to do so will a minister call on a viewer or reader. If a person is interested he may send for the *Bible Correspondence Course*, and a programmed approach to Bible study can be started. If this is successful the person may ask to be baptized, and thus will be inducted into the church. However, once a person becomes baptized and a member of the Worldwide Church of God, he or she must obey all the rules. Tithing of members' before-tax income is compulsory in order to finance the church's operations. During the fifty years when Herbert W. Armstrong was in charge, the membership were left in no doubt of their responsibilities in this regard:

> Not a penny of what you earn, or a penny's worth of the value of what you produce, is yours – it all belongs to God to do with as he directs. God has legally directed that after you have honestly paid him the one little tenth he requires for his creative work, . . . then – AND NOT UNTIL THEN – God has decreed that the other nine tenths becomes legally yours!
>
> That's God's law![92]
>
> The first thing you do when you receive your pay is to give God the 10 per cent that is his in the first place. (In most nations, the

government will already have taken its tax revenues out before you even see your check.)

Remember, though, God's tithes come out of the total increase or adjusted gross income, not on the after-taxes amount.[93]

But LISTEN and HEED! It is not *your* tithe – it is GOD'S – HOLY to Him! IT IS THE FIRST 10th of your income – *before* all else – *before* paying bills. You HAVE NO RIGHT TO IT!

... Christ's chosen apostle has SPOKEN OUT ... DO NOT MAKE EXCUSE![94]

Now a LAW is not a law without a *penalty*. God does not *force* you to tithe. But if you don't there is a penalty! You lose the BLESSING that goes with honest stewardship. You come under a CURSE!

... The man who does not pay God His tithe is a *thief* – and, worse than a criminal robbing a bank, he is *robbing* God ...

And one of the Ten Commandments is 'You shall not steal' (Ex. 20:15). The man who does puts himself immediately *under the law* – under penalty of DEATH for *all eternity* ...

Ignorance of the LAW does not excuse. You may say, 'Well I never *knew* all this!' Well, you are without excuse, for you know it now ...'[95]

From its very small and insignificant beginning in 1934, the Worldwide Church of God has expanded at an extraordinarily fast pace in size, power, wealth and outreach. Throughout the 1950s and 1960s the church membership increased rapidly, reaching a figure of 75,000 by 1972.[96] According to the organization's published figures, the 'Work' expanded 'in power and scope at the rate of 30% per year'[97] between 1934 and 1969. The accounting firm of Arthur Andersen & Co. reported church income for 1983 to be $120,904,000 (this was the first time in almost fifty years that the church published such a report). The same firm reported that by 1988 (two years after Armstrong's death), church membership increased to 92,000 and income to $201.3 million. Income for 1989 and 1990 soared to over $211.5 million, but a Coopers & Lybrand report for 1991 showed a drop in income to just under $200 million.[98] Correspondence that this writer received since 1993 indicates that church income continues to fall, and a recurring opinion as to why this is the case is because people in the church have been slackening off paying tithes and offerings since Armstrong's successor, Pastor General Joseph Tkach, has not implemented the church's tithing law quite as strictly as did Armstrong.

As is the case with the Jehovah's Witnesses, and other closed organizations, discipline is very strict. All those who do not conform to the church's teachings are debarred from fellowship, marked and shunned. This can be very painful and traumatic, because by the time a person has reached the stage of becoming a member, he or she firmly believes the church's claim that it alone is the only legitimate channel of God's Word and work at the present time, and that the orthodox Christian church is a false church ruled by Satan the devil, along with all sects, cults and denominations. Throughout the centuries of spiritual darkness, Armstrong claimed, no priest or minister, nor any church denomination preached God's truth:

> The gospel had not been preached until God raised me up to preach it
> . . . That gospel you never heard from any preacher except from this
> church. You never heard it from Billy Graham. You never heard it from
> any Protestant preacher. You never heard it from any Catholic priest.[99]
> Satan is the god of this world. Now his chief church we know as the
> Roman Catholic Church. And we know she's represented in the 17th
> chapter, the Book of Revelation (as) Babylon the Great, mother of
> harlots. Who are the harlots? All the protestant churches.[100]

This notion of *exclusivity* was mitigated in 1991 by the present administration. Up to that time, Armstrong's teaching was accepted by his successor, and there is evidence of unease and confusion among the membership as to what status their church now has. Reports of the trauma of disfellowshipping and marking are repeated again and again in the literature, and a vast library of discontent and bitterness has been published worldwide.[101] Brenda Denzler, a former WCG member and Ambassador College student, is currently working on a book about the experiences of people who have entered and left the church. She says:

> Many people don't realise what a profound experience WC
> membership can be, or how difficult it can be to leave, once in that
> group. Joining and leaving Worldwide is not like joining and leaving
> the Methodist Church or some other mainstream denomination. For
> many, leaving the Worldwide Church of God can be just as painful as
> the membership itself.[102]

As in most other movements of its kind, dissent and

dissatisfaction developed among the members. In the late 1960s and the 1970s, Armstrong, self-named as 'God's Apostle', felt that he was being called to announce the soon-coming Kingdom of God to all the kings and rulers of the earth. As a result, he spent most of his time flying around the world in his private Grumman Gulfstream II jet visiting kings, princes and heads of state, and banqueting with them in lavish style. Regular reports of these visits were sent to all members and 'co-workers'.[103] Factions which developed within the organization during those years took advantage of his absence to develop their own power structures, and when these clashed in the late 1970s, the result was a series of major crises which shook the movement to its very foundations, eventually changing irrevocably the course on which it had been set.[104] The failure of the Great Tribulation to occur in 1972 or the second coming in 1975 put a strain on the members' credulity; but corruption at the highest level was the catalyst which brought about the first splintering of the Worldwide Church of God. Armstrong's son Garner Ted, once second-in-command and heir apparent to the movement, became involved in a multiplicity of adulterous affairs with Ambassador College co-eds, a number of whom later became ministers' wives, and was for a time in 1972 removed from the ministry. Armstrong reinstated him in 1974, claiming that Ted was divinely called, was 'above the Scriptures' and that his actions as a pastor could therefore not be judged according to the stipulations laid down for Christ's ministers in Paul's epistles to Timothy and Titus. Yet, Armstrong 'disfellowshipped' and banished his son in 1978, not for his immoral behaviour, but when it became apparent to him that Ted was engineering a 'coup' to wrest control of the movement from him. (Garner Ted then founded his own church – the Church of God International, with headquarters at Tyler, in Texas.) The following year the attorney general of California sent in a receiver to the Worldwide Church of God to take control of the assets and financial records of the church. Among the charges in a civil suit brought against the church by a number of members was that Armstrong and his counsel Stanley Rader had siphoned off millions of dollars of church funds annually for their personal use and that there had been a failure to provide an adequate accounting of the church's financial position as required by state laws governing charitable institutions. The church spent scores of millions of dollars of tithe-payers' money fighting the case right up to the US Supreme Court; time and again the church was denied relief in its various petitions to the different courts. Ironically, eighteen months later the attorney general announced that he was dropping the case against the church, not for lack of evidence, but because the law governing the financial operation of non-profit institutions had been changed by the California legislature, significantly reducing the powers of the attorney general in this area.

Other crises which beset the church included: (i) the divorce and remarriage issue: members who were divorced *before* they joind the church were forced to rejoin their first spouse, notwithstanding a happy second marriage with children. This ruling caused dreadful trauma to affected members; (ii) the healing issue: members were not allowed to consult doctors, take medicines or vaccinations, or undergo surgery for any illness, even if this was life-threatening. Inevitably, unnecessary deaths occurred, many of which were of little children; (iii) Armstrong's marriage and divorce: In 1977 Armstrong, against the laws of his own church, married a woman of Cherokee Indian descent whose husband was still living. He was 85 at the time, she was 38. Five years later he divorced her, spending further millions of dollars of tithe-payers money on pre-trial submissions when she contested the case. Further damage was done to Armstrong's credibility when it emerged around this time that he had sexually abused his youngest daughter for over ten years early in his ministry, and that he kept diaries of his habit of masturbation – a practice which he condemned as a perversion and a capital sin in many of his writings for the membership.

Doctrinally, Armstrong taught an unusual or unorthodox kind of religion.[105] Among his teachings were the following:

1. God is not a Trinity – but a Family – of which there are presently two members, God the Father and his divine Son, Jesus Christ. Jesus was *not* the Son in his pre-incarnate state, but was Yahweh, or Jehovah, the God of the Old Testament. He became the Son when born of the Virgin Mary. The resurrected Jesus became the First-born of God's Spiritual Sons.

2. The Holy Spirit is not a *person* in the Godhead, but an *impersonal force*, originating with God, through which God is omnipresent and through which God manifests his power.

3. Man does not *have* a soul, but *is* a soul. The souls of animals are the same as human souls – merely the 'breath of life' (*Nephesh* – Heb.) – all go to the same common grave (Heb. *sheol* ; Gk. *hades*). Thus the soul is not inherently immortal, and the condition of all men after death is one of unconsciousness. They remain as such until the time of the resurrection.

4. The Law of Moses (including the dietary restrictions of Leviticus 2) is, for the most part, still to be observed. Only the ceremonial portions of the Law are dropped.

5. Satan (formerly the archangel Lucifer) now rules the earth, and incites humankind to rebellion and sin, but is destined for eternal defeat and punishing, and will be cast into the 'lake of fire'. Ultimately his fate will be decided by the resurrected saints (members of the Worldwide Church of God).

6. Jesus died while sinless, as a substitutionary sacrifice for those who will accept him in faith as their saviour. He was a *man only* after he, – as the Word – became flesh. He was God (Emmanuel – God with us) only in that he had the perfect character and will of God. As a man he had fallen, sinful, human flesh, fully capable of sinning, all the while having to overcome the sway of sin in his flesh. When he died he ceased to exist for three days and three nights. Then, at his resurrection, he became (fully?) God again – was 'born again', becoming a spirit being, who was not actually flesh and bones, since he was not resurrected in the body in which he died.

7. The *purpose* of man's being put on earth is so that he can be finally *born* into the Kingdom of God, when he will finally *become* God, 'as God is God'; hence, when man is *born of God*, he will be a *spirit*. Just as Jesus Christ was raised from the dead as a spirit, so also the saints will be resurrected as spirits.

8. The blood of Christ does not finally save any man. The death of Christ merely paid the penalty of sin in our stead and wipes the slate clean of *past* sins.

9. Baptism by immersion is required so that man can take advantage of Christ's sacrifice. At that point the 'slate is wiped clean' and past sins are forgiven. After that, the convert is obliged to obey the law. His salvation is conditional on this.

10. Those who have died in ignorance of God's ways will be resurrected in the millennium when they will be given their 'first chance' to receive salvation; however, those who have heard the

truth but rejected it will be thrown into the lake of fire after the third resurrection, and, rather than being punished for ever and ever, will be annihilated.

11. God the Father does not know everything; he did not know that Lucifer and the angels would rebel. He *chooses* not to know, for example, *whether* a man will sin. He did not know whether Adam would sin or not.

12. The seventh-day Sabbath (from sunset on Friday to sunset on Saturday), and the seven annual holy days ordained by God in the Old Testament are to be kept by all who are in obedience to God; Easter, Christmas, various other holidays and also the celebration of birthdays are of pagan origin and are not to be observed by the membership.

13. The wearing of make-up by women was considered to be a sin – worn only by prostitutes – although this doctrine has been changed from time to time.

14. Tithing is required of all members of the Worldwide Church of God – up to three tithes per year, from gross earnings, together with holy day offerings, 'free -will' offerings, and other specified funds made known to the membership from time to time.

Shortly before he died in January 1986, Armstrong appointed Joseph Tkach to succeed him. At first Tkach was careful to give Armstrong honoured treatment in all Worldwide Church of God publications. In a May 1986 *Good News* editorial he stated:

> God used him powerfully to get the Church to a dedicated, concerted *unity* carrying out the *purpose* of our calling, the proclaiming of Christ's Gospel of the <u>*soon-coming*</u> Kingdom of God, and feeding the flock that is the Body of Christ.[106]

The theme of 'passing the baton' was maintained in the early months after Armstrong's death to reinforce the sense of continuity of purpose and ideals; the metaphor, suggesting to the members that when the baton is passed, 'it is not to end a race, but to continue a race with a temporary re-adjustment as the baton is passed from one runner to the next'.[107] The notion that Jesus Christ was directly intervening in church affairs under the new leadership was also sustained: 'Jesus Christ, the living Head of the Church (Ephesians 1:22–3) . . . continues to actively lead and govern the Church through Mr Armstrong's designated successor, Joseph W. Tkach.'[108] Armstrong's use of biblical types to endow an aura of sacredness on the new leader's office was also implemented:

> God used Joshua in a powerful way to lead Israel. Joshua remained faithful to what he had learned under Moses, just as Mr Tkach is determined to remain faithful to what he has been taught under Mr Armstrong. (Joshua 24:31)
> God used Elijah to witness to Israel that they ought to reject false Baal worship (1 Kings 18). Likewise, Mr Armstrong made people aware of the true God.
> But Elijah had a successor, as Mr Armstrong did. His name was Elisha. Elijah put his mantle, symbolising his office and authority, on Elisha (1 Kings 19:19). Mr Armstrong trained Mr Tkach in the use of power and designated him to positions of responsibility in God's work.[109]

A year after Armstrong's death, his memory was still carefully cultivated, and the all-embracing influence which he had on the leadership was emphasized to the membership:

> I knew that there had to be something to it. The powerful, sincere and unrelenting voice of Herbert W. Armstrong convinced my devoutly Russian orthodox father that he should *repent* and change his life . . .
> What an impact Mr. Armstrong had on my life! As God's servant, he brought the message of God's law and way of life, not only to me, but to all those whose minds God would open.[110]

As time went on, subtle changes in emphasis could be noticed in church publications and Armstrong's name began to be invoked less and less, and his writings, once ubiquitous, were coupled as chapters or sections in booklets along with contributions by other church writers. Tkach and his advisers seem to be pursuing a vigorous policy of changing many of Armstrong's key doctrines and apparently attempting to bring them into line with traditional Christian thinking. For while they insist in some cases that 'no change has taken place', quite the opposite, in fact, appears to be true. Among the many changes, the Trinity doctrine was officially adopted by the church in 1993, and in 1994 it was decided to abandon Armstrong's flagship telecast *The World Tomorrow* programme – long considered, with *The Plain Truth* magazine, as the main source of attracting new members – once the current series comes to an end. In 1995 Tkach announced that the Church would no longer demand legalistic observance of the Old Testament Sabbath, holy days, or tithing. Members are now free to work on the Sabbath if circumstances required. Also in that year, the rule forbidding members to abstain from biblically unclean meats was removed.

At the time of writing there appears to be a rising groundswell of membership opinion criticizing Tkach for changing so radically so many of Armstrong's long revered doctrines. Whether they can articulate their opposition adequately, or overcome their fears of punishment by disfellowshipping to the extent that they are able to topple Tkach, is uncertain. Perhaps ominously, one group who went so far as to picket the church headquarters in support of the retention of Armstrong's long-held doctrines was summarily disfellowshipped by the current regime.[111] Long-time stalwart of Armstrong doctrine and one of the longest serving evangelists in the church, Roderick C. Meredith (ordained by Armstrong in December 1952), was disfellowshipped by the present administration in December 1992, allegedly for disagreeing with some of the new doctrinal changes. (He founded the Global Church of God in 1993, attracting away a large segment of WCG tithe-payers.) Some disaffected members to whom this writer has spoken feel that it is only a matter of time before the church fragments, especially since it no longer considers itself to be God's *only* true Church, but merely another *denomination* within the larger Body of Christ.

One thing appears to be commonly agreed among observers and commentators of the Worldwide Church of God. Armstrong could not have picked a man more opposite to himself in terms of charisma, drive, ability to articulate the doctrines and needs of the church, and management style. *Ambassador Report*'s John Trechak quotes a distinguished California psychiatrist who stated that 'in choosing Tkach, Herbert Armstrong was very likely motivated by a subconscious desire to see his successor fail'.[112]

And what about Armstrong himself? For over fifty years he was the vital active force of the Worldwide Church of God, succeeding in keeping the organization together against what appeared to be overwhelming odds. Will his memory go the same way as that of

Charles Taze Russell after his death in 1916, when the Jehovah's Witnesses (then known as Millennial Dawnists) took a new direction under the leadership of Judge Rutherford? Not long after Russell's death, his writings (which had been considered divinely inspired by many within that organization) were allowed to go out of print, and today Witnesses pay only a cursory acknowledgement to the man who founded them, and often have great difficulty in explaining away many of Russell's earlier writings that come back to haunt them when unearthed by diligent researchers.

Already many of Armstrong's writings have been dropped. Even his final book *Mystery of the Ages*, once touted by Tkach as 'probably the most important book in 2000 years', has been withdrawn. Church publications, which up to his death were mostly written entirely under Mr Armstrong's name (though frequently researched by others), now merely acknowledge that a particular chapter had its 'original text written by Herbert Armstrong'. It will be interesting to see, as time passes, to what extent the doctrinal edifice constructed by Armstrong will be maintained, or, will it, too, just as was Russell's before him, be dismantled piece by piece, until 'Armstrongism' – once hated or revered with almost equal passion – is no more?

Notes

[1] G. B. Caird, *A Commentary on the Revelation of St. John the Divine* (London, A. & C. Black Ltd., 1966), 2.

[2] For a thorough exposition of the different views on the millennial kingdom – premillennial, amillennial, and post-millennial, the reader is referred to the following works: John F. Walvoord, *The Millennial Kingdom* (Grand Rapids, MI, Zondervan Pub. House, 1978 ed. first published by Dunham Pub. Co, 1959); I. M. Haldeman, *The Coming of Christ Both Pre-Millennial and Imminent* (Philadelphia, Philadelphia School of the Bible, 1906); Alva J. McClain, *The Greatness of the Kingdom – An Inductive Study of the Kingdom of God* (Chicago, Moody Press, 1968).

For a comprehensive and scholarly history of the rise of millenarianism, the reader is referred to the following works: Walter Schmitals, *Die Apokalyptik: Einfuhrung und Deutung* (Göttingen, Vandenhoeck & Ruprecht, 1973). See English tr. by John E. Steely, *The Apocalyptic Movement, Introduction and Interpretation* (New York,

Abington Press); J. F. C. Harrison, *The Second Coming: Popular Millenarianism 1780–1850* (London, Routledge & Kegan Paul, 1979); Timothy P. Weber, *Living in the Shadow of the Second Coming* (New York, Oxford University Press, 1979); Edwin S. Gaustad (ed.), *The Rise of Adventism: Religion and Society in Mid-Nineteenth-Century America* (New York, Harper & Row, 1974). See also: Ronald Matthews, *English Messiahs – Studies of Six English Religious Pretenders 1656–1927* (London, Methuen, 1936); Cecil Roth, *The Nephew of the Almighty* (London, Goldston Ltd., 1933).

[3] Harrison, *The Second Coming*, 5.

[4] Ibid.

[5] Ibid.

[6] Ibid.

[7] See Appendix I for a breakdown of these historical roots. For an interesting (though mostly subjective) background to the roots of Miller's ideas on millenarianism, the reader is referred to the following mostly biographical and apologetic works on the life and times of William Miller:

Sylvester Bliss, *Memoirs of William Miller* (Boston, Joshua Himes; repr. from the 1853 edn. Boston; New York, AMS, 1971); Elder James White, *Sketches of the Christian Life, and Public Labours of William Miller* (Battle Creek, MI, Steam Press of the Seventh-Day Adventist Publication Association; repr. from the 1875 edn.; New York, AMS, 1971); Joshua V. Himes (ed.), *A Brief History of William Miller the Great Pioneer in Adventist Faith* (Boston, Adventist Christian Publication Society, 1895); Francis D. Nichol, *The Midnight Cry* (Washington DC, Review & Herald Publishing Association, 1944); Robert Gale, *The Urgent Voice: The Story of William Miller* (Washington DC, Review & Herald Publishing Association, 1975). A somewhat more critical account of the same period is given in: Clara Endicott Seers, *Days of Delusion* (Boston, Houghton Mifflin Company, 1924).

[8] Himes, *History of William Miller*, 88.

[9] Ibid., 87, 88. See also White, *Sketches*, 55–7.

[10] Ibid., 182.

[11] Himes, *History of William Miller*, 230, 231. See also White, *Sketches*, 282.

[12] White, *Sketches*, 297, 298.

[13] For an exhaustive and scholarly treatment of the many splinter groups which emerged after 1844 see J. Gordon Melton, *Encyclopaedia of American Religions*, chap. 12: 'The Adventist Family' (Wilmington, NC, McGrath Publishing Co., 1978), 453–500.

[14] See Leroy Edwin Froom, *The Conditionalist Faith of Our Fathers*, 2 vols. (Washington, DC, Review & Herald Publishing Co., 1965).

15 Benjamin Wilson, *The Emphatic Diaglott containing the Original Greek Text of what is commonly styled the New Testament, with an Interlineary Word for Word English Translation based on the renderings of eminent critics and on the various readings of the Vatican Manuscript No. 1209* (New York, International Bible Students Association, 1942).

16 See Arthur C. Piepkorn, *Profiles in Belief: The Religious Bodies of the United States and Canada*, vol. 4, chap. 11: 'Sabbatarians' (San Francisco, Harper & Row, 1979), 133–41.

17 For a detailed history of the development of the Churches of God (Seventh Day), see Richard C. Nickels, *A History of the Seventh Day Church of God* (Sheridan, WY, Published by the author, 1973); idem, *Six Papers on the History of the Church of God* (Portland, Oregon, published by the author, 1977); Joel Bjorling, *The Churches of God, Seventh Day: A Bibliography*: 'Sects and Cults in America Bibliographical Guides' (General Editor: J. Gordon Melton), vol. 8 (New York and London, Garland Publishing Co., 1987).

18 *Time* (27 January 1986).

19 Herbert W. Armstrong, *The Autobiography of Herbert W. Armstrong* (Pasadena, Ambassador College Press, 1973), vol. 1, 16.

20 Idem, 'The history of the beginning and growth of the Worldwide Church of God', *The Good News* (April 1980), 25.

21 Idem, *Autobiography*, 261.

22 Ibid., 27.

23 Ibid., 12.

24 Ibid., 262.

25 Ibid., 263.

26 Ibid.

27 Ibid., 265.

28 Ibid., 13.

29 Ibid., 314.

30 Ibid., 22.

31 Ibid.

32 Ibid.

33 Ibid.

34 Ibid., 24.

35 Armstrong, 'History of the beginning', 26.

36 Ibid.

37 Ibid.

38 Ibid.

39 Ibid.

40 Ibid.

41 Ibid.

42 Ibid.

43 Ibid.
44 Ibid.
45 Herbert W. Armstrong, 'The history of the beginning and growth of the Worldwide Church of God', *The Good News* (May 1980), 24. The reference is to Zechariah 12:7–10.
46 Ibid.
47 Armstrong, *Autobiography*, 366.
48 Ibid., 373.
49 Schmitals, *Apocalyptic Movement*, 36.
50 Herbert W. Armstrong, 'Is a world dictator about to appear?', *The Plain Truth* (February 1934), 1.
51 Idem, 'What is *going* to happen!', *The Plain Truth* (June–July 1934), 1.
52 Ibid., 5.
53 Ibid.
54 Herbert W. Armstrong, *The Plain Truth* (March 1938), 8.
55 Idem, *The Plain Truth* (August 1939), 6.
56 Idem, *The Plain Truth* (September–October 1941), 7.
57 Idem, *1975 in Prophecy!* (Pasadena, Radio Church of God, 1956), 10.
58 Ibid., 12.
59 Ibid., 13.
60 Ibid., 20.
61 Ibid.
62 Herbert W. Armstrong, *The World Tomorrow* broadcast from Radio Luxembourg (Europe, *c*.1955).
63 Idem, *Just What do You Mean . . . the Kingdom of God?* (Pasadena, Ambassador College Press, 1962), 12.
64 Idem, *The United States and British Commonwealth in Prophecy* (Pasadena, Ambassador College Press, 1967), vii, ix, xii.
65 Ibid., 183, 184.
66 Ibid., 185.
67 Ibid., 210.
68 Ibid., 210, 211.
69 Ibid., 211.
70 Ibid.
71 Ibid.
72 Ibid.
73 Dr Herman L. Hoeh, *There Is a Way of Escape* (Pasadena, Ambassador College Press, 1963), 4.
74 Ibid.
75 Ibid., 5; the quotation is from Revelation 12:14.
76 David Robinson, *Herbert Armstrong's Tangled Web* (Tulsa, OK, John Hadden Publishers, 1980), 237. (Robinson was a senior minister in the WCG and a personal friend of Herbert Armstrong.)

[77] Ibid., 239.

[78] Herbert W. Armstrong, 'WHAT EVERY READER NEEDS TO KNOW ABOUT the foundation, history, authority, and doctrines of the Worldwide Church of God', *The Plain Truth* (February 1978), 43 (in US edn. only). See also Armstrong, *Autobiography*, 352, 353.

[79] Armstrong, *Autobiography*, 450.

[80] Ibid., 450, 451.

[81] Ibid., 450.

[82] Ray L. Straub, Letter (under letterhead of Church of God (Seventh Day)) to a Mr John Kessler. (Straub was an elder in that church.)

[83] Armstrong, *Autobiography*, 531.

[84] Armstrong, *Autobiography*, vol. 2, 48.

[85] Ambassador College Press, *This is the Worldwide Church of God* (1972), 17.

[86] Herbert W. Armstrong, *The Mystery of the Ages*: see chap. 'Mystery of the Church' (Pasadena, Worldwide Church of God, 1985), 191–4.

[87] Worldwide Church of God, *The Coming Utopia – Wonderful World Tomorrow* (Pasadena, Ambassador College Press, 1977), 2, 3. See also C. Paul Meredith, *What Will You Be Like in the Resurrection?* (1971).

[88] C. Paul Meredith, *If You Die . . . Will You Live Again?* (Pasadena, Radio Church of God, 1957), 2.

[89] Idem, *IS This the ONLY Day of Salvation?* (Pasadena, Radio Church of God, 1958), 4.

[90] Herman H. Hoeh, 'The resurrection at the Last Day – Who will be in it? When will it occur?', *The Good News* (September–October 1988), 21, 22.

[91] Meredith, *If You Die.*

[92] Herbert W. Armstrong, 'Despite the recession YOU CAN SOLVE YOUR FINANCIAL WORRIES', *The Plain Truth* (March 1983), 8.

[93] Ronald Kelly, 'WILL YOU EVER GET OUT OF DEBT?', *The Plain Truth* (May 1982), 9.

[94] Herbert W. Armstrong, 'CHRIST NOW PUTS CHURCH BACK ON GOD'S FINANCIAL TRACK', *The Good News* (January 1979), 4.

[95] Idem, 'How your financial future is determined', *The Good News* (April 1985), 25.

[96] *This IS The WORLDWIDE CHURCH OF GOD* (Pasadena, Ambassador College Press, 1972), 6.

[97] Ibid., 15.

[98] Photocopies of these financial reports can be seen in Appendix xv and xvi (pp. 895–9, vol. 2) of my doctoral dissertation: Cornelius A. O'Connor, 'A comprehensive analysis of the history and doctrines of the Worldwide Church of God (Armstrongism), together with an

exegetical commentary and a discussion of some of the radical doctrinal changes in the post–Armstrong era of the Church' (unpublished Ph.D. thesis, University of Wales, Lampeter, 1993).

[99]Herbert W. Armstrong, Sermon given to church members, dated 24 July 1976; cited in 'What the Armstrongs say about other churches', *Ambassador Report* (Pasadena, John Trechak, Publisher, 1977), 13.

[100]Idem, Sermon given to church members, dated 7 May 1974; cited ibid., 13.

[101]J. L. F. Buchner, *Armstrongism Bibliography* (Sydney, Australia, published by the author, 1983).

[102]Brenda Denzler, 'Post Traumatic Stress Disorder (PTSD) and the Armstrong experience' (unpublished: PO Box 1005, Newton, Kansas 67114); cited in *Ambassador Report* (October 1985), 4.

[103]See Armstrong, *Autobiography*, ii, 441–61.

[104]For a fully documented account of these crises within the church see O'Connor, 'Comprehensive analysis', 117–227.

[105]The doctrines of the Worldwide Church of God, together with comprehensive primary source references, are discussed in ibid., 228–619.

[106]Joseph W. Tkach, 'Our work is cut out for us', *The Good News* (May 1986), 1.

[107]'Passing the baton', *The Good News* (May 1986), 12.

[108]Ibid.

[109]Ibid., 13.

[110]Joseph W. Tkach, 'God's work was his life', *The Good News* (January 1987), 1.

[111]*Ambassador Report* (September 1990), 3.

[112]John Trechak, *Ambassador Report* (September 1989), 4.

Appendices: The writer would like to acknowledge the assistance of Ms Carole Jones MA in drawing the charts. Source: *The Watchman Expositor*, 10, No. 7 (1993) (Arlington, Tx, Watchman Fellowship Inc.).

Appendix I

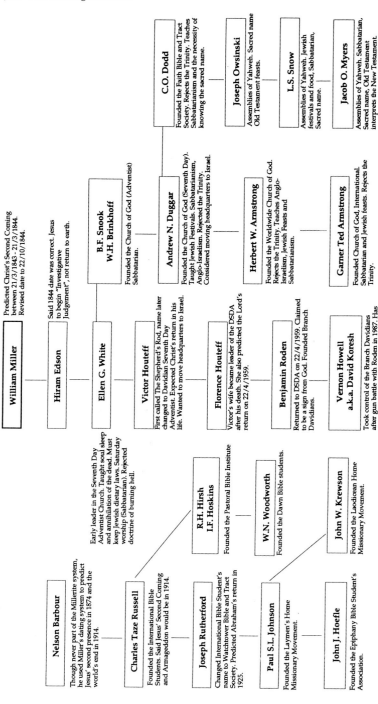

Appendix II

Worldwide Church of God
Splinter Groups

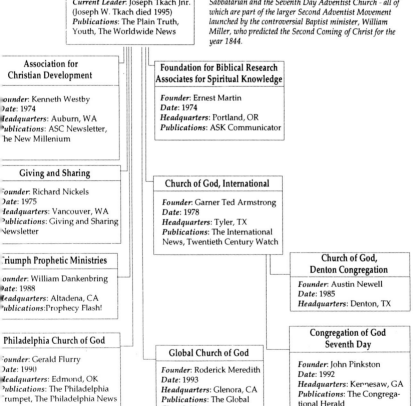

Worldwide Church of God

Founder: Herbert W. Armstrong
Date: 1934
Headquarters: Pasadena, CA
Current Leader: Joseph Tkach Jnr.
(Joseph W. Tkach died 1995)
Publications: The Plain Truth,
Youth, The Worldwide News

Note: The Worldwide Church of God is itself a break-off of the Church of God (Seventh-day), with which Herbert Armstrong was a minister. The Church of God (Seventh-day) is directly related to the Church of God (Adventist) Sabbatarian and the Seventh Day Adventist Church - all of which are part of the larger Second Adventist Movement launched by the controversial Baptist minister, William Miller, who predicted the Second Coming of Christ for the year 1844.

Association for Christian Development

Founder: Kenneth Westby
Date: 1974
Headquarters: Auburn, WA
Publications: ASC Newsletter, The New Millenium

Foundation for Biblical Research Associates for Spiritual Knowledge

Founder: Ernest Martin
Date: 1974
Headquarters: Portland, OR
Publications: ASK Communicator

Giving and Sharing

Founder: Richard Nickels
Date: 1975
Headquarters: Vancouver, WA
Publications: Giving and Sharing Newsletter

Church of God, International

Founder: Garner Ted Armstrong
Date: 1978
Headquarters: Tyler, TX
Publications: The International News, Twentieth Century Watch

Triumph Prophetic Ministries

Founder: William Dankenbring
Date: 1988
Headquarters: Altadena, CA
Publications:Prophecy Flash!

Church of God, Denton Congregation

Founder: Austin Newell
Date: 1985
Headquarters: Denton, TX

Philadelphia Church of God

Founder: Gerald Flurry
Date: 1990
Headquarters: Edmond, OK
Publications: The Philadelphia Trumpet, The Philadelphia News

Global Church of God

Founder: Roderick Meredith
Date: 1993
Headquarters: Glenora, CA
Publications: The Global Church News

Congregation of God Seventh Day

Founder: John Pinkston
Date: 1992
Headquarters: Kennesaw, GA
Publications: The Congregational Herald

9

The Lord of the Second Advent – the deliverer is here! [1]

SARAH M. LEWIS

> The Second Coming of Christ will occur in our age, an age much like that of the First Advent. Christ will come as before, as a man in the flesh, and he will establish a family through marriage to his Bride, a woman in the flesh, and they will become the True Parents of all mankind. Through our accepting the True Parents (the Second Coming of Christ), obeying them and following them, our original sin will be eliminated and we will eventually become perfect. True families fulfilling God's ideal will be begun, and the Kingdom of God will be established both on earth and in heaven. [2]

Members of the Unification Church believe that the Messiah has made his [3] second coming and is on earth at present. The quotation sums up the Unification Church belief that Christ will be born as a man in the flesh, and that through his marriage the True Parents will be created. Through following them the sins of humanity will be eliminated and God's kingdom of heaven, both on earth and in the spirit world, will be established. Before looking further at these beliefs and at Sun Myung Moon's declaration of messiahship it is necessary to look at Unificationist theology as a whole. It is only then that Moon's messiahship can be placed in its proper context and truly understood.

1 God and creation

God in Unification thought is an invisible essence composed of dual characteristics, spirit and energy, and all existence is generated by these. In Unification thought creation is *projected out of* God; creation is the outward form of the invisible essence of God. God, like humanity, exists through a reciprocal relationship between the dual characteristics of subjectivity and objectivity (positivity and negativity, masculinity and femininity) and internal character and external form. The dualities of subjectivity and objectivity are complete opposites yet are complementary units. They may be manifested in a number of ways, for example as stamen and pistil in the plant world and as male and female in the animal world. Internal character and external form may be manifested as internal mind, which is invisible, subject and gives direction, and external body which is visible, object and responsive.

2 God and creation – the give-and-take action

According to Unificationism, the energy necessary for existence is generated by what is called a 'give and take' action. This 'give and take' action is understood as a relationship between God and humanity and between individuals. When God created Adam and Eve they were meant to sustain a vertical give and take relationship with him, and a horizontal relationship with each other. Creation functions through this give and take action. The relationship with God resulting from the give and take action is called the 'Four Postion Foundation' which is the basis for establishing the Kingdom. When subject and object perform a give and take action, they become one and thereby a new object for God. There are then four beings: the origin (God), the subject (mind), the object (body), and the resulting union (ideal person).

3 Creation – the three blessings

The four position foundation is complete when humanity fulfils the three blessings given to it by God. Adam and Eve were the first recipients of the three blessings, but they failed to fulfil them. The first blessing is an individual's ability to perfect her or his character. A perfected character is achieved when a person's mind and body (the divided form of God's dual essentialities) are united through a give and take action; thus a four position foundation centred on God is established. The fulfilment of the first blessing sees the establishment of the four position foundation on the individual level. The second blessing is the ability to multiply and produce the Ideal Family, centred on God.

Having fulfilled the first blessing, Adam and Eve should have formed one unit through marriage; they should have procreated thus establishing the four position foundation on the family level. The establishment of the first True Family would have led to the establishment of a perfect society, nation and world, therefore inaugurating God's Kingdom of Heaven on earth. The third blessing is the right of dominion over creation, thus establishing the four position foundation on the universal level. In the same way that humanity was created to give joy to God, the rest of creation was to give joy to humanity. Humanity has the potential to harmonize with the remainder of creation in oneness. *Divine Principle* states that, 'the Kingdom of Heaven is the world resembling a man with his individuality perfected in accordance with the essential character and form of God'.[4]

4 The fall

In Unification thought God created Adam and Eve as the first human ancestors. They were to live together as brother and sister until they were spiritually mature. They were to develop through the three stages of formation, growth and completion. They were then to marry with God's blessing and become the True Parents of humankind, establishing God's kingdom of heaven on earth. However, Eve was tempted by Satan then Adam by Eve, resulting in the fall of humanity. The Unificationist interpretation of the fall is that it was the result of a sexual relationship between Eve and Satan and then between Eve and Adam. Adam and Eve became bonded with Satan, forming a four position foundation with him instead of God. This led to the beginning of original sin that can only be eradicated by the Messiah. At the fall the world is said to have become divided into Cain-type and Abel-type areas, later becoming manifest as Communism and Democracy.

5 Jesus

Jesus, in Unification thought, came to eradicate the sin of Adam and Eve, to reverse the fall. Since it was God's intention that Adam and Eve should marry and produce children to establish God's kingdom, it follows that this too was Jesus' mission. Jesus, for Unificationists, was to fulfil the three blessings that had originally been given to Adam and Eve. He was to achieve individual perfection, marry and procreate and gain dominion over creation. It is believed that Jesus fulfilled the first blessing, but his crucifixion meant that the last two blessings remain unfulfilled.

Jesus in Unification thought was not divine. There is no belief in the doctrines of the eternal generation of the Son, the Virgin Birth, the Incarnation or the Trinity. Jesus was a man, chosen by God to act as the central figure, the Messiah, of humanity. Jesus was failed by Mary, John the Baptist and the Jewish people and crucified before he could complete his role as Messiah. When Jesus urged on the cross: 'Father, if it be possible, let this cup pass from me',[5] he was, according to Unificationists, pleading with God to allow him to live; he knew that if he died his mission would be left incomplete.

The Unification Church teaches that only married couples may enter the kingdom of heaven. Jesus died unmarried and for him to be allowed into heaven it has been necessary for Moon to conduct a wedding ceremony for Jesus. In Unification Church thought Jesus is now married to an old Korean woman and has been able to enter heaven in the spirit world.[6]

6 The crucifixion

Although the Unification Church does not accept the crucifixion as a part of God's original plan, it teaches that God brought it into existence as a secondary plan. God offered Jesus to Satan 'in place of the people who could otherwise be controlled by Satan because of their faithlessness'.[7] The crucifixion does hold some salvific value, that of spiritual salvation. Had the Jews followed Jesus and become one with him, body and soul, they would have been saved both spiritually and physically. However, they did not accept Jesus as the Messiah and upon his crucifixion Jesus' physical body became invaded by Satan. Since Jesus' physical body was taken by Satan and put to death he was able to offer only spiritual salvation; physical salvation cannot be offered by a messiah who has lost his physical body. Thus a new messiah is needed; a messiah who has his physical body; a messiah who is alive and able to establish *physically* the kingdom of heaven through marriage and procreation. One important point to note here is that in Unificationism the Christ fulfils an office. The term 'Christ' is not inseparable from the person of Jesus; the Christ is the Messiah; the Messiah is no longer Jesus.

7 The resurrection

Unificationism does not deny the resurrection but has a different interpretation of it to historic Christianity. The Unification Church teaches that Jesus' spiritual body appeared to the disciples, and although this was a 'bodily resurrection', it was not a physical resurrection.[8] Jesus' spirit was raised and it was his spirit body the disciples saw raised; there was no physical resurrection. Since the resurrection lies at the core of Christianity, and is often seen as proof of Jesus' divinity, there seems to be a clear gulf between Unificationist and Christian teaching on this point.

8 The Lord of the Second Advent

The 'Lord of the Second Advent' is the name given by the Unification Church to the new Messiah. Unification Church theology merges Taoism, Christianity, Confucianism, Shamanism, Buddhism, numerology, physics, and anti-Communism in order to fuel its lengthy and complicated arguments. *Divine Principle* teaches,[9] through pre-Christian and post-Christian historical parallels and numerological deductions, that the Messiah will be born between the years 1917 and 1930 and, adhering to Revelation 7:2–4, that he must be born in the East. Moon was, in fact, born in 1920, in Korea.

There are three qualifications that, for Unificationism, the new Messiah must hold. First, he must stand on the foundation of Jesus; that is, that the circumstances surrounding the second Messiah must mirror those that surrounded Jesus. Second, he must bring new revelation that will replace existing revelation. Third, he must fulfil the three blessings. It would appear that Moon has these qualifications; at least functionally he has always performed the role of Messiah. The circumstances surrounding Moon's life may be interpreted to parallel those that surrounded Jesus. There is great emphasis within the Unification Church on the fact that both Jesus and Moon appeared in an obscure setting; that is that they were born of women and did not descend from the clouds. Both Jesus and Moon met with countless difficulties, accusation and rejection. Moon did bring new revelation in the form of *Divine Principle*, that is believed to supersede the Bible and to explain the mysteries of the universe and the parables and symbols of the Bible. Finally, Moon is believed to have fulfilled the three blessings: individual perfection (Moon is without sin, although he has the free will to sin), procreation (through his natural and 'adoptive' children) and dominion over creation (through gaining adoptive children at the Blessing ceremonies and also through establishing a number of organizations[10] that are supported by many scholars, including non-Unificationists).

Unificationists argue that when we look for the Messiah we should be looking for someone as ordinary as Jesus; Jesus was merely a carpenter, yet was chosen to be the Messiah; it is no more unusual for a person such as Moon to take over this role. J. Wells, a Unificationist, argues that it would not be out of the question for God to choose an Oriental as the Messiah. He notes that it is a primary role of the Messiah to unite all nations, and Wells does not think that a white man would be capable of this.[11]

9 The messianic secret

Nowhere in *Divine Principle* does it state that Moon is the Messiah, but it is a natural conclusion that is easily reached. Parallels may be drawn between the possible reasons behind Jesus' messianic secret, evident in Mark's gospel, and the secrecy that has surrounded Moon. In both instances there is a strong emphasis upon the enlightenment of the select few and the temporary exclusion of those outside the movement. Both could similarly be explained through the desire to educate those who had already made a firm commitment to the movement, before embarking on the education of the unconvinced masses. Similarly, both could be explained through a desire not to be viewed with suspicion as a (politically) harmful movement.

10 Heavenly deception

The secrecy surrounding Moon's messiahship has always been strong within the Unification Church. M. Durst, a Unificationist, notes that the Unification Church has been accused of 'heavenly deception', that is, of not disclosing the part played by Moon within the church. N. Spurgin, also a Unificationist,[12] states that it was actually a Unificationist who coined the phrase 'heavenly deception'. She claims that Orientals within the Unification Movement do not give such a high priority to honesty. Instead, they value loyalty, and this ideal is alien to Western society. Spurgin believes that once the Unification Church began to be persecuted, members feared disclosing their identity. Faced with the prospect of violence, members would say that they were from a Christian group in general, and not specifically the Unification Church. On heavenly deception Durst states, 'such is now clearly and expressly against our policy and our instructions to members of the church'.[13] However, it has been drawn to my attention that Unificationists witnessing in a town in Wales in January 1995 would not divulge the name of their organisation until pressed.

11 Moon's declaration of messiahship

In July 1992, Sun Myung Moon publicly declared himself the Messiah. He declared, 'My wife . . . and I are the True Parents of all humanity . . . we are the saviour, the Lord of the Second Advent, the Messiah'. He noted that,

> God has been carrying out His providence to send the Messiah as the second perfected Adam who has subjugated Satan, to establish a perfected Eve who will represent all women. God has done this, because it was when Satan caused Eve to fall that human history came to be permeated with sin. The establishment of God-centred family ethics and the education of our children lie at the innermost core of my teachings as the person who has declared for himself the responsibilities of the Messiah.[14]

The inclusion of Hak Ja Han Moon in the messianic expectations indicates the growing awareness of the female within Unification thought, at least exoterically. Until recently Hak Ja Han's role within the Unification Church was unclear and she ranked behind Moon in the movement. Although Moon will probably always be viewed as the leader proper, the high esteem in which Hak Ja Han is held by Unificationists is obvious. For example, she is fondly, and in a very natural manner, termed 'Mother' by

Unificationists, in the same way as Moon himself is referred to as 'Father'. Yet, although Moon originally implied that the role of the Messiah, in the same way as the role of the True Parents, was a joint one, and applied to both him and his wife, he later made it clear that he alone is the Messiah. There is a constant problem when attempting to make *any* statement or to reach *any* conclusion concerning the role of women in Unification thought; it is always necessary to attempt to distinguish between exoteric and esoteric doctrine. In Unificationism the term 'Messiah' is always followed by the pronoun 'he', never 'he and she' or 'they'. We may conclude from this that in reality Moon remains in a higher position than his wife and the messiahship is really a masculine one. This view is strengthened by the way Unificationist writings almost always use exclusive language and assume that human beings can be covered by a term like 'mankind'.

Many Unificationists are still unwilling to confirm the Declaration to non-members; or to enter into any discussion about it. One member explained to me that the secrecy element had been in existence for so long that many members are still in the process of becoming accustomed to the fact that it has been broken. For many years Unificationists have feared attack and it became both natural and necessary for them to hide their beliefs from outsiders. Unificationists will still find it difficult to proclaim Moon's messiahship, but it now seems necessary for them to try. The new teaching on the matter emphasizes:

> Now we can go back and proclaim the Messiahship in our own tribe and in our own home. We shout it out and speak it more freely than we have eaten in our past life time. More than we moved our mouths to chew food, we should speak the proclamation this time. Father wants us to move our mouths. It is not your own life about which Father is concerned, but the hundreds of thousands of lives which must be saved through you.[15]

And: 'Talk and talk, even in your sleep, talk about the Messiah and the proclamation of True Parents'. In 1992, 'Father proclaimed the messiahship, not to ignorant people, but to people of the top status in the world. We must now teach simply: the Messiah is here; we must follow him to prosper.' 'Now two

thousand years later, at the Second Advent, the Lord of the
Second Advent as the True Parents will bring in and restore
hundreds of thousands and even millions of families on the
horizontal level.'[16]

Adam and Eve had no foundation with which to connect to
God. Centring on Satan, Adam followed Satan, Eve followed
Adam, Cain followed Eve and Abel followed Cain; there was no
true love or true lineage. In complete contrast we now have
Moon as Adam following God, Hak Ja Han as Eve following
Adam, Cain following Eve and Abel following Adam. The two
paths are the complete opposite of one another; the first is hell,
the second is heaven. Unificationism teaches that true lineage
develops from the love between a husband and a wife. So the
purpose of salvation is to put Adam and Eve into their true
position. The lineage must be changed and filled with true love.
The Messiah comes as a new Adam, to establish a family with a
new Eve, a literal bride. The same theory is applicable to Jesus.
Jesus was to unite with a literal bride; the marriage between them
would have established them as the True Parents of humanity.
The vital difference is that Moon has a bride whilst Jesus did not
(when he was alive). The Messiah must be part of a couple, and
not a single individual. The True Parents are to create a physical
lineage as well as engrafting 'adopted' children into their family.
These children will 'inherit God's blessing and learn the tradition
of true love'.[17] The True Family is the 'redemptive unit' from
which other God-centred families will extend. This unit is
essential, which is why we need the type of Messiah who is able to
instigate it; a living, physical messiah, who is able to produce off-
spring. Moon, born sinless, is in a position to grant salvation and
this is done through the Blessing ceremony. It is essential to
salvation, and is the only method of eradicating the original sin
that infests humanity. The blessed couples begin their own
families; these families are a part of the new lineage; original sin
is no longer transmitted, the sin is not inherited, although
humanity still retains the free will to sin.

12 The Blessing ceremony

It is only through the Blessing that the kingdom of heaven will be
established. Thirty-six thousand couples were blessed in Seoul in

August 1995, with others blessed via satellite links with several countries of the world.[18] Each such event is seen to depict Moon's ability to gain followers through their own free will. Yet it is worth noting that many non-Unificationist couples were invited to Seoul to be blessed by Reverend and Mrs Moon; they were assured that their attendance and participation would not be taken as representative of any adherence to Unification Church doctrine. Through their holy mass weddings, the Unification Church believes it is creating a new heavenly family tradition. It is trying to heal the broken relationships that have arisen not only in the family but also in society and the whole world. It is hoped that, by the end of this century, 3.6 million couples will be blessed at one time.

With the Unificationist belief that the kingdom of heaven can only be established through the establishment of True Families at the Blessing ceremony, the event is clearly of vital importance. It is taught that Adam and Eve's disobedience is restored when Unificationists are matched to a partner by Moon and his Blessing Committee and not through making the choice themselves based on romantic attraction. The True Family then becomes the mediator between God and the rest of humanity.

Sun Myung and Hak Ja Han Moon preside over the Blessing ceremonies. 'The True Parents take upon themselves all of our sinful nature when they administer the Blessing'.[19] With their words and actions they are believed to be engrafting those they bless onto their own family, and by extension God's family. It is the role of the Messiah to move humanity away from Satan towards God and God has given the Messiah the authority to forgive sins. To this effect in 1970 Moon stated:

People have inherited Satanic blood and have become substantial beings who have nothing to do with God's blood lineage. We are completely opposite to the realm of God's love, and this must be indemnified. Man's original sin must be removed; the blood lineage from original sin must be removed; the blood lineage from Satan must be changed. But fallen people cannot do it by themselves; therefore the messiah is necessary.[20]

At the Blessing, therefore, original sin is removed. The blessed couples become God's sons and daughters. After the Blessing,

Unificationists live in God's realm and receive God's inheritance. Moon terms the spouse of a Unificationist their 'second messiah' and their children their 'third messiah', as through them they will be connected to God's original ideal.

13 The reappearance of the second coming

Since the Declaration, the reason for the messianic secret has become more apparent, and allows us to conclude that until this time Moon had apparently been building the foundation upon which to make the declaration. In January 1993 Moon delivered a speech to Unificationists in America entitled 'The Reappearance of the Second Coming and the Completed Testament Era'.[21] The speech was said to mark a culminating point in Moon's global ministry. The significance of the title of the *reappearance* of the second coming is that this second coming is not the first second coming. The Unification Church teaches that the Second Advent of the Messiah actually took place at the end of the Second World War, but the world was not ready to accept him so his declaration had to be delayed and a new foundation prepared.

Jesus is now placed on the same level as the Buddha, Confucius and Muhammad, as a prophet. Sun Myung Moon, as the Lord of the Second Advent, is the true Messiah. Moon notes that, 'We can be in a better position than Jesus in this respect.' Similarly, he urges, 'If I love God representing the whole, and if I myself become one whom God can present to the whole world and be proud of without shame, then I would become a person who is better than Jesus himself.'[22] The Unification Church assumes that Moon is now accepted all over the world and by extension that God is being accepted all over the world; subsequently that unification is near. 'We are on the way to the unified world. We tend to think that we must keep working like this for another hundred years. No, the unified world is quite within our vision now, it is very near, much nearer than we think.'[23] Unificationism teaches that the most important thing now is to: 'Pay no attention to anything else; just hold on to Reverend Moon.'[24] The secrecy that Unificationists have, until now, been only too willing to uphold, must be deleted. Now, they have been informed that God wants them to proclaim who they are: 'we should be as David proclaiming his name before Goliath.'[25] The Lord of the Second Advent will not only come as the central figure for Christianity, but will also play the role of the Buddha whom Buddhists believe will come again; the 'True Man' awaited by Confucianists; Chung Do Ryung, whom many Koreans await; and any other central figure of all other religions.

14 The role of the Unification Church as a Christian church

At the fortieth anniversary of the Unification Church in 1994, Moon made a statement that clearly outlined the role of the Unification Church. He said,

> Now, at this fortieth anniversary milestone, the Unification Church has completed the course of separation from Satan. We are entering the new era when, in a realm of brightness, we can attend and experience the reality of God freely. The Unification Church has received the protection of the Heavenly will, following the tradition set up by the True Parents. It will realize the righteous way of true love that invests for the sake of others, and accomplish the purpose of God's creation on the earth.[26]

The importance of the Unification Movement is clear from this extract, and it is in his speech on the reappearance of the second coming, that Moon unveils his belief in the *exclusivity* of the Unification Church and actually states that only Unification Church members will be saved whilst all those outside the movement are satanic: 'but we Unificationists are the only ones going to heaven. All of Satan's side is going to the other direction, to hell.' Moon continues, 'The world will decline and perish, but Reverend Moon and the Unification Church will not. We will stay and prosper by doing God's will.' It is implied that even Christianity, at least the form in which we know it, is not the way to salvation but must be, and is being, absorbed into Unificationism. Moon was quoted in *Time* magazine as urging, 'God is now throwing Christianity away and is establishing a new religion, and this new religion is Unificationism.'[27] Similarly, 'The Christians are the ones who hate us most; they hate us because Satan is in them.'[28] Christianity is also perceived as a stepping-stone: 'But this Christianity isn't the Kingdom of God. Christianity is just the midway position. It must be decided whether Christianity belongs to God or Satan.'[29] It is open to question whether Christianity is necessary to Unificationism. Unificationists do not really need to know Jesus; not all Unificationists enter from the Christian tradition; to acknowledge Moon's position as Messiah is the only requirement for salvation through Unificationism. It is difficult to decide whether Unificationism is a new Christian interpretation of the scriptures, or post-Christian. Moon notes, 'Until our mission with the Christian Church is over, we must quote the Bible and use it to explain the Divine Principle. After we receive the inheritance of the Christian we will be free to teach without the Bible.' Similarly,

> The Divine Principle . . . is truth in its fullest meaning, but not the Bible word for word. The Divine Principle clearly shows how the Bible is symbolic and how it is parabolic . . . The Bible is based upon the truth. The Divine Principle gives the true meaning of the secret behind the verse.[30]

Unificationism stresses that the contradictions within the Bible are clarified by *Divine Principle*. If we are now, as Unificationism professes, in the Last Days, *Divine Principle* and Unificationism as a whole represents the Completed Testament Age. In this sense, the apparent contradictions between Unificationism and Christianity are in fact *clarifications*. *Divine Principle* is exposed as the most true, fullest and most recent interpretation of Christianity as it has been developed and finally revealed by God. All that needs to be realized, says Unificationism, is that the revelation of the Unification Church is the new and final interpretation of Christianity.

Unificationism is clearly exclusivist. It *is* taught within the church that everyone will be saved, but this is not because the church is universalist. It is because it believes that eventually everyone will choose to join the Unification Movement; even Satan will not be able to help but join. I term this 'exclusive universalism'.

15 Recent changes

With the evolution of the Unification Movement over the last two decades, and more specifically the last couple of years, there has been a definite change in doctrinal emphasis, towards conservatism, although this is not uniformly the case. At a conference[31] in November 1993, Mark Brann, the former British leader of the movement, made no reference to Moon as Messiah, referring instead to each individual person as being a messiah, or at least as having the potential to aspire to this. Similarly, he noted that there is not to be only one set of True Parents, but that all couples should work at being True Parents.

Professor Eileen Barker has recently spoken of the natural changes faced by New Religious Movements when they cease to be 'new'.[32] She argued that the beliefs and practices of movements and their relationship to society have been modified over the last two decades. This is certainly true of the Unification Church. The movement is also displaying signs of internal tension, a phenomenon common to New Religious Movements. Moon, at the head of the movement, is making the clear claim that he is the Lord of the Second Advent; the Messiah. Yet, at the same time, British (and perhaps other) leaders are reinterpreting Moon's declaration to conclude that the whole of humanity is in the messianic position, not solely Moon. It would appear that there is disagreement between Moon's own theology and what appears sensible to some of the intellectuals below him. It is very likely that there is disagreement between the Korean and the Western leaders of the movement, with the Korean leaders emphasizing Moon's messiahship and the Western leaders displaying a reserve typical of their culture. It is possible that those who dilute Moon's claims of messiahship feel a certain amount of embarrassment and are unable to accept themselves that an elderly Korean man is the second coming of the Messiah. Or, perhaps, in our age of science and technology the idea of *any* literal second coming is difficult to accept and profess. It could, however, be that those who dilute the significance of Moon's position as Messiah are merely doing so in order for the theology to appear more palatable to those under their instruction; and specifically to those outside the Unification Movement.

It would certainly appear that the Unification Church is

working to become accepted as an ordinary movement within Christianity and not as the radical anti-Christian cult it once appeared. Barker argues that the Unification Church has moved from the millennial expectation of 1967 to a more utopian outlook where the Messiah must be followed, and finally now to a reformist outlook where members are more important. Yet this evolution of beliefs and practices is not catered for in *Divine Principle*. It is as if the movement is abandoning its original beliefs to conform to contemporary social expectations, and perhaps to prepare for the death of Moon. There is the possibility that this will result in the collapse of the original Unification Church and the principles for which it has always stood.

16 The possible results of Moon's death

Regarding Moon's death Salonen, a Unificationist, states,

> What will happen will depend on the nature of his death and the internal state of the church at the time. But the basic teaching will not change. It is realized within the church that Reverend Moon is important for his guidance and insight, but after his death God will continue his work through a different channel.[33]

Salonen's comment may seem surprising in that it suggests the death of Moon will not greatly impede the future and expansion of the Unification Church. If Moon is viewed as the Messiah it may be assumed initially that his death will pose a great problem. However, it is important to remember that in the Unification Church death is viewed as a natural progression from life and not as a great disaster or loss. There is believed to be interaction between the physical world and the spirit world, and in the latter the dead person remains active and dynamic. It could be argued, therefore, that Moon's work will continue in the spirit realm. A Unificationist from London once suggested that when Moon dies he will be followed by a new messiah. If this new messiah dies with the work incomplete another will follow, and so on until the whole of humanity has been grafted into the Perfect Family and God's kingdom of heaven on earth is established. It has also been suggested that Moon's eldest son will take over the leadership of the Unification Church if Moon dies before he has established

God's kingdom of heaven on earth. It might also be that the Korean members will fight for power and that this will result in the division of the Unification Church into factions. Another Unificationist has suggested that Hak Ja Han will be in contact with her husband in the spirit world and will lead the Unification Church on behalf of them both on earth. The latter possibility, that of Hak Ja Han taking over the leadership, makes the most sense both theologically and practically since Hak Ja Han holds one half of the messiahship. Yet, however much the importance of Hak Ja Han is emphasized and however sensible her taking over the leadership seems, it is very unlikely that it will actually happen. It is very unlikely that the male leaders of the movement will allow a woman to have control over them. In my own opinion, the most likely result upon the death of Moon will be that the Korean male leaders will fight for power.

Unificationism emphasizes that this time is unique because *Divine Principle* has been disclosed. Moon has stated, 'This period of providence comes *only once in history* [my italics], no more. There will be no other time you can receive directions directly from your master, and work with his heart.'[34] Views such as these give the feeling that Moon is not dispensable, and suggest that the Unification Church is able to exist in only one form and at only one time and that is with Sun Myung Moon as the leader. Upon further reflection, however, it could be the case that Moon's mission *is* complete and that he has been a great success. Moon has done what God required of him and in that sense it would not matter if he died. It is now up to the Unification Church in general to continue to engraft the remainder of humanity into the Unification Movement, and our task to join. Moon came, appeared as the Messiah, and was accepted by those who became his followers. Even though he will die before the whole world is Unificationist, he will have succeeded in that he has established the Unification Church, and has paved the way for its expansion and the subsequent unification of the world. The Unification Church will remain the only true way to salvation and salvation will always continue on this level within the boundaries of the Unification Church. Non-Unificationists may well argue that, if Moon dies before the whole world has been engrafted into his Perfect Family, his mission has been a failure, in the same way that Unificationism views Jesus' mission as a failure. However, if

Jesus had married and established a Perfect Family and *then* died, he would probably have retained his messianic position. If Moon dies a natural death, his death will not constitute a failure. He will have completed his task in being the Messiah in that he has provided humanity with its True Parents and begun the chain of the Perfect Family. Moon has been successful in a way that Jesus was not; he has restored the divine lineage into his own family. He has also extended this divine family through engrafting people onto himself and Hak Ja Han, thus establishing the kingdom of heaven.

17 Resurrection-death and eternal life

Unificationism has a unique view of 'heavenly life' and one that has few roots in Christianity. Its interpretations are dependent upon the existence of a 'spirit realm' that mirrors the physical world. Kim[35] writes, 'By the principle of polarity, the counterpart of the physical world must exist.' The physical world was created for humanity's physical body, so a spirit world was created for its spirit body.

In the same manner that the physical body is said by Unificationism to develop through the three stages of formation, growth and completion, the spirit-person also develops in parallel stages. A spirit-person in the formation stage is still imperfect and is known as a 'form-spirit'. A spirit-person in the growth stage is more developed 'and shine[s] with reflective light',[36] and is known as a 'life spirit'. A spirit-person in the perfection stage is the most advanced and is known as a 'divine-spirit'. A divine-spirit is a person of perfected heart; at one with God. A person becomes a divine-spirit when she or he accepts the Messiah at the second coming. A divine-spirit dwells in heaven, either on earth or in the spirit world. Spirits who have not even reached the form-spirit stage dwell in hell; hell is not a place distinct from earth in Unification thought, rather earth as it is now. Form-spirits dwell in the formation stage of the spirit world and life-spirits dwell in paradise, the place preceding heaven.

It is taught that people are only able to perfect themselves and be resurrected whilst alive on earth in a physical body. If a person dies before achieving this perfection she or he must return to earth to fulfil the responsibility that was left unfulfilled. This is achieved through the spirit-person working through other peoples' physical bodies. When a person on earth lives according to God's will and establishes a foundation suitable for spiritual communication, an inadequately developed spirit-person will return to earth and begin give and take with the spirit-self of the physical person. Unificationism explains, 'the physical self of the person on earth becomes the physical self for the returning spirit person as well. In this sense, the person on earth becomes the "second coming" of the returning spirit person.'[37] Similarly, life-spirit-level spirit persons who are in paradise must return to earth and co-operate (establish give and take) with faithful persons on earth.

Holding no belief in physical resurrection, Unificationism denies that the dead will be physically resurrected upon death or at a particular point in the future. Resurrection within Unification thought is the *passing from spiritual death to spiritual life*; it is eliminating spiritual death, turning to God and gaining life through him. Even if a person is physically alive, if she or he is under Satan's control, she or he is dead. Resurrection, therefore, does not refer to physical life and death, but to the life and death of a person's spirit-self.

The spirit-self was created to live for eternity, so upon the death of the physical body the spirit-self separates from it and lives eternally in the spirit world; the physical body disintegrates into the earth. Unificationism argues that when Adam and Eve 'died' at the Fall, it was the death of their spirit-selves, rendering them incapable of communicating with God; clearly they continued to live physically. Unificationism turns to the situation in the Garden of Eden to discover the true interpretation of resurrection. God, it argues, warned Adam and Eve that they would die if they ate the forbidden fruit. Once they had eaten it they did not die *physically*, so, says Unificationism their death must have been a *spiritual* one. Death is not physical; God had always intended human beings to age and die physically. Adam and Eve and their descendants were not to be immortal in their original physical forms. They always had the ability to live eternally *spiritually* so their death would be spiritual if they were unable to sustain a give and take relationship with God. Resurrection is the restoration of humanity from the dominion of Satan to God's dominion. Humanity is dead as it has derived from Adam and Eve's satanic lineage; when it is restored to God it will be alive. According to Unification thought, there is no outward change in a person once she or he has been resurrected; the transformation is purely spiritual. Resurrection, according to the Unification Church, will not happen physically when Christ returns; it is an ongoing process as a part of God's dispensation for restoration.[38]

18 Conclusion

For the Unification Church the deliverer is here! The potential for change, for the transformation of humanity, for the establishment of the kingdom, came when Moon was chosen by God as the Messiah. Moon, as the Lord of the Second Advent, the Messiah, comes to reverse the Fall. Adam and Eve were to fulfil the three blessings, they were to establish God's kingdom of heaven on earth. Their Fall resulted in the destruction of the family unit and the creation of original sin. Jesus was not able to fulfil the role of Second Adam as he was crucified before he could marry his Second Eve. Moon is the Third Adam and his wife is the Third Eve. The kingdom began when Moon and Hak Ja Han married in 1960.[39] They come to restore God's ideal of creation; they come to establish a Perfect Family, thus inaugurating God's kingdom of heaven on earth.

Complete resurrection, according to Unificationism, should have taken place in Jesus' time if he had been accepted as the Messiah. Now, complete resurrection may only take place at the second coming, and the ultimate catalyst for the resurrection of the whole of humanity is the Lord of the Second Advent. The present age is termed the Dispensational Age of Completion Stage Resurrection at the Completed Testament Age and will fulfil the Old Testament and New Testament ages. Unificationism claims that our age is one of increasing spiritual activity that verifies that the Messiah has undertaken his mission; people are apparently receiving revelations concerning the second coming and preparing the way for the new Messiah, who is on earth at present.

Notes

[1] I am grateful to Professor Paul Badham, Dr Gavin Flood and Ray Carew for their comments.

[2] HSAUWC, *Unification Theological Affirmations* (1976).

[3] I use a masculine pronoun even though the Messiah is a couple, male and female, as the Unification Church always speaks of the messiahship in masculine terms.

[4] *Divine Principle* (HSAUWC, 1973), 31–46.

[5] Matthew 26:39; Mark 14:36; Luke 22:42.

[6] G. D. Chryssides, *The Advent of Sun Myung Moon* (Basingstoke, Macmillan, 1991), 124.

[7] W. Bergman, 'The Mission of Jesus', in D. Bryant (ed.), *Proceedings of the Virgin Islands Seminar on Unification Theology* (The Rose of Sharon Press, Inc., New York, 1980), 99.

[8] A. Wells, 'Unification Christology', in F. K. Flinn (ed.), *Christology* (Paragon House Publishers, New York, 1989), 51.

[9] *Divine Principle*, 516ff.

[10] Examples are the Inter-Religious Federation for World Peace, the Professors World Peace Academy and, most recently, the Women's Federation for World Peace.

[11] Quoted in R. Quebedeaux and R. Sawatsky (eds.), *Evangelical-Unification Dialogue* (Barrytown, New York, The Unification Theological Seminary, 1979), 125.

[12] Cited ibid., 85.

[13] M. Durst, *To Bigotry, No Sanction* (Chicago, Regery Gateway, Inc., 1984), 163.

[14] S. M. Moon, 'Becoming the Leaders in Building a World of Peace' (speech given on 24 August 1992, at the Little Angels Performing Arts Center, Seoul, Korea), 5.

[15] S. M. Moon, 'The Crossing Point of Good and Evil', speech delivered in Korea (16 July 1972).

[16] Ibid., 53, 58.

[17] *Unification News* (February 1993), 2ff.

[18] The target number of couples to be blessed in this last ceremony was 360,000. When I spoke with a leading Unificationist in March 1996 he explained to me that Moon had continued to bless couples throughout the months following the main Blessing, and that the target had only just been reached.

[19] C. H. Kwak, 'The Blessing' (speech, October 1978), 14, quoted in B. Colford, 'Practical Responses to Evil: A Unification Perspective' (speech given at the Inter-Religious Federation for World Peace, Seoul, Korea, 28 April–2 May 1994), 6.

[20] S. M. Moon, 'Change of Blood Lineage: The Real Experience of

Salvation by the Messiah', in *God's Will and the World* (New York, HSAUWC, 1985), 39, quoted in Colford, op. cit., 6.

21 S. M. Moon, 'The Reappearance of the Second Advent'. Speech given in Belvedere International Training Center, New York (10 January 1993).

22 S. M. Moon, 'The Crossing Point of Good and Evil'. Speech delivered in Korea (16 July 1972).

23 S. M. Moon, 'Reappearance of the Second Advent', 57.

24 S. K. Han, in J. Allan, *The Rising of the Moon* (Leicester, Inter-Varsity Press, 1980), 45.

25 Ibid., 53.

26 S. M., Moon, 'The Movement that Can Receive the Benefit of Heavenly Fortune', speech given at the HSAUWC 40th Anniversary Banquet, Seoul, Korea (1 May 1994).

27 (30 September 1974), 68, quoted in J. Bjornstad, *The Moon is Not the Son* (Minneapolis, Bethany Fellowship, 1976), 71.

28 From a speech by Paul Rose MP, House of Commons, 23 February 1977 (HMSO), quoted in Allan, op. cit., 33.

29 Sudo, 'Foundation for the Messiah', *120 Day Training Manual*, 61, quoted in I. Yamamoto, *The Puppet Master* (Chicago, Inter-Varsity Press, 1977), 56.

30 Master Speaks, March and April 1965, MS-7, p.1, quoted in Bjornstad, *The Moon is not the Son*, 114.

31 Women's Federation for World Peace (WFWP).

32 INFORM (Information Network Focus on Religious Movements), December 1993. Also lecture at the University of Wales, Lampeter, January 1995.

33 Y. O. Kim, *Unification Theology* (New York, HSAUWC, 1980), 264.

34 Master Speaks, 1971b:10, quoted in D. G. Bromley and A. D. Shupe, Jr., *'Moonies' in America* (Beverly Hills, Sage Publications, 1979), 100.

35 *Unification Theology and Christian Thought* (New York, Golden Gate Publishing, 1976), 33.

36 Ibid., 34.

37 Ibid., 121.

38 Ibid., 109.

39 There is a problem here in trying to reconcile the idea that Moon and Hak Ja Han fulfil the role of the Messiah with Moon's statement that the declaration of the messiahship should have been made at the end of the Second World War. This discrepancy leads me to conclude that the nature of the messiahship as both masculine and feminine is a recent addition to the theology.

Further reading

Allan, J., *The Rising of the Moon* (Leicester, Inter-Varsity Press, 1980).

Bjornstad, J., *The Moon is Not the Son* (Minneapolis, Bethany Fellowship, 1976).

Bromley, D. G. and Shupe, A. D. Jr., *'Moonies' in America* (Beverly Hills, Sage Publications, 1979).

Bryant, D. (ed.), *Proceedings of the Virgin Island Seminar on Unification Theology* (New York, The Rose of Sharon Press, Inc., 1980).

Chryssides, G. D., *The Advent of Sun Myung Moon* (Basingstoke, Macmillan, 1991).

Colford, B., 'Practical Responses to Evil: A Unification Perspective', speech given at the Inter-Religious Federation for World Peace, Seoul, Korea, 28 April–2 May 1994.

Durst, M., *To Bigotry, No Sanction* (Chicago, Regery Gateway, Inc., 1984).

Flinn, F. K. (ed.), *Christology* (New York, Paragon House Publishers, 1989).

HSAUWC, *Unification Theological Affirmations* (London, 1976).

——, *Divine Principle* (Surrey, 1973).

——, *Unification News* (New York, February 1993).

Kim, Y. O., *Unification Theology* (New York, HSAUWC, 1980).

——, *Unification Theology and Christian Thought* (New York, Golden Gate Publishing, 1976).

Moon, S. M., 'Becoming the Leaders in Building a World of Peace', speech given on 24 August 1992, at the Little Angels Performing Arts Center, Seoul, Korea.

——, 'Proclamation of the Messiah', speech given in New York, January 1993.

——, 'The Movement that Can Receive the Benefit of Heavenly Fortune', speech given at the HSAUWC 40th Anniversary Banquet, Seoul, Korea, 1 May 1994.

Quebedeaux, R., and Sawatsky, R. (eds.), *Evangelical-Unification Dialogue* (Barrytown, NY, The Unification Theological Seminary, 1979).

Yamamoto, I., *The Puppet Master* (Chicago, Inter-Varsity Press, 1977).

10

Old ideas in new forms: millennial movements in the Republic of Turkey

DAVID SHANKLAND

1 Introduction

Let us say that a traveller to Turkey arrives for the first time at Atatürk Airport, situated just outside Istanbul on the European side. Taking the coast road, they will first see the outskirts of a shanty town: a collection of rather bedraggled but brightly painted low concrete apartment blocks amidst scattered hastily built huts. Then, as the road curves to the left along the coast proper, they will see a brand-new Turkish Printemps department store complete with air-conditioning and the latest fashions. Passing through the old Byzantine gate and the newly restored city walls, they leave a ramshackle fishermen's co-operative on the edge of the Bosphorus to their right, pass modern apartment blocks and offices, then, finally, they arrive at Pera, the heart of old Istanbul, a city resounding with the filth, tradition and pulse of two thousand years and the sure knowledge of being the economic and social heart of modern Turkey.

The visitor may conclude, rightly, that much of the old has remained to mix with the new, in often entrancing ways. In fact, to leave intact so much of the old was not the aim of the original founders of the Turkish Republic. They sought Turkey's development, but they aimed also to turn Turkey into a modern nation-state modelled closely on those of Western Europe of that time, and to rid themselves of much of the remnants of the Ottoman Empire. Further, they believed in egalitarian universal progress: unostentatious, industrious, honest and peaceful, the whole administered by a powerful state. A key factor within this programme was secularism: the desire to remove religion from public and political life, to make belief a matter of purely individual conscience. This recent past, so full of dramatic reforms, means that Turkey today raises fascinating questions for the student of religion in the modern world, questions to do with the place of Islam in modern secular democracies, the possibility of successful deliberate social engineering and, not least, wonderment at the sheer scale of the changes to the social and legal fabric of the country. It is worth looking at these bold, perhaps uniquely long-lived, social changes a little more closely.

Before we do so it is perhaps worthwhile to outline the main arguments of this chapter: in spite of the drastic modernization programme of the Kemalists, they did not manage to alter substantially much of the basic cosmology of the Turkish people; the great mass of the Turkish population are Muslim, and they remain so in spite of the weight of social change. One of the most interesting questions which stems from this conclusion is, in what ways has their traditional belief been able to adapt, survive and redevelop itself to cope with the threat of the new? The idea of the 'coming deliverer', the defining characteristic of a millennial movement, is a particularly interesting way of looking at this question because it plays an important but muted part in Islam as a whole. One might expect that, given such a comparatively minor role and the dubious reception that millennial claims are often given by theological leaders, they would have a successively less important role as the Faith is reformulated in response to modernism.[1] Curiously enough, this is not the case: though they often assume a slightly unexpected aspect, millennial movements are alive and well in Turkey.

2 The foundation of the Republic

Atatürk, the first president of Modern Turkey, during fifteen tumultuous years between the foundation of the Republic in 1923 and his death in 1937 was faced with the task of rebuilding a country shattered by the loss of an empire, capitulation and occupation by the Allies at the end of the First World War. He first defended Anatolia against its enemies, in the process defeating an invading Greek army. Then, with a group of supporters, he introduced a series of laws which one by one dismantled the laws, mores and pomp of the Ottoman state and replaced them with a republic. The capital of the country was moved from Istanbul to Ankara. Sovereignty was transferred from the Sultan, who had ruled over Istanbul for eight generations, and vested in the Grand National Assembly at Ankara. Islamic (*Şeriat*) laws were replaced with new laws compiled from the Swiss civil, the Italian commercial and the German criminal codes. Islamic brotherhoods (*tarikats*) were banned. The old education establishments (*medrese*) were replaced with secular schools. The Arabic alphabet, in which Turkish had been written up until that time, was replaced with a slightly modified Latin version, and foreign words, particularly those deriving from Arabic and Persian, systematically purged from the daily language. Women were given the vote, and encouraged to enter the civil service and other professions on an equal basis with men, and it was forbidden to discriminate against people on the basis of their religion.[2]

The victors of any revolution are dogged by the unpleasant fact that social life is so extraordinarily complex that it is very difficult to predict the long-term effect of any particular measure. This is as true for religious reforms as any other. In Turkey today, whilst the original framework of the secular laws is still in place, evidence of a reconfirmation and recreation of Turkey's Islamic past is all around: mosques are being constructed apace, often modelled on the Ottoman, imperial style with dome and minaret. There are increasing numbers of women wearing the veil, bearded men sombrely looking out from their place on the mosque steps carefully examine the passing tourists, whilst bookshops selling canonical literature and Islamic newspapers are doing a brisk trade. Islamic brotherhoods, whilst never quite ceasing their activities entirely, are playing an increasingly prominent part in public life. These developments are most obvious during the month of Ramadan, when the mosques light up their minarets with signs celebrating the auspicious days of the fast, shops close their doors for trade during the day, and the television channels devote much of their air-time to religious programmes.[3]

Even the state has not been independent of this resurgence in religion. The years since the first democratic elections, held in 1950, have seen a succession of official concessions to the practice of Islam. Indeed, whilst it could once be said that the state was the upholder of the secular basis of the Republic, now it can truly be asserted that it upholds both secularism *and* Islam: through a central directorate attached to the prime ministry, it co-ordinates the number of visas and the pilgrimage to Mecca, the *hac*, it runs a special vocational (*imam-hatip*) school in every sub-province, in which a substantial part of the curriculum is devoted to Islamic teachings, it employs civil servants to act as prayer leaders (*imam*) sufficient for a mosque in almost every village, it checks and certifies that mosques face toward Mecca, and publishes an enormous amount of eschatological literature.

The vibrancy of the Islamic brotherhoods, discussion groups for religious affairs, the television programmes and channels devoted to Islam, mean that any analysis of an Islamic movement has a great number of possible variants to choose from: simply put, Turkey is full of debates about Islam. One of the most dominant and most successful, however, is a particular constellation of ideas put forward by Mr Necmettin Erbakan. Erbakan is the leader of the only large political party whose doctrines are specifically founded on religious principles. Interestingly enough, his religio-political philosophy is also distinctly millennial in character.

3 Why is Erbakan important?

Religion has a curious, anomalous position in Republican Turkey's political life. The mass of Turkey's people so clearly wish the government to support religion that no party has been able to win a majority without making it quite explicit that they are sympathetic to its practice. However, as none of the main parties have had the inclination to move outside the broad framework of citizenship created by Atatürk, they have always claimed to be secular and *also* supported religion – not, it should be pointed out, the return of Islamic law, but almost every other aspect of its belief and practice. This willingness to compromise greatly explains why the religious revival has occurred within the secular laws of the Republic rather than breaking them asunder.

Outside this mainstream compromise, however, there have always been small parties which have been more openly, explicitly in favour of Islam, and Erbakan has long been the most successful of these Islamic political leaders. Whilst sometimes the small parties have been closed down by the constitutional court,

Erbakan has avoided this fate partly because he is more wily, and partly because he seemed unable ever to gather more than 10 per cent of the total votes cast by the electorate. Indeed, citing this statistic, for decades intellectuals dismissed the possibility of a serious Islamic political threat. Recently, this attitude has appeared insufferably complacent. The Welfare Party, headed by Erbakan, has been going from triumph to triumph: winning Ankara and Istanbul municipalities in the local elections of 1993, and then, in the general elections held on 24 December 1995, taking control of most of the provinces in Anatolia, providing them with the largest number of representatives in the Grand National Assembly. They did not actually come to power, because other parties combined together to prevent them from doing so.[4] The fact remains, however, that they came close to forming a government, and the chances are that at the next general election they will have an even more forceful attempt at doing so. Erbakan, and his political philosophy, are thus very important indeed.

4 Erbakan's philosophy

In Turkey, the pronouncements of political leaders are given great importance: the television evening news often consists largely of extracts from the leaders' speeches of that day, their press conferences are widely reported, and at election times the leaders move around the country in convoys, holding huge rallies in provincial centres. Erbakan is a master of the simple language with which politicians appeal to the mass of the people on these occasions, using colloquialisms, sharp witty comments about the other leaders, frequent recourse to Islamic rhetoric and straightforward, firm assertions about what must be done.

Being so down to earth, even homely, in his conversation, Erbakan is sometimes laughed at by other politicians for being simplistic, out of touch with the complexities of the modern world and old-fashioned. However, Erbakan's popular style is in some ways an advantage. It means that his ideology comes across sharply, clearly defined with none of the compromises, twists and turns which characterize debate in more intimate circumstances. Further, given his recent success, he is demonstrably not out of touch with the mass of the Turkish people, and can now claim quite legitimately that the boot is on the other foot.

In his speeches, Erbakan accuses Turkey's leaders, quite bluntly, of being frauds and crooks, and asserts that Turkey is in a position of servitude *vis-à-vis* the rest of the world, a world which is run by Zionists. He accuses all Turkey's parties, whether of the right or the left, of being party to this situation. By 'servitude' he does not mean physical control, but rather that the level to which Turkey has become indebted to the World Bank means that it has in effect lost its independence. He also asserts that the World Bank is controlled by a group of Zionists in New York: they, therefore, and Israel, whom he claims has declared its intention to make Turkey one of its provinces, are the winners. The losers, he claims, are the workers, who have to slave to meet the interest payments on the massive national debts. This, when it is added to income tax, social, and health insurance that they also have to pay means that they receive the benefit of only one-sixteenth of their true wages.

Erbakan calls for great, fundamental upheaval with the aim of replacing the existing regime with his alternative programme. First, he appeals to nationalism, saying that for two centuries, and especially since the Second World War, Turkey has been seduced by the West, whereas previously, during the time of the Ottoman Empire, it lit up the world with its achievements. He refers this shift in orientation as a return to a 'national viewpoint': *milli görüs*. Further, he claims that the Welfare Party will impose a new scheme of things: the *adil düzen*, the just order.

In a booklet published by the Welfare Party in Ankara, Erbakan states that his 'just order' will necessitate the introduction of a number of measures which he says 'combine the best aspects of the capitalist and the socialist systems'. These include substituting a production tax for income tax, instituting state control of investment and manufacturing and, a point to which Erbakan refers again and again, that there will be an absolute ban on interest. He accuses the international financial institutions of handing out money without ascertaining first of all whether it is linked with the productive capability of the country or the project concerned, or whether they will be able to pay the interest, thus causing a fatal disjunction between production and capital. Instead of interest, therefore, he intends to allow credit only to projects whose capacity for success has been carefully examined, and to permit the money lent to be recouped through sharing the profits which ensue. Erbakan concludes by saying that when these measures are implemented, they will allow Turkey to overtake the level of development in the West. This is at the heart of his exhortations: Turkey is undeveloped, deprived of the fruits of modernization by a corrupt order. Imposition of a new system, above all the banning of interest, will allow Turkey to make up the lost ground, and even overtake Europe's industrial level in five years.[5]

5 Millennial ideas

The term 'millennial', as perhaps is true of any term which is used widely across different fields of learning, can be interpreted to mean many different things. Within the social sciences, and particularly within social anthropology, it has been used to describe a particular phenomenon within unindustrialized communities to indicate the expectation of the sudden coming of a period of plenty, a belief that, after a particular happening or occurrence, all their problems will vanish. The instantaneous, magical cure-for-all element in Erbakan's philosophy, appealing to those who have fared worst in Turkey's industrialization, or partial industrialization, is exactly pertinent to this usage: Erbakan offering affluence greater than that of the most successful countries of Western Europe, even Germany, in return for believing in his vision. All that his followers must do is to follow him, and riches will be theirs in this, not the next world. Thus, in effect, the millennial movement is employing wishful thinking combined with religious belief to cut short what is the technical, and highly complicated, process of modernization.[6]

Within Islam, 'millennial' movements are usually given a more conventional designation, one which does not have any specific connotations of modernization or development. They are taken to be that part of a movement or ideology which refers to the coming of a saviour who will rescue his followers from the evils of the age, whatever age, and provide them with a golden period of comfort. Often, this person is held to be a religious leader, *imam*, who has departed or vanished, but who will ultimately return. This returning, or 'occluded', *imam* is known as *mehdi*. Sometimes, his coming has overtones also of Armageddon, the final days of human existence when the sinners and the faithful will be judged, but it may also mean, more prosaically, the return of the lamented lost leader to rescue his flock from their time of difficulty.[7]

Just how much sanctity may be vested in a leader is one of the main differences between the Shi'ite and the Sunni community of believers within the Islamic world. Sunni tenets tend to hold that the will of the community to choose their leader is more important than their line of descent. Shi'ite communities, however, privilege sanctity through inheritance much more. This difference goes back to a schism very early on within the history of Islam and is now a key factor in separating the Shi'ite and Sunni forms of the faith. The Shi'ite population revere in particular the line of descent of religious leaders emanating from Ali, the Prophet's son-in-law, and different Shi'i populations may have as their particular religious patron the fifth, sixth, seventh or twelfth *imam* in the original line descended from Ali.[8]

In Turkey today, whilst most of the population is Sunni, there is also a significant Shi'ite minority. Whilst the mutual exchanges of peoples with Greece after the First World War led Turkey to become almost entirely Muslim, it still did not create a homogenous population. Today, broadly about 15 per cent of the population is Kurdish, and 85 per cent Turkish. The population is also split between Alevi and Sunni. Sunni are the orthodox majority, the Alevi are Shi'ites, though of a particular mystical bent, and consist of perhaps 20 per cent of Turkey's population. The religious crosses the ethnic divide, making a fourfold basic categorization of the people within modern Turkey: Alevi Turk, Alevi Kurd, Sunni Turk and Sunni Kurd. There is a significant indigenous minority, the *Laz* on the Black Sea coast, and many much smaller immigrant groups such as the Circassians (*Cerkez*) from Russia, but it is not misleading for our purposes to visualize Turkey as consisting broadly of these main groups, as long as it is remembered that this is a simplified statement of a more complicated reality.[9]

6 Alevi and Sunni

The Alevi doctrines differ substantially from those of their fellow Sunni believers. For most Sunni people, the minimum requirements to be a good Muslim are primarily to fulfil the 'five pillars' of the faith: to believe in the one God, to pray five times a day, to go to the pilgrimage to Mecca, to pay alms and to fast. They maintain also that the Qur'an is the word of God, revealed to the world through Muhammad, infallible and immutable. In addition, they usually hold that it is auspicious to pray in a mosque where possible, and maintain the importance of good moral behaviour, associated in Turkish with the word *ahlak*. The Alevi, in contrast, believe that it is more auspicious to pray in a group, face to face, with both men and women together, than to pray in a mosque and that the Qur'an can be expressed through esoteric songs and laments sung by a minstrel at these collective prayer ceremonies. They also take a much more flexible approach to the 'five pillars' than the Sunni, believing that neither the fast nor alms, nor the pilgrimage, are essential to achieve religious fulfilment. Doctrinally, the Alevi are known as a *Ghulat* sect,[10] and are sometimes vilified for their extremely flexible approach to the orthodox canons of the faith by the Sunni people. In brief, however, it is fair to say that what makes the Alevi extreme is their enormous emphasis on the esoteric importance of religious satisfaction at the expense of the more normal, exoteric requirements of the Islamic faith.

A further, and crucial, difference between the Alevi and the Sunni is that the Alevi associate their heritage with the Shi'ite canon. According to a sacred text which many communities use, the *Buyruk*, 'decree', the way to practice the Alevi form of the faith was revealed to the Alevi by Ali. He passed his knowledge down to his children, Hasan and Hūseyin, but they were betrayed, resulting in Hūseyin's massacre at the Kerbala. Within Alevi villages, collective rituals, in which these traditions are celebrated, are led by hereditary leaders who themselves may trace their position back to Ali. These holy leaders are regarded as qualitatively different from the rest of the Alevi population by virtue of being possessors of *keramet*, a favour from God bestowed upon them in their ability to perform miracles.[11]

In traditional Alevi society, then, there are hereditary holy figures to whom responsibility for the spiritual and ritual leadership of the community is given. Today, much is changing: migration to the cities is affecting the cohesion of their villages, the holy leaders are losing their influence, baffled perhaps by the complexity of change in the modern world which leaves them, as the oldest members of the community, out of touch, and the younger generation are often ignorant of the complexities of Alevi traditional mores.[12] The idea of a saviour of the community survives, however, though it is not a religious figure in whom they vest this accolade, but rather a repeated, though often muted idea, that Atatürk himself is their *mehdi*. Thus, by no means all, but certainly some Alevi take a religious idea, one inherent within their culture, and press it into service in a secular setting. What is the sociological explanation for this defining of one of the greatest secularizers of the modern world as a religious leader?

7 The Alevi and Atatürk

Until very recently, the Alevi have been a rural people, largely inhabiting a belt beginning at Ankara and moving down to the south-east of Turkey, thus occupying an area approximately between Iran, Syria and central Anatolia. The Ottoman state, based in Istanbul, was frequently at odds with the Shi'ite movement in Iran, and the Alevi were therefore caught in between: subjects of the Ottoman Empire, but nevertheless due to their religious sympathies being suspected of being unreliable. As the centuries passed, the difference between Sunni and Shi'i became ever more clearly defined, rendering the Alevi more obviously unorthodox, culminating in the seventeenth century in terrible massacres of their number by the Ottoman troops. Whilst there is as yet no reliable history of the Alevi movement, it appears that throughout the eighteenth and nineteenth centuries, animosity was less marked and the Alevi tribal communities in central Anatolia began to settle, still uneasy with central authority, unforgetting and unforgiving of their tragic past, and still running their own affairs as much as possible. Their position within Islam remained profoundly uneasy: so much so that they seriously questioned amongst themselves whether they are not in fact in many ways closer to Christianity than to Islam, quoting, for example, the fact that they have a trinity, Allah, Muhammad and Ali, just as the Christians have theirs.

When, after the demise of the Ottoman Empire, Atatürk emerged as a possible leader of the resistance movement against Allied occupation, he toured Anatolia looking for support for his cause. The Alevi claim that they were crucial to him at this delicate stage of his operation, passing him from village to village across the land and ensuring that he had sufficient support for his cause to be successful. Whilst this might be to some extent apocryphal, the period from the foundation of the Republic until the first elections is remembered by the Alevi as a particularly peaceful and happy stage in their history, when they were able to become members of the modern Turkish nation without fear of persecution.

This attribution of the period of Atatürk's rule as a golden age within the history of the Alevi provides a clue as to why they revere him so much. It is not just that he was a great war leader who provided them with protection against the Sunni pressure that they otherwise would have had to suffer. Rather, they found that the particular, inner-looking esoteric interpretation of Islam which they favour coincided largely with the Atatürk's conception of the relationship which should exist ideally between a person and their religion: one where the inner self may be satisfied by piety or worship, but where the outer rules of religious observance were not of paramount importance. To the Alevi, Atatürk therefore became a social and philosophical figure with whom they could identify as well as a statesman: truly an appropriate figure for them to apply their conception of the *mehdi*.

By way of illustration, these sentiments are summed up in the following song, 'The One Haci Bektash, the Other Atatürk', which I collected during fieldwork in Anatolia in 1990, composed by an Alevi minstrel for the hundredth anniversary of Atatürk's birth. I should explain that Haci Bektash is one of the most important saints of the Anatolian Alevi, supposed to have lived in the thirteenth century.[13] By comparing him to Atatürk, the minstrel is indicating the two most important influences in his life. Note also the penultimate line, where Atatürk (using his first name 'Mustapha') is directly compared to Ali: the emphasis is in the original, and the translation is mine.

> They who bring freedom to the Turkish people
> The one Haci Bektash, the other Atatürk
> They who made revolutions bringing forth freedom
> The one Haci Bektash, the other Atatürk

> The alphabet reforms, women's rights
> Enemies who used to share this earth
> Come together, hand in hand
> The one Haci Bektash, the other Atatürk
>
> Seven hundred years ago Bektash Veli
> The celebrated hundredth year of Atatürk
> The one Mustapha, *The Other Ali*
> The one Haci Bektash, the one Atatürk

8 Conclusion

In this chapter, we have looked chiefly at two communities, the Alevi Turks and the Sunni Turks, and examined the way in which they have mixed old ideas with new in their treatment of millennial ideas. Erbakan is the representative of one particular view: he does not claim to be a saint, nor do his followers, almost invariably Sunni, regard him as one. Rather he hopes to be the voice of an impoverished community, to fulfil their dreams of greater affluence by changing the existing order. Among Turkish Alevi, however, it is possible to find millennial movements which still emphasize the person rather than the movement, in this case Atatürk, the founder of the Turkish Republic. Each perspective is appropriate to the traditional philosophy of their respective sect. Ideas, it seems, particularly in the field of religion, never actually disappear entirely but re-emerge and mingle with the themes of later epochs.

In sum, the Turkish case helps us to understand how seemingly minor aspects of the religious and ideological past of a community can still shape their contemporary thoughts, even in their secular lives. Thus they can assist us to contextualize political movements within the important cultural and religious paradigms of that society, and may indeed shed interesting light on the long-running question of the way in which human beings create and conceive of their relationship with the spiritual and material world.

Notes

[1] Such has been the argument of E. Gellner over many years: cf. *Muslim Society* (Cambridge, Cambridge University Press, 1989).

2 The best account of the reforms is still B. Lewis, *The Emergence of Modern Turkey* (Oxford, Oxford University Press, 1962). See also Lord Kinross, *Ataturk: A Biography of Mustafa Kemal, Father of Modern Turkey* (New York, William Morrow, 1965).

3 For a recent set of essays on Islam in Turkey see R. Tapper (ed.), *Religion in Modern Turkey: Religion, Politics and Literature in a Secular State* (London, IB Tauris, 1991).

4 Cf. D. Shankland, 'The end of Turkey's Social Contract? Thoughts on the recent general election', *Government and Opposition*, 31 No. 3 (1996).

5 N. Erbakan, *Adid Ekonomik Duzen (Just Economic Order)* (Ankara Refah Partisi, [c.1989]).

6 Cf. I. Jarvie, *The Revolution in Anthropology* (London, RKP, 1964) for a pioneering attempt to interpret millennial movements in this fashion.

7 See P. Khoury and J. Kostiner (eds.), *Tribes and State Formation in the Middle East* (Berkeley, CA, University of California Press, 1990). On the sociology of leadership in Islamic communities, particularly I. Lapidus, 'Tribes and state formation in Islamic history', 25–47. Cf. also M. Van Bruinessan, *Agha, Shaikh and State* (London, Zed Books, 1992), 249, for a note on the *mehdi* in the east of Turkey.

8 For a historical account of the Shi'ite/Sunni divisions see G. Von Grunebaum, *Classical Islam*, tr. Katherine Watson (London, George, Allen & Unwin, 1970), ch. 2.

9 Cf. P. Andrews, *Ethnic Groups in the Republic of Turkey* (Wiesbaden, Dr Ludwig Reichert, 1989).

10 M. Moosa, *Extremist Shi'ites: The Ghulat Sects* (New York, Sycracuse University Press, 1988) for a discussion of these.

11 For a more detailed account of the Alevi relationship with Sunni Islam see D. Shankland, 'Social change and culture: responses to modernization in an Alevi village in Antolia', in C. Hann (ed.) *When History Accelerates* (London, Athlone Press, 1994), 238–54.

12 Cf. D. Shankland, 'Diverse paths of change: Alevi and Sunni in rural Anatolia in culture and economy', in P. Stirling (ed.), *Changes in Turkish Villages* (Huntingdon, Eothen Press, 1993), 46–64.

13 Cf. K. Birge, *The Bektashi Order of Dervishes* (London, Luzac and Co., 1965).

Further reading

Andrews, P., *Ethnic Groups in the Republic of Turkey* (Wiesbaden, Dr Ludwig Reichart, 1989).

Birge, K., *The Bektashi Order of Dervishes* (London, Luzac and Co., 1965; 1937).

Erbakan, N., *Adil Ekonomik Duzen (Just Economic Order)* (Ankara, Refah Partisi, n.d. *c.*1989).

Gellner, E., *Muslim Society* (Cambridge, Cambridge University Press, 1989).

Jarvie, I., *The Revolution in Anthropology* (London, RKP, 1964).

Khoury P. and Kostiner, J. (ed.), *Tribes and State Formation in the Middle East* (Berkeley, CA, University of California Press, 1990).

Kinross, Lord, *Ataturk: A Biography of Mustapha Kemal, Father of Modern Turkey* (New York, William Morrow, 1965).

Lewis, B., *The Emergence of Modern Turkey* (Oxford, Oxford University Press, 1962).

Moosa, M., *Extremist Shi'ites: The Ghulat Sects* (New York, Syracuse University Press, 1988).

Shankland, D., 'Diverse paths of change: Alevi and Sunni in rural Anatolia in culture and economy', in P. Stirling (ed.), *Changes in Turkish Villages* (Huntingdon, Eothen Press, 1993), 46–64.

——, 'Social change and culture: responses to modernisation in an Alevi village in Anatolia', in C. Hann (ed.), *When History Accelerates* (London, Athlone Press, 1994), 238–54.

——, 'The end of Turkey's social contract? Thoughts on the recent general election', in *Government and Opposition*, 31 No. 3 (Summer 1996).

Tapper, R. (ed.), *Religion in Modern Turkey: Religion, Politics and Literature in a Secular State* (London, IB Tauris, 1991).

Van Bruinessan, M., *Agha, Shaikh and State* (London, Zed Books, 1992).

Von Grunebaum, G., *Classical Islam*, tr. Katherine Watson (London, George, Allen & Unwin, 1970).

11

When prophecy fails: messianism amongst Lubavitcher Hasids

SIMON DIEN

'I believe in perfect faith in the coming of the Messiah, and even though he may tarry, nevertheless I shall wait for his coming every day' (Maimonides' twelfth principle of faith): a belief in the advent of *Mosiach* (the Messiah) is an integral part of Jewish teachings. The twelfth-century Jewish scholar Maimonides[1] in his *Mishneh Torah* compiled the thirteen principles, which are now recited after the morning prayers, during the prayers after meals, during the wedding ceremony and on festivals and fast days. Not only is there an obligation to believe in the advent of the Messiah, but also actively to await his arrival. As Maimonides states, 'And all those who do not believe in the Messiah or do not await his coming, not only do they deny the truth of the words of the prophets, but they reject the truth of the entire Torah and our master Moses.'

According to biblical teachings, the *Mosiach* will arise and restore the kingdom of David to its original state, rebuild the *Bet Hamikdosh* (Holy Temple) in Jerusalem and gather the dispersed of Israel. In addition, the messianic era will mark the end of evil and sin (Ezekiel 37); bring universal awareness, perception and knowledge of God (Isaiah 11:9); bring all humanity to worship God in unity (Zephariah 3:9); bring universal peace and harmony (Isaiah 2:4); bring on the resurrection of the dead (Isaiah 26:19); and eradicate illness and death (Isaiah 25:8). Although opinions vary, the resurrection of the dead will occur about forty years after the messianic arrival.

In the *Mishneh Torah* it says:

A man will arise from the house of David who is devoted to the study of Torah and the observances of the *Mitzvot* (commandments) like

David his ancestor, in accordance with the written and oral Torah. If he will prevail upon all of Israel to walk in the way of the Torah and repair the breaches of its observances and if he will fight the wars of God, he is presumed to be *Mosiach*. If he succeeds in the above, builds the *Bet Hamikdosh* on its site, and gathers in the dispersed remnants of Israel he is definitely *Mosiach*.

It goes on to state that *Mosiach* is a being of flesh and blood born of human parents. The history of Judaism is replete with false messiahs.[2] Perhaps the best example of that is Sabbatai Sevi (1626–76), the Turkish false Messiah,[3] who started the largest messianic movement known in Jewish history.[4] Sevi was a manic depressive with messianic delusions. He aroused great messianic hopes in Jews across the world which soon ended in despair as the would-be Messiah converted to Islam.[5] In the wake of this movement, Hasidism developed in Eastern Europe in the eighteenth century. Its founder was the Baal Shem Tov.

Hasidism singled out the inner state of the worshipper, rather than his understanding of the tradition, as the primary value in the service of God. An emphasis was placed on *Devukut*, the idea that one should be attached to God at all times and one's thoughts should always be on him. It taught spirituality through corporality, meaning that everyday activities such as eating and drinking could be used to praise God and in turn elevate the physical body spiritually. It is important to emphasize that although Hasidism is often spoken of as a sect within Judaism, it is not a sect in the true sense of denomination. The Hasidism never seceded from the main body of traditional Judaism. The Hasidism are Orthodox Jews who emphasize a different aspect of the tradition. Originally, they stressed feelings over and above the intellect. However, as Hasidism spread they came closer to institutionalized Orthodoxy. Today, for Hasids, the meticulous following of Talmud and the study of Torah are the main ideals of religious life.

A unique facet of Hasidism and the way in which Hasidism differs from other orthodox groups is the idea of the *Zaddik* or *Rebbe*, a perfectly righteous man who leads the Hasidic group. Hasidism hold that only the *Zaddik* can attain *Devekut* all the time, hence the Hasid has to attach himself to a *Zaddik* through whom he can become attached to God. The concept of *Zaddik* was introduced by the successor of the Baal Shem Tov, Rabbi Dov Baer of Messeritch (1710–71). The *Zaddik* was believed to work miracles and act as a channel for divine energy to flow into the world. Hasidism sought his blessings for all their undertakings and told many stories about his wonderful deeds.

Hasidism spread rapidly in Poland and was introduced to Lithuania by Rabbi Schneur Zalman (1746–1813), who founded the Lubavitch movement there (named after the town in Russia where the movement started). Throughout the nineteenth century the Lubavitch battled under the banner of Hasidism to secure economic and political benefits for Jews. The vast majority of Lubavitchers were wiped out in the Holocaust. The sixth Lubavitch *Rebbe*, Rabbi Joseph Isaac Schneerson (1880–1950), organized communities outside Russia. In 1940 the movement settled in New York and a Lubavitch centre opened in Stamford Hill, London, in 1959.

Lubavitch is a worldwide movement of about 200,000 Hasidic Jews. The movement's centre is in Brooklyn, USA, where its leader, Menachem Schneerson, lived until his death on 12 June 1994. During his lifetime his followers proclaimed him as *Mosiach*. Studies of contemporary messianic movements are rare, and our knowledge of messianic movements is largely based on historical accounts, with some notable exceptions.[6] This chapter is an account of a modern-day messianic movement and contains ethnographic material obtained in the Stamford Hill Lubavitch community during fieldwork from 1990–4.[7] It provides a good test of cognitive dissonance theory,[8] which suggests that intensification of a religious belief will occur when disconfirming information is presented, as long as the disconfirmed belief is deeply held, the believer has made public his or her own commitment to the belief and he or she is in contact with other believers who can provide support for the prediction. Evidence from history,[9] and field observation[10] provide confirmation for this theory.

1 The Stamford Hill community

Stamford Hill is an inner-city area in East London, with a population of around 27,000 people in an area of three square miles. There are about 1,000 Hasidic families living there, about

200 of them Lubavitchers. Lubavitch is just one of a number of Hasidic groups in the UK. The others include Satmar, Visnitz, Bratzlav and Ger. They are all ultra-Orthodox Jews with their own *Rebbe*. Although there is some association with other Hasidic groups and occasional intermarriage, there are frequent tensions. The Satmar publicly criticize the Lubavitchers' proclamation that their leader is the *Mosiach*, and believe that their adaptation to modernity has been too enthusiastic. Today, less than half the population of Stamford Hill are Jews, mainly lower middle-class tradesmen, religious teachers and small businessmen. The other minority groups living in Stamford Hill include West Indians, South Asians and some Irish, Greek and Turkish families.

Lubavitch is distinguished from other groups by its emphasis on 'conversion', the bringing back of non-Orthodox Jews to Orthodoxy. Members of the community conduct mass campaigns to reclaim 'stray' Jews. In fact about 70 per cent of the Stamford Hill Lubavitch community are *Ballei Teshuvah* (non-Orthodox Jews who have become Orthodox). These campaigns consist of large meetings where Rabbis preach, *Mezuzot* campaigns in which the Lubavitch go round the streets checking that local Jews have *Kosher Mezuzot* (scrolls of parchment in a case) on their doors and, most striking, the *Mitzvah* (good deed) tank, a truck going round the streets of Stamford Hill inviting male Jews to put on *Tefillen* (phyllacteries) and females to light the *Shabbat* (Sabbath) candles. These activities are seen as being as important part of doing the '*Rebbe*'s work' and is in line with the teachings of the *Rebbe* who emphasized the importance of performing *Mitzvot* (good deeds) to hasten the arrival of the messianic era. Lubavitchers are keen to incorporate modern technology into their everyday lives, especially new communication technology such as faxes, arguing that these facilitate the spread of the *Rebbe*'s teachings. The movement centres around Lubavitch House, a large building with a steel façade which contains a synagogue, school, swimming pool and library. It is here that Stamford Hill Lubavitchers congregate and decisions about the movement are made.

Daily life within the group is strictly determined by the Talmud, the rabbinical collection of legal, ethical and historical writings. Although the language spoken at home is usually English or Yiddish, the sacred texts are written in Hebrew.

Minimum standards of observance for all the community include: strict *Kashrut* (food must be ritually pure; milk must neither be drunk not cooked with meat) together with Sabbath and festival observance. For men there is regular attendance in the prayer house and daily study of the sacred texts, with suits, unshaven sideburns, beard and a covered head. For women, an enthusiastic attitude to child-bearing is expected, with modest dress including covered hair (married women cut their hair short and cover it with a wig called a *Sheitel*), regular prayer (not always in the synagogue) and some religious learning.

Marriages within the community are arranged by a *Shidduch* (arranged marriage-maker). Couples are expected to adhere to the laws governing family purity, especially the time of *Nidah* (ritual impurity when a woman is menstruating). Families tend to be large with the average number of children being eight. Children are educated in single-sex Jewish schools and there is sexual segregation from the age of three. This segregation continues throughout adult life and functions to protect the sanctity of the family. The domestic role of women is stressed, particularly their role in guaranteeing the purity of food and the household and in bringing up the children. Young men generally go on to study at a *Yeshivah* (seminary) where some become rabbis. In fact, about 25 per cent of the Stamford Hill adult male community are rabbis. Other favoured occupations include small businesses, especially those serving the wider Orthodox community with food stores, religious teaching and other religiously linked professions such as *Mohels* (circumciser) and *Shohet* (slaughterer).

Interaction with the outside world is strictly limited to business purposes. The justification for not mixing with non-Jews is that, through friendship and intimacies, the temptation to stray from the law could be irresistible, and thus self-imposed segregation is seen as a precaution.

2 The *Rebbe*

Every room in a Lubavitch house has several pictures of the *Rebbe* on the walls, both as a young man and as a nonagenarian. The process of becoming a member of the Lubavitch is characterized by an increasing orientation to the *Rebbe* and an interest in his teachings. Lubavitch stresses a familiarity with the lives, works and teachings of earlier *Rebbe*s. Much time is spent studying their discourses. The heritage of the movement is seen principally through the works of the *Rebbe*s and among important gatherings of the Lubavitch are those that commemorate the lives of these *Rebbe*s. Children are taught to revere the *Rebbe*. Lubavitchers relate to him in everyday conversation with great frequency and discuss his teachings, directives and his extraordinary powers of perception and wisdom. Miracle stories about him abound in the community. Though the *Rebbe* himself discouraged such talk, his adherents have for decades circulated countless anecdotes of their leader's miraculous abilities. A recent book written by his followers entitled *Wonders and Miracles* describes a number of miraculous tales about him. Where possible, his directives were transmitted to Lubavitch communities throughout the world by radio links, and – on the Sabbath days and holy days when broadcasting is forbidden – those present would attempt to memorize his words and pass them on to their communities.

Menachem Mendel Schneerson was born in the Russian town of Nikolaev in 1902 and was named after his grandfather, the third Lubavitcher leader, himself the grandson of Rabbi Schneur Zalman, the founder of the Lubavitch movement. His followers make a number of claims about him. On the day that he was born, Rabbi Sholem Dov Ber, the fifth leader of the Lubavitch dynasty, sent no less than six telegrams with detailed instructions regarding the infant, informing his mother to always wash the baby's hands before he ate, so he never ate in his life without first washing his hands. When he was only two years of age he was asking the four questions of the *Seder* (Passover Service) table.[11] At two-and-a-half he could pray like an adult. From early childhood, the *Rebbe* displayed prodigious mental activity and had to leave his Jewish school because he was so far ahead of his classmates. His father engaged private tutors for him. By the time of his Bar Mitzvah he was considered an *Illuy* (a Torah prodigy). Four years later he was ordained as a Rabbi by virtue of his mastery of the entire Talmud and codes of Jewish law. One famous story recounts how, at the age of nine, he dived into the Black Sea to save the life of another boy who had fallen from the deck of a moored ship.

At the age of twenty-seven he married Chaya Moussia, the second daughter of the sixth Lubavitcher *Rebbe*, and he studied diligently under his father-in-law. He spent some time in various countries, including Russia, Poland, Germany and France, before arriving in the United States in 1941. During this period he took courses at the University of Leningrad, Berlin and the Sorbonne in Paris where he studied electrical engineering.

From 1941, until his recent death, the *Rebbe* lived at his residence, '770' Eastern Parkway, a synagogue and community centre in Crown Heights, Brooklyn, and led the movement from there. Although he never visited Israel, and had not left Brooklyn for the past forty years, he was very interested in Israeli politics. Sometimes, senior Lubavitchers downplay these stories but they do not deny the truthfulness of the accounts. I was told by one Lubavitcher in 1990:

> Yes, he is a truly miraculous person. He can speak 10 languages, he is 90 years of age but only sleeps one hour a day. He can give Torah for hours on end without stopping. No-one else of his age can do this. On a weekly basis he visits the grave of the sixth Lubavitcher *Rebbe*, Yosef Schneerson, and communes with his soul. He faces the headstone and opens a small Hebrew prayerbook of psalms and biblical verses. He recites prayers and after some time opens a large bag. This holds hundreds of recent letters and notes and the *Rebbe* reads them one by one. Each request from a Jew bears the author's name and that of his mother. Hasidism believe that this information establishes the soul's link with the earthly existence. Many of the petitions are written in Hebrew but other languages are represented. They concern personal issues such as health, the family and livelihood. For instance, it may say, 'I Moshe, son of Leah, pray that my son Shemeuli will recover quickly and fully from his illness.'

Up until several years ago it was possible to get a private audience with the *Rebbe* (called *Yehidus*). This ceased about six years ago. Until his first stroke in March 1992, visitors could meet the *Rebbe* at a ceremony called 'dollars' where several thousand people would file past the *Rebbe* on a Sunday morning at his residence in Brooklyn. Each would ask the *Rebbe* for a blessing, usually for health, marriage, business or education. Each person received a dollar which symbolized charity. Visitors would come from all over the world and would often queue up for several hours before seeing the *Rebbe*.

In 1990, I visited the *Rebbe* for 'dollars'. It was a wet Sunday morning in November. I remember waiting outside '770' for about four hours, seeing numerous people coming out clutching a dollar in their hands. In the road outside his residence were stalls selling paintings, engravings and pictures of the *Rebbe*, sometimes for exorbitant prices. There were also stalls specializing in encasing the dollar in plastic. After several hours my turn arrived to speak to the *Rebbe*. I was aware that I could only spend a short time with him. A non-Lubavitcher man stood by the *Rebbe*'s door (I assume a guard) to show people in. When I first glanced at him I was struck by his long white beard and his staring eyes. He was wearing a long black coat and Trilby hat and had a somewhat leaning posture. He smiled at me and asked if I spoke Yiddish. I answered no. I told him that I wanted a blessing for a *Shidduch* (marriage) with my girlfriend. He asked me whether she was Jewish and I answered in the affirmative. He gave me a blessing and two dollars, one for me and one for her. I then left, feeling that for the short moment I was with him I had had his undivided attention.

Numerous stories are told about these visits: Mr Suffrin went to visit the *Rebbe* in Brooklyn in order to receive a blessing for his disabled son for whom he wanted to arrange *Shidduch*. The *Rebbe* gave him a blessing and two dollars, one for himself and one for Israel. Mr Suffrin's wife told him that the *Rebbe* meant him personally to take the dollar to Israel. This he did. While riding on a bus in Tel Aviv, he spoke to the man next to him. This man asked what had brought him to Israel. As Mr Suffrin responded he fainted. When he came round Mr Suffrin asked him what had happened. The other man was in a state of shock. He himself had recently visited the Lubavitcher *Rebbe* for his disabled daughter for whom he wanted to find a *Shidduch*. The *Rebbe* had similarly given him two dollars, one for himself and one for Israel. Ultimately, the son and daughter met and married.

According to another story, in 1971 an Israeli journalist visited the United States. He decided to visit the *Rebbe*. When his turn came to enter the *Rebbe*'s room, he handed the *Rebbe* a hand-written request. The *Rebbe* looked at this closely and remarked, 'I recognise the handwriting, you must have written to me before.' The journalist was shocked. 'You must be mistaken', he said, 'I have never written to the *Rebbe* in the past.' Again, the *Rebbe* looked at the writing and said, 'You have written to me in the past.' Still the journalist disagreed. The *Rebbe* took a folded piece of paper from his desk drawer and repeated the statement. He passed the paper to the journalist, who turned pale. The letter was in his handwriting, but it was not his signature. Then he remembered. Four years earlier, in the Six Day War, one of his friends had suffered a hand injury and asked him to write a letter to the *Rebbe* on his behalf, which his friend had signed. Over the four-year period, hundreds of thousands of letters had passed through the *Rebbe*'s hands, but for some reason the *Rebbe* had kept this letter in his desk drawer.

Numerous comments were made by Lubavitchers about his astounding memory. Many believed that he knew every Jew in the world, even if he had never met them before and had the power of *Rauch Ha Kodesh* (divine providence). He was the spiritual guide of the Lubavitch in all matters. Many people wrote to him about matters such as health, divorce, marriage and business and each week he would receive thousands of faxes and letters from people all over the world (Jews and non-Jews). Although not everyone received a letter in return, it is believed that the *Rebbe* personally read every letter. Many people would receive a letter in return, often containing a biblical quote, a blessing and advising that they should check their religious artefacts.

A major article of ritual clothing is the *Tallit* (prayer shawl). According to the book of Numbers, the children of Israel were commanded to have fringes at the corners of their garments. These fringes served as a constant reminder of God and his laws. The *Tallit* has four corners, at each corner there are eight strands, totalling thirty-two strands in all. Mr Levy, a thirty-year-old Lubavitcher from Stamford Hill, wrote to the *Rebbe* about continuous toothache which he had had for several months. Although he had consulted several dentists over this period, nothing abnormal was found and in despair he wrote to the *Rebbe*. The *Rebbe* responded by asking him to check his *Tallit*. He examined his prayer shawl to find that one of the strands was distinctly worn. He replaced his *Tallit* and, shortly afterwards, the toothache disappeared. He emphasized the connection between the thirty-two strands and his thirty-two teeth (between the spiritual-physical worlds) and how spiritual disorder could result in physical disorder.[12]

Stories are frequently told about the *Rebbe*'s powers of prediction. He was considered a prophet by his followers. As one Lubavitcher recounted:

> The *Rebbe* has made a number of correct predictions. He accurately predicted the fall of the communist regime in Russia. In the year 5751 (1989) the *Rebbe* explained that this year could be interpreted as an acronym for the phrase, 'This will surely be a year of miracles'. This year was highlighted by the collapse of regimes that had stifled Jewish expression. During this year these nations began to allow freedom of religious practice. However, I feel his greatest prophecies concerned the Gulf War of 1991. In January of this year he stated that, 'There is no safer place in the world today than Israel. Heaven forbid that anyone living in Israel should think of leaving at this time, on the contrary, whoever is planning to visit Israel should go without fear and should let others know of his trip as well, for this will raise the confidence of the Jewish people throughout the world.' Despite the concern over the safety of Israel from Jews in the Diaspora, the *Rebbe*'s predictions were in fact confirmed and only one person died in Tel Aviv from a Scud missile, compared to several in Saudi Arabia.

3 The *Mosiach* campaign

In the early 1980s, Lubavitch began a 'We want *Mosiach*' campaign to popularize the belief that the arrival of the Messiah was imminent. This campaign increased in momentum over the next few years, with frequent advertisements appearing in Jewish newspapers about the topic of *Mosiach*. One popular advert entitled 'Draw your own conclusion', stated,

> These are amazing times. The Iron Curtain tumbled. Iraq is humbled. The people of Israel emerge whole from under a rainstorm of murderous missiles . . . An entire beleagured population is air-lifted to safety overnight . . . A tidal wave of Russian Jews reaches Israel . . . Nations around the world turn to democracy . . . Plus countless other amazing developments that are taking place in front of our eyes. Any one of these phenomena by itself is enough to boggle the mind. Connect them all together and a pattern emerges that cannot be ignored . . . The Lubavitcher *Rebbe* emphasises that these remarkable events are merely a prelude to the final redemption. The era of Mosiach is upon us. Learn about it. Be a part of it. All you have to do is open your eyes. Inevitably, you will draw your own conclusion.

Although the *Rebbe* never openly encouraged messianic fervour, he did little to condemn it. Although *Mosiach* was always a favourite topic for the *Rebbe*, on 11 April 1991 he changed from his usual *Sichah* (discourse) to an injunction: 'What more can I do to motivate the entire Jewish people to . . . actually bring about the coming of Mosiach. All that I can possibly do is to give the matter over to you now, immediately . . . I have done whatever I can; from now on you must do whatever you can . . .' Lubavitchers were stunned by this injunction and started organizing teachings and directives about the messianic redemption. The *Rebbe*'s talks on *Mosiach* were published and classes were organized to teach messianic topics. *Mosiach* became a major topic of discussion, and soon Lubavitchers talked of the *Rebbe* himself being the *Mosiach*.

Shortly afterwards, the *Rebbe* not only spoke about yearning for the coming of *Mosiach* but also about his imminent arrival: '*Mosiach*'s coming is no longer a dream of a distant future, but an imminent reality which will very shortly become manifest . . .' In September 1991, the *Rebbe* stated that, only if Jews believed with absolute certainty that the Messiah would come as redeemer, would such an event occur. As the Jewish New Year was approaching, he said, 'When the divine service of the Jewish people over the centuries is considered as a whole, everything that is necessary to bring about the redemption has been accomplished. There is no valid explanation for the continuance of the exile . . .'.

The *Rebbe*'s statements had a profound effect on the Stamford Hill Lubavitchers. *Mosiach* became a major topic of conversation, as was life after the redemption. Issues such as the types of food we would be able to eat after the redemption and whether we would have bodies after the resurrection were discussed. After a short time, Lubavitchers discussed not just the imminent arrival of the *Mosiach* but that the *Rebbe* was the *Mosiach*. A *Mosiach* campaign was launched. As one Rabbi stated,

> As part of this campaign to bring *Mosiach* we make use of books, seminars and lectures. There was a time when *Tefillen* was a forgotten thing by many Jews. In the 1960s Lubavitch started a campaign to reintroduce these into Jewish life. The campaign revolutionized their use. Similarly the *Mosiach* campaign is part of Jewish education. At the

end of the day this a major part of Jewish theology. There is nothing wrong with using modern day technology to propagate the idea of *Mosiach*. Today only one person fulfils the criteria for *Mosiach*. This is the Lubavitcher *Rebbe*. He has brought more Jews back to Judaism than any other leader and himself is a descendant of King David. If pressed all Lubavitchers will say he is *Mosiach*. There is no other candidate. We are nearly out of our predicament now . . .

In 1992, the *Mosiach* campaign escalated in Stamford Hill. There was an explosion of books about *Mosiach* such as *Highlights of Mosiach* and *Sound the Great Shofar*. Lectures and seminars were held on messianic topics. Posters were placed in houses and shops and stickers were placed on cars stating '*Mosiach* is coming soon, let's be ready.' Above the stickers was a large picture of the Lubavitcher *Rebbe*. At a number of effective public meetings Messianic ideas were discussed. In April 1992 there was a *Mosiach* awareness caravan tour. A motorcade of three especially prepared caravans, otherwise known as 'Mitzvah (good deed) tanks', embarked on a tour around Britain to provide information about the the concept of *Mosiach* and its significance for Jewish life and belief. It was launched by the mayor of Hackney, while a Hasidic band offered musical entertainment. A public discusssion was held in the grounds of Lubavitch House which focused on a number of messianic issues, including one talk entitled 'Taking the first step towards miracle making'. The mobile unit carried books, brochures, tapes, education material and religious articles such as *Tefillen, Mezuzot* and *Shabbat* candlesticks.

One twenty-year-old Lubavitcher stated,

On their current assignment, the *Mitzvah* mobile staff will endeavour to communicate the idea that belief in *Mosiach* is a central theme within Judaism and that anticipation for *Mosiach* has always been integral to Jewish belief, life and observance. The Lubavitcher *Rebbe* has asked that the Jewish people should study what the Torah teaches about *Mosiach* and, further to prepare ourselves for the imminent arrival of *Mosiach*. This will signify the commencement of a new historical epoch when the world will change for the better on every level. The signs on the caravans will announce '*Mosiach* is about to change the world for good' and 'Your *Mitzvah* can make a world of difference.'

4 The *Rebbe*'s illness

In March 1992 the *Rebbe* suffered a stroke which rendered him speechless and paralysed on the right hand side. Despite his profound incapacity to look after himself, his followers described the stroke as mild. Following this he was unable to give dollars but his followers continued to write to him asking for blessings. His secretary would read the letters to him and he would gesticulate an answer by moving his head up or down. In Brooklyn, he would be seen frequently, although unpredictably, at prayer service sometimes twice a day and sometimes less than once a week. In order to ensure that his followers would be present when he came out, his followers carried '*Mosiach* bleepers'. When he came on to the platform of the Synagogue in '770' a message would be flashed on the bleeper – 'MHM is on the platform' (meaning *Melech Ha Mosiach*, king *Mosiach* is on the platform). The bleepers were supposedly programmed to flash the number 7–7–0 the moment the *Rebbe* revealed himself as *Mosiach*. When the bleeper sounded, hundreds of Lubavitchers would be seen running towards '770' to see the *Rebbe*. One Lubavitcher said, '*Mosiach* could come any day, we hope today he will reveal himself.' Other followers waited patiently in the synagogue in the hope that he would come out. Sometimes they would wait all day to no avail.

At the times when he was seen, the curtains would suddenly be pulled back and the *Rebbe* would be seen sitting on a chair, his secretary close to him. Immediately, there would be a chorus of *Yechh Adoneinuu Moreinu, Rabenu Melech Ha Mosiach Leolam Vaed* (Long live our master, our teacher and our *Rebbe*, king *Mosiach*, forever and ever). As this was sung, the *Rebbe* would smile and move his left arm about.

On a daily basis, a message was faxed to the Lubavitch House in Stamford Hill informing his followers about what went on that day. For example, on 5 July 1993 it stated:

Monday, the *Rebbe*'s *Mincha* [afternoon prayer] was about 2.15pm and *Ma'ariv* [evening prayer] was about 9.40pm. After *Mincha* the *Rebbe* was on the porch about three minutes and after *Ma'ariv* about two minutes. *Yechi Hamelech Hamisiach* was sung. The *Rebbe* participated by moving his lips, nodding his head and drumming his fingers.

In Stamford Hill, the *Rebbe*'s illness was frequently discussed. Publicly, Lubavitchers stated that the *Rebbe* would recover and his stroke was a significant event which would usher in the messianic era. Talk of a *Mosiach* increased and the fact that the *Rebbe* could not talk did nothing to detract Lubavitchers from their messianic beliefs. There was increased discourse about *Mosiach*, more meetings, adverts and books about messianic topics. Belief that the *Rebbe* was *Mosiach* intensified.

A number of explanations were given for the *Rebbe*'s illness, often based post hoc on biblical and Talmudic sources. They deployed the writings of Maimonides to argue that the *Rebbe* himself had chosen to become ill and had taken on the suffering of the Jewish people. Maimonides had described 'a man of pains and acquainted with sickness . . . indeed he has borne our sickness and endured our pains.'[13] One *Rebbe* explained how he could be healed:

> The soul of the *Rebbe* represents the group soul of the Jewish people. His suffering represents the suffering of every Jew. It is like a body and a head, the *Rebbe* being the head of the Jewish body. The two cannot exist independently. If the body is sick it can give rise to a headache. If the brain does not work, how can the body function? If every Jew does not perform good deeds the Jewish body will become sick and in turn the *Rebbe*. If more Jews perform these deeds the *Rebbe* will recover.

Lubavitchers attempted to restore the health of the *Rebbe* by the recitation of psalms. Every day Lubavitchers were encouraged to say extra psalms. Shortly after his first stroke a *Sefer Torach* (a scroll containing the text of the Torah) was written in New York, and every Lubavitcher was asked to donate a pound towards a letter. The aim of writing this was to perfect the *Rebbe*'s soul and in turn his body. The same Lubavitcher continued:

> All Jewish souls are tied to the *Rebbe*'s soul. In the *Torah* there are six hundred thousand words (three hundred and twenty eight thousand complete words and two hundred and seventy two thousand incomplete words). In the world there are six hundred thousand general souls (each divides up into many more souls). These general souls are linked to the *Rebbe*'s soul. By writing a perfect *Torah* the *Rebbe*'s soul becomes perfect again and this will affect his body. The *Rebbe* must first undergo a descent into the realm of evil to redeem the

souls of sinners. This descent on the spiritual plane is associated with physical sickness.

But, alas, the *Rebbe* had another stroke on 10 March 1994, almost two years after his first stroke. This time he was rendered comatose. From then until his death on 12 June 1994 he was on a ventilator and never regained consciousness. There was much consternation in the Stamford Hill community and the *Rebbe*'s sickness was the focal talking point. Despite various newspaper reports alleging that the *Rebbe* was 'brain dead' or 'without brain function', his followers continued to declare him as *Mosiach*. When questioned about the meaning of the *Rebbe*'s second stroke, the answers given were categorically '*Mosiach*' and that, 'We are on the threshold of a Messianic era.' Messianic propaganda increased in intensity. Extra meetings were held where Psalms were said. Thousands of his follwers slept in the hospital where the *Rebbe* lay, reciting psalms in the hope that he would arise.

During this period, I interviewed several Lubavitchers about his illness. Although no one publicly discussed the possibility that he could die and who his successor would be (the *Rebbe* had no children to succeed him), privately several people admitted their concerns about his possible death. One person said,

> I know the *Rebbe* is a great man, but he is human after all and is about ninety three years of age. I think he could die. I hope for the sake of Lubavitch that he does not but we must face this possibility. If he died how will Lubavitchers account for his death and what will happen to their messianic beliefs?

Publicly, however, the 'party line' was that his illness signified the imminent arrival of the messianic era and forthcoming redempton. One eminent rabbi stated,

> The *Rebbe* is now in a state of concealment. The Jews could not see Moses on Mount Sinai and thought he was dead. They built the golden calf and had a vision of him lying dead on a bier whereas he was in fact alive but was in a state of concealment. He is in a state of *Chinoplet*, a trance-like state where the soul leaves the body. The Soul of the *Rebbe* has to go down to the lower realms to drag up the souls of

the sinners. He must do this before he declares himself as *Mosiach*. The spiritual energy required to bring *Mosiach* is very great and his body is depleted of energy. It is only now that we have the medical technology to keep him alive. We should not be sad. The attitude to adopt is one of *Simcha* (Joy). We are of course sad that the *Rebbe* is suffering but must be joyful, that he is undergoing a process of transformation to reveal himself as *Mosiach*.

Even though Hasidism emphasizes joy in the face of adversity, during the three months leading up to his death people were very subdued. A notice was distributed in Lubavitcher houses relating to how people should act at this time. It emphasized that Lubavitchers should learn the *Rebbe*'s teachings, perform *Mitzvot*, give charity, support one's neighbours and recite psalms.

Even when the *Rebbe* was comatose and attached to a ventilator, his followers continued to write for blessings. His secretary would stand over his sickbed and read them to him. New miracle stories appeared such as the one following which was circulated around the community shortly before the *Rebbe*'s death. Dr Fink, one of the *Rebbe*'s physicians, was travelling up a hill in New York. The car in front of him had a trailer attached. Suddenly the trailer came loose and started to roll backwards. Dr Fink saw a vision of the *Rebbe* standing in front of his car holding the trailer up, giving the physician enough time to escape. It was reported that Dr Fink had never met the *Rebbe* before he went into a coma.

Every day, faxes were received from Beth Israel Hospital in New York, where the *Rebbe* lay, documenting the *Rebbe*'s medical condition. Slight improvements were taken as signs of his imminent recovery and ascension to the messianic role. Over the last month of his life his medical condition deteriorated considerably. In May 1994 he had pneumonia, from which he recovered, and several days before his death he had a cardiac arrest and was resuscitated. Still his followers did not give up hope and claimed he would get up from his sick bed and proclaim he was the Messiah.

However, this was not to be the case. The *Rebbe* died on 12 June 1994. His death was reported in the major tabloids, on the radio and television. *The Times* newspaper reported the event as follows:

> The death of the *Rebbe* Menachem Schneerson, seventh leader of the
> Lubavitcher rabbinic dynasty, brings to a close a remarkable career
> which had culminated in his followers' claim that he was about to be
> revealed as the messiah. His face, with its piercing blue eyes and black
> fedora, was familiar throughout photographs in thousands of shops,
> offices and homes in the Jewish world. During his fifty five year
> stewardship the Lubavitch movement was transformed from a
> practically moribund branch of Hasidism to a powerful and
> international movement, deploying all the resources of modern
> communication technology to spread its message.

A message was faxed from '770' to the Stamford Hill community
at the time of the *Rebbe*'s death. This said, 'Blessed be the divine
Judge', meaning that God had ordained that the *Rebbe* should die.

I arrived at the Lubavitch House several hours after the *Rebbe*
had died, having heard the news on a local radio station. The
atmosphere was subdued. I was struck by the small number of
people there and was told that most of the community had at
very short notice flown to New York for the funeral. Some were
praying, others saying *Tehillim* (psalms), while other Lubavitchers
stood in groups talking. I could see no one crying. After an hour
more and more people assembled in the synagogue and I was
able to discuss with them what had happened. There was a
distinct lack of leadership, no one knew exactly how to proceed.
'Do we sit *Shiva*?' (seven days of mourning), asked one man.
'The *Rebbe* is not our immediate family.'

Some answered that it was necessary to sit *Shiva*, for several
hours only, others suggested a day and others said one week.
Everyone agreed that at the time of the funeral they would do
Keriah (rend garments), and someone was appointed to perform
this task. As the day proceeded, more and more people assembled
in the synagogue and attempts were made to link the Lubavitch
House by satellite with NBC American news channel, which was
due to broadcast the funeral live.

Right up to his funeral, there was still a feeling of hope
expressed by those present. 'The *Rebbe* could still arise and
proclaim himself as *Mosiach*', said one student. With this hope in
mind, a group of Lubavitchers read *Tehillim* (psalms) loudly.
About an hour before the funeral, a commentary on Genesis 49
was distributed, describing how, just as Judah is being buried, he
will arise, implying the same thing would occur with the *Rebbe*.

Jacob says the time will come when the kingship of the house of David will appear at its lowest, deepest end, and Judah no longer strong as a lion, but femininely weak, and one will think it has reached its final stage where Judah's virility will almost have disappeared, and then – just then – when the undertakers of world history will already have ordered the coffin for Judah's body apparently coming to its end, it will manfully arise and to it all the weak of the nations will come.

With the room full to the brim with Lubavitchers, some stood reciting psalms, some observed the funereal procession on satellite, and yet others tore their clothes. On satellite, a group of Lubavitchers could be seen dancing and singing, in the anticipation of his resurrection and the imminent redemption. Suddenly one man shouted out that he could hear the *Shofar*[14] (ram's horn) which announced the arrival of *Mosiach*. After the burial, some Lubavitchers left, others continued to say *Tehillim*.

The following morning, everyone was asking why he had died and what it meant for the arrival of *Mosiach* and the future of Lubavitch. Two days after his death a statement was made by Rabbi Yehuda Krinsky, a spokesman for the worldwide Lubavitch movement. This emphasized how much good work has been done by the *Rebbe* and how Lubavitchers now had the job of bringing forth the coming of the redemption. In it he stated,

By sharing with us his vision, his hopes and his promise, and by making us active participants in the perfection of God's world, the *Rebbe* has empowered us in a way that every parent can hope to empower his and her children. Handicapped as we are now by the loss of his physical presence . . . we rededicate ourselves to continue to acomplish that which our beloved *Rebbe* taught us through his life's work for a humanity uplifted by good, and a world sanctified and redeemed by God.

It was advised that everyone should sit *Shivah* for one week, read Psalm 93 (equivalent to the *Rebbe*'s age) and read the section from *Tanya*[15] called *Igaret Hakodesh*, where it states, 'The spiritual presence of a Zaddik is greater then his physical presence.'

I discussed his death with a number of people in the community. Several themes emerged from these discussions. Many Lubavitchers expressed the idea that he would be resurrected.

Most emphasized that he still had a major presence in the world, and that without the hindrance of his physical body his spiritual presence was even greater. Some admitted that they were wrong about him being *Mosiach*. Everyone expressed the feeling that they must continue to hope and pray for the messianic arrival and redemption.

> The *Rebbe* was higher spiritually than any other man. He must be resurrected although we do not know when. It could come at any time. We must carry on hoping for Mosiach to come.[16]

> All Lubavitchers believe that the *Rebbe* is *Mosiach*. We should still believe this. It is not impossible that the *Rebbe* will be resurrected. The *Rebbe* himself said that the great Zaddikim would come back before the redemption. When he returns, he will have the same body of a ninety three year old man. The *Rebbe* has greater power now. His spiritual presence is greater now in all the worlds. People still write to him asking for a blessing, although of course they do not get a reply, but there is a response. Things are happening.[17]

> The fact that the *Rebbe* has died is important for non-Jews. They believe in the resurrection. They could not understand the concept that *Mosiach* could be a dying man.[18] For them the Messiah is resurrected. Since the *Rebbe* has died and will be resurrected they will believe us.[19]

> I have always been sceptical about the *Rebbe* being *Mosiach*. He was a great man. Now he is dead I feel he has greater power. People do not know what to say at the moment here. There are no guidelines. Also there is a political problem about who will lead Lubavitch. I have several thoughts about the topic of the *Rebbe* and *Mosiach*. First, God possibly misled the *Rebbe* into saying *Mosiach* is imminent. I do not really believe this. Second, the *Rebbe* misled his followers, again I do not believe this. Third, the *Rebbe* misread the situation, I do not believe this. Why would he say *Mosiach* is imminent if it was not true? His death is a matter of cosmic significance. It means something. There is an air of expectancy in Stamford Hill. We do not know what will happen. Some people are still mourning, for example lighting candles. I feel the mourning must be channelled into following the *Rebbe*'s teachings. There is some dissension about the ideas of resurrection. According to Jewish teachings, resurrection of the dead will only occur once the *Mosiach* has come and we are in the period of redemption. It is not accepted that it will occur in the reverse order. I think people are wrong about this aspect.[20]

Over the next couple of weeks a number of public meetings were held for men and women and a number of leaflets were distributed. At one meeting on 3 July 1994, forty eminent Rabbis attended, but, according to one man who attended, no satisfactory answers were given: 'We felt cheated by the Rabbis. All we got was information about *Mosiach*. Now there is silence. No one can answer why the *Rebbe* died.'

In the Lubavitcher junior girls school, the week after the *Rebbe*'s death was devoted to discussing why it occurred and what to do now. During one assembly one of the teachers stated:

Concerning *Mosiach*: up to now we thought that we knew the script, the series of events which were going to happen in the process of the revelation of *Mosiach*. The *Rebbe* never actually told us a script, but we thought we should make it up. Now we realise we do not know the script. We should try to understand that this is not surprising. The coming of *Mosiach* is the drawing of the infinite into the finite, this is very difficult. It is quite beyond ordinary reason. It is understandable that we do not know the steps which lead to this.

In response to the question, 'Why did God do this?' he replied,

We cannot understand God and His ways. This is not surprising, since we are limited and God is infinite. Some things are very painful – but we trust in God that they are for the best. When the redemption comes we will thank God for all the difficulties he gave us now, for then we will realise their positive effect. God loves us and only does things for our good.

Shortly after his death, the organization running Lubavitch, *Aggudut Chassedei Chabad*, sent a letter to every Lubavitcher community. It stated that Lubavitchers were not to publicize that the *Rebbe* is *Mosiach*, and any behaviour to this effect such as public dancing in anticipation of the coming redemption, was not permissible. Talk of resurrection decreased, although privately many Lubavitchers continue to believe that the *Rebbe* is *Mosiach*, and will arise out of his grave and redeem his people. Four months after his death, the *Rebbe* is still an important topic of discourse, people are talking about how much they miss him. Lubavitchers, however, are getting on with their everyday lives. One Rabbi told me,

Things have changed. We thought we knew the agenda but now we know we do not. Only God knows this. The head of our community has publicly stated that we must not publicize that the *Rebbe* is *Mosiach* and we should no longer sing *Yechi Adenenu*. However, in this community most people still believe that the *Rebbe* is *Mosiach*. We believe but we do not publicize.

Since his death, Lubavitchers have been flying out to the *Ohel*, the *Rebbe*'s tomb. Queues of people wait in line to deposit small pieces of paper with their requests for a blessing written on them. Others write to the *Rebbe*'s secretary with their requests. He takes them to the tomb and reads them to the *Rebbe*. There are a growing number of miracle stories about people who have visited his grave. For instance:

Mr Rabin was in great financial despair, recently having gone bankrupt. He went to the *Ohel* and left a request for a blessing to save his business. Shortly after he returned home he unexpectedly received a letter from a distant relative informing him that they were willing to give him money to save his business.

5 Conclusion

What are the implications of the above for cognitive dissonance theory? According to this theory, religious beliefs are highly resistant to change. When presented with disconforming information, rather than giving up the beliefs, there is a process of reinterpretation and belief intensification. When the *Rebbe* became ill, rather than believing that he could not be *Mosiach*, the illness was reinterpreted in theological terms increasing the messianic belief. Lubavitchers felt more strongly that the *Rebbe* was *Mosiach*, and this was a prelude to the messianic arrival. This was exemplified by increased discourse about *Mosiach*, more meetings, books and adverts. Even following his death, the greatest disconfirming evidence, many still believe that he is *Mosiach*. The data confirm Festinger's theory. For Lubavitchers, although he is physically dead, he is more than ever spiritually alive, and plays a major part in their everyday lives.

Notes

1 Moses Maimonides (1136–1204) was a Spanish rationalist philosopher who lived in Fostat, Egypt. In his code of Jewish law, the Mishneh Torah (1180), he discussed a number of messianic issues.

2 See S. Sarot, *Messianism, Mysticism and Magic* (Chapel Hill, University of Carolina Press, 1982).

3 Sabbatai Sevi (1626–76) was a Turkish false messiah whose following extended throughout the Jewish world. He suffered from episodes of mood swings and when he was in an elated state proclaimed himself the Messiah. He prophesied that the year 1666 would signal the onset of the Messianic era. He was imprisoned by the Turkish Sultan and forced under threat of death to convert to Islam.

4 See Gershom Gerhard Scholem, 'Some reflections on Jewish theology' in *Conference on the Jewish Tradition and Experience* (Santa Barbara, CA, Center for the Study of Democratic Institutions, 1973).

5 Ibid.

6 E.g. L. Festinger, H. Riecken and S. Schachter (eds.), *When Prophecy Fails* (Minneapolis, University of Minnesota Press, 1956) and J. Lofland, *Doomsday Cult* (New York, Irvington, 1977).

7 The information in this chapter was obtained while I was living in the Stamford Hill Lubavitch community as a participant observer. I am a non-Orthodox Jew, but while living in the community was expected to perform rituals.

8 Festinger, Riecken and Schachter, *When Prophecy Fails*.

9 Ibid.

10 Festinger, Riecken and Schachter, *When Prophecy Fails*, and J. A. Hardyck and M. Braden, 'Prophecy fails again: a report of a failure to replicate', *Journal of Abnormal and Social Psychology*, 65 (1962), 136–41.

11 Traditionally, at the Seder, the Passover Service, the youngest child in the family asks four questions, beginning with, 'How does this night differ from all other nights?'

12 In my paper, 'Letters to the *Rebbe*: millennium, messianism and medicine among the Lubavitch of Stamford Hill', I have examined how Lubavitcher ideas about the body and sickness derive from the Lurianic Kabbalah, and how physical disorder reflects spiritual disorder. *The International Journal of Social Psychology*, 38 No. 4 (1992), 262–72.

13 Isaiah 52–3.

14 According to Jewish belief, the arrival of *Mosiach* will be signalled by the sound of a *Shofar*, a ram's horn which is traditionally blown on *Rosh Hashanah*, the Jewish New Year festival.

15 The major text of Lubavitch is the *Tanya*, which is a synthesis of

rational and mystical ideas. One section called *Igaret Haskodesh* emphasizes that, even when a *Rebbe* is dead, his spiritual presence in this world is greater than when he was alive.

[16] The words of a forty-year-old Lubavitcher.

[17] The words of an eighteen-year-old Lubavitcher.

[18] Jesus had to die prior to the resurrection.

[19] The words of a sixty-five-year-old Rabbi.

[20] Unattributed quotation.

Further reading

Dien, S., 'Letters to the *Rebbe*: millennium, messianism and medicine among the Lubavitch of Stamford Hill', *The International Journal of Social Psychiatry*, 38 No. 4 (1992), 262–72.

Festinger, L., Riecken, H., and Schachter, S. (eds.), *When Prophecy Fails* (Minneapolis, University of Minnisota Press, 1956).

Hardyck, J. A., and Braden, M., 'Prophecy fails again: a report of a failure to replicate', *Journal of Abnormal and Social Psychology*, 65 (1962), 136–41.

Littlewood, R. and Dien, S., 'The effectiveness of words: religious healing among the Lubavitch of Stamford Hill', *Culture, Medicine and Psychiatry* (1995), in print.

Lofland, J., *Doomsday Cult* (New York, Irvington, 1977).

Sarot, S., *Messianism, Mysticism and Magic* (Chapel Hill, University of North Carolina Press, 1982).

Scholem, G., *Sabbatai Sevi: The Mystical Messiah* (London, Routledge, 1973).

Sound the Great Shofar: Essays on the Imminence of Redemption (Brooklyn, SIE, 1992).

Stone, A., *Highlights of Mosiach* (Brooklyn, SIE, 1991).

Tanya (Stamford Hill, Kehot Publication Society, 1981).

Index